THE COMMUNIST PARTY OF INDIA AND THE INDIAN EMERGENCY

THE COMMUNIST PARTY OF INDIA AND THE INDIAN EMERGENCY

DAVID LOCKWOOD

SAGE Series in Modern Indian History

Volume XVII

Series Editors:
Bipan Chandra
Mridula Mukherjee
Aditya Mukherjee

www.sagepublications.com
Los Angeles • London • New Delhi • Singapore • Washington DC

First published in 2016 by

 SAGE Publication India Pvt Ltd
B1/I-1 Mohan Cooperative Industrial Area
Mathura Road, New Delhi 110 044, India
www.sagepub.in

SAGE Publications Inc
2455 Teller Road
Thousand Oaks, California 91320, USA

SAGE Publications Ltd
1 Oliver's Yard, 55 City Road
London EC1Y 1SP, United Kingdom

SAGE Publications Asia-Pacific Pte Ltd
3 Church Street
#10-04 Samsung Hub
Singapore 049483

Published by Vivek Mehra for SAGE Publications India Pvt Ltd, typeset in 10/13pt Berkeley by Zaza Eunice, Hosur, India and printed at Chaman Enterprises, New Delhi.

Library of Congress Cataloging-in-Publication Data Available

ISBN: 978-93-515-0578-5 (HB)

The SAGE Team: Rudra Narayan, Vandana Gupta, Megha Dabral and Rajinder Kaur

Other Volumes in the Series:

Bulk Sales

SAGE India offers special discounts
for purchase of books in bulk.
We also make available special imprints
and excerpts from our books on demand.

For orders and enquiries, write to us at

Marketing Department
SAGE Publications India Pvt Ltd
B1/I-1, Mohan Cooperative Industrial Area
Mathura Road, Post Bag 7
New Delhi 110044, India

E-mail us at **marketing@sagepub.in**

Get to know more about SAGE

Be invited to SAGE events, get on our mailing list.
Write today to **marketing@sagepub.in**

This book is also available as an e-book.

Contents

List of Abbreviations

AIADMK	All-India Dravida Munnetra Kazhagam
AICC	All-India Congress Committee
AIRF	All-India Railwaymen's Federation
AITUC	All-India Trade Union Congress
CC	Central Committee
CEC	Central Executive Committee (CPI)
CFSA	Congress Forum for Socialist Action
CNS	Central News Service
Cominform	Communist Information Bureau
Comintern	Communist International
CPI	Communist Party of India
CPI(M)/CPM	Communist Party of India (Marxist)
CPSU	Communist Party of the Soviet Union
CWC	Congress Working Committee
DIRs	Defence of India Rules
DMK	Dravida Munnetra Kazhagam
ELI	Export-led Industrialisation
FICCI	Federation of Indian Chambers of Commerce and Industry
ICS	Indian Civil Service
INA	Indian National Army
INC	Indian National Congress
INTUC	Indian National Trade Union Congress
ISI	Import-substituting Industrialisation
JPM	'JP' (Jayaprakash Narayan) Movement
JNU	Jawaharlal Nehru University
JS	Jan Sangh
MISA	Maintenance of Internal Security Act
NC	National Council (CPI)
NDF	National Democratic Front

NFIR   National Federation of Indian Railwaymen
NSF   Nehru Study Forum
PB   Polit Bureau
PMO   Prime Minister's Office
PSP   Praja Socialist Party
RSS   Rashtriya Swayamsevak Sangh

Series Editors' Preface

The SAGE Series in Modern Indian History is intended to bring together the growing volume of historical studies that shares a very broad common historiographic focus.

In more than 60 years of independence from colonial rule, research and writing on modern Indian history have given rise to intense debates, resulting in the emergence of different schools of thought. Prominent among them are the Cambridge school and the Subaltern school. Some of us at the Jawaharlal Nehru University (JNU), along with many colleagues in other parts of the country, have tried to promote teaching and research along somewhat different lines. We have endeavoured to steer clear of colonial stereotypes, nationalist romanticisation, sectarian radicalism and rigid and dogmatic approach. We have also discouraged the *flavor of the month* approach which tries to ape whatever is currently fashionable.

Of course, a good historian is fully aware of contemporary trends in historical writing and of historical work being done elsewhere, and draws heavily on the comparative approach, that is, the historical study of other societies, states and nations, and other disciplines, especially economics, political science, sociology and social anthropology. A historian tries to understand the past and make it relevant to the present and the future. History, thus, also caters to the changing needs of society and social development. A historian is a creature of his/her times, yet a good historian tries to use every tool available to the historian's craft to avoid a conscious bias to get as nearer to the truth as possible.

The approach we have tried to evolve looks sympathetically, though critically, at the Indian national liberation struggle and other popular movements, such as those of labour, peasants, lower castes, tribal people and women. It also looks at colonialism as a structure and a system, and analyses changes in economy, society, and culture in the colonial context, and also in the context of independent India. It focuses on communalism and casteism as major features of modern Indian development. This volume in the series will tend to reflect this approach as well as its changing and developing features. At the broadest plane, our approach is committed to the enlightenment values of rationalism, humanism, democracy and secularism.

The series will consist of well-researched volumes with a wider scope, which deal with a significant historiographic aspect even while devoting meticulous attention to details. They will have a firm empirical grounding based on an exhaustive and rigorous examination of primary sources (including those available in archives in different parts of India and often abroad); collections of private and institutional papers; newspapers and journals (including those in Indian languages); oral testimony; pamphlet literature; contemporary literary works. The books in this series, while sharing a broad historiographic approach, will invariably have considerable differences in analytical frameworks.

The many problems that hinder academic pursuit in developing societies—for example, relatively poor library facilities, forcing scholars to run from library to library and city to city, and yet not being able to find many of the necessary books, inadequate institutional support within universities, a paucity of research-funding organisations, a relatively underdeveloped publishing industry and so on—have plagued historical research and writing as well. All this had made it difficult to initiate and sustain efforts for publishing a series along the lines of the Cambridge History Series or the history series of some of the best US and European universities. But the need is there because in the absence of such an effort, a vast amount of work on Indian history being done in Delhi and other university centers in India and also in British, US, Russian, Japanese, Australian, and European universities, which shares a common historiographic approach, remains scattered and has no *voice*. Also, many fine works published by small Indian publishers never reach the libraries and bookshops in India or abroad. We are acutely aware that one swallow does not make a summer. This series will only mark the beginning of a new attempt at presenting the efforts of scholars to evolve autonomous (but not indigenist) intellectual approaches in modern Indian history.

Bipan Chandra
Mridula Mukherjee
Aditya Mukherjee

Acknowledgements

I would like to acknowledge my intellectual debt to Nigel Harris and Aditya Mukherjee in establishing the theoretical foundations of this book. I would like to thank my wife Sue and my son Karl, Graham Willett, my father and my colleagues at Flinders University for their abiding support. Thanks should also go to the hardworking staff of the Archives on the Contemporary History of India (P. C. Joshi Archive) at JNU and the Nehru Memorial Museum and Library in Delhi.

Introduction

This book examines an episode in Indian political history—the Emergency imposed by the Indira Gandhi government between 1975 and 1977.

In June 1975, the Indian prime minister, Indira Gandhi, declared 'Emergency' in India. Key constitutional liberties were suspended, leaders of opposition parties were arrested and the normal functioning of democracy (including the press) virtually shut down. A chorus of condemnation rained down on the Congress government, from within India and abroad. But *one* political party supported Indira Gandhi's action—the Communist Party of India (CPI).[1] In fact, the CPI had critically defended the Gandhi government against the tide of opposition—in the street, in the central and the state parliaments, in workplaces and in universities—that had been rising at an alarming rate over the preceding two years. The CPI did this in the face of total political opposition from the Right, the Centre and the rest of the Left. In return, it received no political pay-off, in terms of ministerial positions or electoral alliances and precious little acknowledgement (let alone thanks) from the Congress leadership. Why then did the CPI take up this lonely and much-criticised stand?

Answering that question is the purpose of this book. The glib answer, often put forward by contemporary analysts at the time, was that the Party was either obeying the advice of its Soviet patron (in order to advance the Indo-Soviet alliance) or seeking political gain (as the last party standing during the Emergency). But the CPI had gone against Moscow's behests in the past—and the Kremlin was quick to drop Indira Gandhi after her election loss once the Emergency was over. As for political influence, none was forthcoming where Congress was concerned.

This book will take a different approach—one that analyses the Emergency as a crucial turning point in India's political and economic development and recognises that it was the CPI's analysis of Indian society and the forces arraigned within it, developed over the previous decade or so, that caused it to take such a position in 1975. It attempts to look at the Emergency through the prism of the CPI and, simultaneously, at the CPI through the prism of the Emergency.

The book is written from a Marxist perspective. To begin with, I will introduce three organising ideas from that perspective, which may help the reader in following the argument of the book. They are historical materialism, the state and the bourgeois revolution.

Historical Materialism

The book is based on an orthodox version of historical materialism. It proceeds from the assumption that the level of development of the productive forces provides the basis for the existence of a particular set of production relations (the economic structure), which in turn gives rise to a legal and political superstructure.[2] The economic structure exists, *because* it has the ability to advance productive power—that is, to promote the tendency of the productive forces to develop. On the relationship between forces and relations of production, Marx wrote that '[a]t a certain stage of development, the material productive forces of society come into conflict with the existing relations of production....' The latter restricts (or 'fetters') the development of the former.[3] Historical advance then, is a continuing process of productive force development, production relation fettering and eventual change in the latter forced through by the former. This kind of change affects the nature of social classes and their relationship to each other. Specifically, it affects which class will be dominant within a set of production relations.

From the late 1960s onwards, India began to feel a major rise in the level of the productive forces brought about by the application of new technology to the production process and the consequent changes in the relations of production—including the state—which we have now come to know as 'globalisation'. The economic advances that made the creation of a world market possible also began to eat away at the role of the state in the economy from this time. The trade and investment flows of a global economy no longer corresponded to the historical boundaries between nations.[4] National economies began to dissolve into a global division of labour. The governments of national states, including the Indian government as we shall see, tried to control this process—but, in the end, they succumbed. As will be made clear in the course of this book, India, in 1975, was on the brink of this transition.

The State after Colonialism

The nature of the state and its relationship with the forces that surrounded it, in particular with the Indian bourgeoisie, was crucial to developments in India after 1947. The nature of the Indian state and the Indian bourgeoisie was particularly important for the Indian Left—and, as I shall explain a little later, for the CPI.

Much has been written on the state in post-colonial societies—particularly on the question of its autonomy from other social forces.[5] For many Marxists, that autonomy has constituted a special case: owing to the imperialist process and the colonial inheritance, the post-colonial state emerges stronger, more autonomous and more dominant than states elsewhere. Thus, can the standard Marxist theory of the state, as a tool of the ruling class or sections thereof, be squared with the post-colonial experience—when it clearly was not.

Hamza Alavi wrote in 1972 that, since the colonial state had to 'exercise dominion over *all* the indigenous social classes in the colony', the state that the colonial power left behind was 'overdeveloped'—that is, stronger and more autonomous than the norm.[6] Its autonomy is enhanced by its mediating role between the 'competing but no longer contradictory interests and demands' of 'the indigenous bourgeoisie, the Metropolitan neo-colonialist bourgeoisies, and the landed classes.'

Alavi immediately sets about further strengthening the autonomy of his post-colonial state. It is not, for example, controlled by the indigenous bourgeoisie, which finds itself 'enmeshed in bureaucratic controls'. Indeed, in Pakistan, 'The influence of the business community on the conduct of public affairs is primarily through its direct contact with and influence on the bureaucracy itself.' It is not controlled by the 'neo-colonialist bourgeoisies' (past or emerging imperialist powers). If it were, suggests Alavi, this 'would have the implication that independence is a mere sham' (something that Alavi clearly does not believe). Again, in Pakistan, 'None of them [the "competing Metropolitan bourgeoisies"] has complete command over the bureaucracy nor do they command it collectively.' As for the landed classes, 'landlords as a class ... cannot be said to have command over the bureaucracy.' In short:

> None of the three proprietary classes [the indigenous bourgeoisie, the metropolitan bourgeoisies and the landlords] ... exclusively command the state apparatus; the influence and power of each is offset by that of

the other two.... But they make competing demands on the post-colonial state and on the bureaucratic-military oligarchy which represents the state.

Alavi continues that, from its relatively autonomous position, the post-colonial state can take up 'a new and relatively autonomous *economic* role'. It 'directly appropriates a very large part of the economic surplus and deploys it in bureaucratically directed economic activity in the name of promoting economic development'.

This, surely, is the main point. For here, Alavi alludes to (but does not fully answer) the question that his propositions on the post-colonial state beg: Why does the state seek autonomy and what does it use it for?[7] What is the purpose of 'bureaucratically directed economic activity'? Entirely left out of Alavi's account is the idea that the state may have its own interests which it pursues despite and even in opposition to the interests of other classes. For this reason, his analysis (and he is not alone) is vitiated by his insistence that, relatively autonomous or not, the state works for 'the three proprietary classes' in order 'to preserve the social order in which their interests are embedded'—that is, capitalism. I shall return to this theme later. But as a preliminary observation, it is worth pointing out that the twentieth century alone was littered with examples where states did no such thing. They pursued state interests regardless of the interests of the propertied classes.[8] It is the state's pursuit of power—and the economic forces that it demands—that makes it seek autonomy. The post-colonial situation gave it an increased opportunity to do so. India, after 1947, was one example of such a state and we will turn to India in due course.

More recently, Tariq Amin-Khan has endorsed the autonomy of the post-colonial state, while at the same time clinging to a more familiar story of capitalist domination. Thus, 'we can characterise the Indian state as having relative autonomy *albeit under the sway* of the indigenous bourgeoisie.'[9] There was a 'critical juncture' when the post-colonial state could have changed the course, along the lines of 'the former Soviet Union and China's early economic/industrial development'. That it did not do so reflected the lack of 'national leaders who pursue a self-reliant path of economic and social development'. Nehru, Amin-Khan tells us, 'did not adapt his policy to reflect the lessons learned from the 1917 revolution'.[10] So, the Indian State ends up subordinated to metropolitan capital and imperialism.[11] But at the same time, it is dominated by Indian capitalists.

The power of the Indian state 'has been curtailed from the period of colonial rule and immediately following decolonization'.[12]

Little of this accords with India's post-1947 reality. Contrary to the theorists cited here, it is my contention that, for most of the twentieth century, in most industrialising economies, the role of the state cannot be properly understood if it seen as a tool or an instrument of some other social force, or as a mediator between competing social forces. The state is an actor with its own interests and its own ways of pursuing them. At times, these have coincided with those of capital—at times, they have not. For Marxists, it is *this* reality that has to be squared with Marxism.

Most Marxists argue that the state is a part of the legal and political 'superstructure', the nature of which is determined by the 'relations of production'—the economic structure or 'base'.[13] In this scheme, state autonomy presents a problem since it appears that a part of the super-structure is dictating to the economic base in its own interests. It is this problem that has produced, within Marxist theory, the verbal gymnastics of 'partial autonomy', 'relative autonomy' and the state pursuing 'the general interests of the system' (of which its upper parts seem to be unaware). It has also produced an inability to explain the vigorous and dominating activities of states in the twentieth century. The difficulty can only really be tackled within Marxism by re-examining the assumption that the state is a part of the superstructure.

Marx certainly made that assumption, and it is accepted by the over-whelming majority of Marxists.[14] But an immediate difficulty arises here because there is no sense in which a *particular* economic structure erects the state as a suitable superstructure for the continuation and development of that economic system. The state in capitalism, for example, does not arise with the capitalist system; it predates it. In *The Origin of the Family, Private Property and the State*, Engels is not describing a state specific to capitalism, but the rise of the state in general, as a product of the struggle between classes—which, of course, predates capitalism by a lengthy his-torical period.[15] I will argue that the state, rather than being a part of the legal and political superstructure, is in fact a production relation itself.[16] So, in a set of production relations that make up an economic structure, it is possible that state production relations can dominate. And were that to be the case (as it has been, and, in a very few cases, still is), the economic structure and the society it gives rise to would be dominated by the priorities of the state. In the post-colonial situation, those priorities revolved around state-directed economic development. Nayar points out that for the state: 'it is not only higher standards of living that are the "ultimate" or "long-term" fruits of economic development but also, most importantly and visibly, national power and national status in the international state system.'[17]

The Bourgeois Revolution

The importance of the above, in the Indian context, lies in the fact that India was, under the British, a society dominated by the state production relation. Bipan Chandra argues that the colonial state 'is not a super-structure erected on the economic base; it is part of the economic base of colonialism.' The post-colonial state sets out with 'the tradition of a strong state role in the control and shaping of the economy ... the post-colonial state is an important part of the economic base itself.'[18] This was the India that Congress inherited. The Indian bourgeoisie enrolled itself in the anti-colonial struggle under the command of the Congress leadership. When the latter was transformed into a new state, the bourgeoisie was temporarily content to accept its domination of the production relations.[19]

The Congress state, therefore, initiated the bourgeois revolution in India.[20] A study of bourgeois revolutions, of both the 'classical' variety (England, America and France) and those 'from above' (German and Italian unification, the Meiji Restoration)[21], reveals that the foundations of a bourgeois revolution and of a capitalist economy are not laid by the bourgeoisie itself. The bourgeoisie may not be fully formed before a bourgeois revolution and may not emerge immediately in its wake. In advanced countries, it took the bourgeoisie a considerable historical period to develop.[22] Bourgeois revolutions, then, are 'not ... revolutions consciously made by capitalists, but ... revolutions which promote capitalism'.[23]

The emergence of the first shoots of capitalism was very often a by-product of the need of state 'to maximise both their military investments and the efficiency of those investments'.[24] In this way, given the lack of a fully fledged bourgeoisie in the vanguard of the struggle against militarily inefficient feudalism, the state sponsored both the development of the bourgeoisie and the initial stages of the bourgeois revolution. In fact, by the late nineteenth century, the state's revolution from above, pursued for military ends, became a much more common historical phenomenon than the revolutions of the English, American or French type. Engels described it as a part of 'the new age of revolution from above'.[25]

In 1947, the leadership of the Indian National Congress (INC) inherited a strong state. Far from attempting to dismantle it, they completed the job of making it theirs.

The British state in India had been both a ruler and a proprietor. It owed no allegiance to any social class in India and bent its knee only to its political masters in London. It had, during the course of two world wars, gathered unto itself a fearsome set of state powers, both political and economic. Given the popularity and apparent efficacy of state intervention in the aftermath of those wars, it did not let those powers go. But the British state could not carry out the bourgeois revolution in India. At times, particularly at times of war, it encouraged industrialisation in India and this gave the Indian bourgeoisie a start. But at other times, pressed by competing economic interests at home, or when India's strategic importance outweighed all other considerations, it did not. As Shashi Joshi points out:

> The colonial state became the 'engine' of modernisation of Indian society ... As a result the state apparatus turned out to be an 'advanced' one, while the corresponding processes in society not only 'lagged behind' but also acquired a measure of complexity not witnessed by the history of western countries.[26]

In the end, the economic and political structures of the British empire in India became a fetter on the development of India's productive forces. For the forces to develop, those fetters had to be broken—and they were broken by the national movement for freedom, with Congress in the lead.

The fact that the state structure left behind by the British was not taken apart root and branch by the new authorities does not imply that 'nothing happened' in August 1947, or that the Indian state was then a 'tool' of foreign imperialism or indigenous capitalists, or both.[27] In fact, as British rule in India declined, a new state was forming within the shell of the old. Achin Vanaik tells us that 'by 1947 [the Congress] had become a kind of parallel government or government-in-waiting'.[28]

This was possible because British rule was not based on pure suppression of the Indian masses or pure repression of anti-colonial resistance. It was rather, 'semi-hegemonic' (in the Gramscian sense), that is, not able to exercise total domination and, therefore, requiring a social base in Indian society and needing co-operation from significant sections of it.[29] To obtain these, the colonial state had to be based on 'the creation of certain civil institutions and on the rule of law, a certain amount of civil liberties, and a certain toleration and civil behaviour towards its opponents'.[30] Thus, the British were engaged in a 'continuous effort to create channels, institutions and opportunities for cooption of their opponents'.[31] Co-option may have been the aim. But the process contained within it a clear danger:

> [E]ach successive retreat from local or provincial power on the part of the British administration in the quest for new forms of collaboration only served to strengthen the potential hand of the very forces in Indian society which sought its ultimate removal.[32]

The Congress strategy was to occupy every democratic and semi-democratic space that the British opened up.[33] The Congress leader, K. M. Munshi declared in the early 1930s:

> The real object of Congress, therefore, is to prepare the country for a new life by gaining greater control over all forms of social organisation, governmental and non-governmental.[34]

The strategy had a dramatically corrosive effect on the British state in India, as between bouts of repression, each reform presented new opportunities for Congress to undermine British authority. Morarji Desai, preparing to take up the position of Home Minister in the Bombay Congress ministry in 1937, told the Governor, 'Yours is a disappearing Government, ours is the incoming one.'[35] According to Reginald Coupland, power extended from the Congress ministries to the Congress itself: after 1937, 'all the committees of primary party members, great and small, became quasi-official organs overnight'—and started issuing 'orders' to the administration.[36] Nehru was justified in telling the National Planning Committee in 1939, 'Now the Congress is to some extent identifying itself with the state.'[37]

Congress strategy not only initiated the transformation of the state, but brought about changes in state officials. The object here was 'to undermine the hold of the colonial state on the members of its own state apparatus, destroy their morale, promote "rebelliousness" among them, and to neutralise or win them over to the national cause.'[38] The effect this had on British officials can be gauged from Wavell's description, after the Quit India campaign, of 'the weakness and weariness of the instrument still at our disposal in the shape of the British element in the Indian Civil Service'.[39]

Amongst Indian state officials, a change in ideas as well as in mood was evident. Gupta argues that, while Indians in the Indian Civil Service (ICS) were inclined to 'play safe' during mass upheavals, during quieter periods 'their role can be shown to have been in support of liberal nationalist points of view'.[40] During the Congress ministries, says Mahajan, 'the tendency of Indian officials to look up to the Congress had been apparent, but by 1945 the Indian services were assertively nationalist.'[41] Even after the resignation of the ministries in 1939, for non-Congress supporters, 'playing safe' meant preparing for a probable return of Congress to power.[42] To make matters worse, the 'British element' in the ICS was declining, while the Indian one increased. By 1929, 20 per cent of the total posts were occupied by Indians, rising to over 40 per cent in 1939. By 1945, 'Indian ICS officers had moved up through steady promotion to occupy a dominant position within the colonial structure.'[43] The national movement was also able to penetrate the armed wing of the state, aided by a combination of the Indian troops' experience overseas and the debacle of the Indian National Army (INA) trials.[44] As a result of this strategy, by the end of the war, the British government was by no means certain of the continuing loyalty to the colonial state of either the ICS or the Indian armed forces.

Just as with the state that preceded it, the new Congress state was controlled by no social class. It pursued interests of its own. But here, post-colonial state analysts make a further mistake. In keeping with their insistence on the state's location in the superstructure and its (ultimate) subservience to other classes, they conclude that this state that was coming into being—which was identified with Congress and the national movement—was dominated by the Indian bourgeoisie.[45] This is wrong on two counts. Firstly, the Indian bourgeoisie was simply not strong enough—either in terms of economic clout or popular support—to dominate the national movement. What actually occurred was a realisation on the part of big business of its need for a political leadership and a mass base if independence were to be achieved. Both of these were provided by the Congress leadership during the independence struggle.[46] The situation after independence is summed up by Vanaik:

> The autonomy of India's economy and polity is essentially the creation of the state, not of the Indian bourgeoisie. On its own this bourgeoisie could never have succeeded in achieving what clearly was (in hindsight) its general interest—a substantially self-reliant and relatively insulated economic system.[47]

Secondly, because (as we have established) the state was so important in India in 1947, in terms of power, it mattered more than anything else who inherited that state from the British. As Bipan Chandra points out, the British controlled India not because they owned the means of production, but because they controlled the state.[48] And the state inheritance was gifted by the British to the Congress leadership. Just as the state played a crucial role in building colonialism, it would play a similarly important role in 'destructuring' it.[49]

Who then was the Congress?

It is well established that the Congress leadership was dominated by urban professionals, often educated in British institutions (whether in India or in Britain) and 'steeped for the most part in the values of bourgeois liberalism'. These men and women 'came to oppose British rule in the name of the most advanced bourgeois democracy, represented by Britain itself'.[50] At the first Congress session in 1885, out of about 80 participants, 80 per cent spoke English, 45 per cent had attended colleges and over 25 per cent had taken higher degrees.[51] While Gandhi's efforts successfully transformed Congress into a mass movement at the bottom, sociologically speaking, its top leadership ranks remained relatively stable. Nearly half of the members of the All-India Congress Committee in 1923 were listed as 'professionals' or 'public workers'—the latter being a term for full-time political activists. The number had dropped slightly (to a third of the members) by 1956.[52] Nevertheless, after independence:

> [A]t the elite levels of the national party organization there is a massive shift to dominance by middle-class professionals, especially lawyers.[53]

This trend was also evident in the new state's political administration. Almost all the members of independent India's first government came from a background in law. By the time they reached office, most of them were full-time political workers. In India's first three Lok Sabhas (1952, 1957 and 1962), the percentage of Congress members who were professionals or 'public workers' never fell below 58 per cent.[54] Nigel Harris comments:

> The articulate political arena is almost wholly dominated by the educated middle class, which, since the role of the State as employer is so great, is clustered round the State. Thus, the middle class represents a primary vested interest in the State and its expansion—they are all 'socialists'.[55]

The new politicians and their state counterparts were no longer imbued simply with bourgeois liberalism. In the period initiated by the First World War, exacerbated by the Depression and reinforced by the Second, other ideas had found favour—and not just in India. Societies in crisis, whether through war or economic collapse, began to turn to the state as an organised, efficient and fair, if stern, agency to get them out of it. This was in marked contrast to the final decades of the nineteenth century when international trade and peace seemed to be the road to salvation (and when capital seemed to be outstripping states in terms of power).[56] But, the First World War set a great example of what could be achieved by a strengthened state and a mobilised population and it seemed that there was no going back.

This new state, in Europe and beyond, produced a new elite of 'engineers, planners, technocrats, high-level administrators, architects, scientists and visionaries', empowered by state intervention and schooled in the war-time virtues of planning and efficiency.[57] This elite emerged in the inter-war period, more powerful in some economies than in others. Where it was backed by armed force—in Russia, Italy, Germany and Japan—it brought into being the state-run war economies of the 1930s and 1940s. Elsewhere, it settled into an accommodation with the established ruling classes (at least until 1945). The ideas behind it remained common currency long after the guns fell silent.

In India, those ideas—mostly in a non-authoritarian form—were tailor-made for the Congress elite, given its ideological preferences and its social origins.[58] In the post-colonial situation, Harris contends:

> Along with the demands to develop the needs of defence and the techniques of modern industrialism, the whole adds up to a powerful compulsion towards *étatisme*. The native capitalists are usually too weak to resist

the process, and in any case, where foreign capital continues to operate in the independent economy, they need the State to protect them. That need is purchased at a high price—the line between 'Indianisation' (or Ceylonisation, Egyptianisation, etc.) of business and its nationalisation becomes very fine.[59]

The transformative role of the state and the necessity of state intervention and control were accepted by the Congress well before 1947.[60] War-time controls after 1939 would give the new government a firm base from which to start. Nehru told the National Planning Committee in 1940:

> War has compelled planning though this planning is for the specific purpose of destruction. When the war ends, this planned economy and State control cannot be given up and there appears to be no possibility [of] a reversion to pre-war capitalism.[61]

By 1947, such a view was by no means confined to the Congress leadership or even to its mass membership. It was hugely popular on a global scale. This was reflected in the fact that the (British) Government of India, itself endorsed central economic direction and planning.[62] This, in turn, meant that the members of the ICS (steadily becoming Indianised), whether supporters of Congress or of the British, were steeped in this kind of thinking. There was no major overhaul of the (Indian) bureaucracy after 1947 and its numbers grew substantially under the premiership of Jawaharlal Nehru. The Rudolphs conclude:

> [C]ivil servants were the vanguard of the lobby for an industrial strategy, collaborating in the creation of basic and heavy industry under the second and third five-year plans. They brought into being the third actor in the Indian economy, the state sector, which rivalled and then surpassed private capital and organised labor. As the 'new class' of a semisocialist state, they were among its principal beneficiaries.[63]

In the years from 1947 to 1991, the Indian state remained strong.[64] Economically, it played 'a large and leading role in reshaping the economy in a self-reliant direction, especially on the basis of planning, public sector and large scale expenditure'.[65] It is important to remember that, while in part the state's role was a response to mass demands for an improvement in the people's lot, the state also pursued development in its own interests. Baldev Nayar points out that states also aim 'most importantly and visibly [for] national power and national status in the international state system'.[66] This was particularly urgent for non-industrialised economies:

> This, in essence, is the *modernisation imperative*: … 'Modernise or be sub-jugated.' … For the non-industrialized country there is no escape from the modernisation imperative, there is no other alternative, there is no other choice.[67]

This kind of development demands industry, and heavy industry especially. As Nehru told the Avadi Congress session in January 1955: 'We want heavy industry because without it we can never really be an independent country.'[68] And this, in turn necessitated generalised industrialisation. Nehru told the Lok Sabha in March 1956:

> The more technical armies and navies and air forces get, the more important becomes the industrial and technological base of the country … apart from the army, navy and so on, you have to have an industrial and technological background in the country.[69]

Economic independence was also required: 'independent control over the direction of the economy by the nation itself and not by foreign powers and agencies.'[70]

Nayar stresses that these policies are undertaken by states regardless of the individual wishes of the states or leaders concerned. In the Indian case:

> [M]odernisation is undertaken despite the prospect of rootlessness and alienation that it holds for man … Gandhian schemes of village self-sufficiency are unacceptable to national statesmen.[71]

From the earlier discussions, some conclusions follow. If it can be accepted that the state is, in the Marxist sense, a part of the economic base, we can surmise that independent India was a state-dominated society. Not in a 'totalitarian' sense, but simply in the way that the state's preoccupations took priority. The interests of the state—a combination of economic development, economic independence and military security—were paramount. The interests of the Indian bourgeoisie were not. Indeed, under the state's tutelage, the pressure of state priorities on Indian business was considerable:

> State intervention had a decidedly regulatory cast: Instead of asking business what it could do and how the state could help, the state itemized

what private business could not do and then raised numerous barriers to what it could do.[72]

The Government's 1948 and 1956 Industrial Policy Resolutions went further in this direction than the bourgeoisie had hoped or liked.[73] By the 1980s, the state had 'powers of direct ownership and control in the economy to an extent unparalleled in Indian history'.[74] Vanaik concluded shortly before the 1991 reforms that 'probably no other developing country has such an array of public controls over the private industrial sector'.[75]

As noted earlier, the Congress state emerged as a strong institution, dominating the classes around it, as the Congress leadership had dominated the national movement. It was the state that set its seal on the programmes for economic development. The fact that this development nurtured Indian capitalism does not diminish the state's leading role. It simply confirms the common interest, at that stage, of state and capital, in pursuing the development of the productive forces.

The reason that this arrangement remained relatively stable for nearly three decades—and the reason that the bourgeoisie accepted it—was that, in the initial stages of India's bourgeois revolution, the interests of the Indian state and Indian capital at one with each other. The consolidation of a national economy with appropriate infrastructure and its defence against competitors was the common interest of both the state and capital. But it should not be forgotten that the final aim of the bourgeois revolution is to ensure the domination of capital as a production relation rather than the state. The aims of the state and capital are, in the long run, different.[76]

This book is largely concerned with the point at which those aims started to diverge.

The first chapter outlines the political position of the CPI from 1947 (Indian independence) to 1966 (when Mrs Gandhi became Prime Minister). It pays particular attention to the communists' changing appraisal of the Indian revolution, the Indian bourgeoisie and the Congress. The second chapter charts Congress economic policy from the death of Nehru in 1964, through the Congress split in 1969 up to the eve of the Emergency in early 1975. That is, from the mild reforms in response to the beginnings of globalisation under Prime Minister Shastri through the return, under electoral pressure, to Leftist policies. Chapter 3 examines the relationship of the CPI to the Congress during this period, explaining how the Party arrived at its position of 'unity and struggle' with the Congress by the early

1970s. Chapter 4 deals with the Emergency proper and Chapter 5 with its excesses, especially in the areas of family planning and slum clearance. A preliminary examination of the role of Sanjay Gandhi is conducted at this point. In both these chapters, the role of the CPI is considered, as it moved from initial support of the Emergency to criticism and finally to the demand that the Emergency be withdrawn. The Party itself conducted a debate about its role and the theoretical basis of its political positions from 1969 to 1977, which forms the basis of Chapter 6. During that discussion, the old questions of the stage of the revolution, the nature of the Indian bourgeoisie and the relationship of the Party to the Congress emerged once again. Chapter 7 reinserts the Indian events into the world economy and outlines the effect of the latter on the bourgeois revolution in India and on the CPI's version of it, that is, the national democratic revolution.

Notes

1. The Communist Party in India had been brought forth out of various socialist and communist groups in 1925. Before the Second World War, it spent most of its existence in illegality, periodically dispersed by British repression.
2. See Karl Marx, 'Preface', *A Contribution to the Critique of Political Economy* (New Delhi: People's Publishing House, 2010 [1859]), 20–21. My account of historical materialism owes a great deal to G. A. Cohen, *Karl Marx's Theory of History* (Oxford: Clarendon Press, 1991).
3. Marx, 'Preface', 21.
4. Nigel Harris, *Of Bread and Guns: The World Economy in Crisis* (Harmondsworth: Penguin, 1983), 20.
5. Nicos Poulantzas, for example, wrote of a '*state bourgeoisie* in certain developing countries' (Nicos Poulantzas, *Political Power and Social Classes* (London: NLB, 1975), 334). See also Hamza Alavi, 'The State in Post-Colonial Societies: Pakistan and Bangladesh', *New Left Review* I, no. 74 (1972) at www.hamzaalavi.com; John S. Saul, 'The State in Post-Colonial Societies: Tanzania', *The Socialist Register, 1974* (London: Merlin Press, 1974); Colin Leys, 'The "Overdeveloped" Post Colonial State: A Re-evaluation', *Review of African Political Economy*, www.roape.org; W. Ziemann and M. Lanzendorfer, 'The State in Peripheral Societies', *The Socialist Register, 1977* (London: Merlin Press, 1977); Tariq Amin-Khan, *The Post-Colonial State in the Era of Capitalist Globalization: Historical, Political and Theoretical Approaches to State Formation* (New York: Routledge, 2011).
6. Hamza Alavi, 'The State in Post-Colonial Societies', www.hamzaalavi.com—from which all the following citations are taken.
7. John Saul picks up, 'Alavi's rather bland statement that [the state] deploys surpluses "in the name of promoting economic development."' He asks, '[W]hat … is the nature of the oligarchy's distinctive interest which any "autarky" it may win permits it to advance and defend?' (Saul, 'State in Post-Colonial Societies', 352–53).

8. For an extensive treatment of this question see Nigel Harris, *The Return of Cosmopolitan Capital: Globalization, the State and War* (London: IB Tauris, 2003).

9. Amin-Khan, *Post-Colonial State*, 140; author's emphasis.

10. Amin-Khan, *Post-Colonial State*, 134–36. One wonders which of the lessons of 1917 Nehru should have taken up: Urban insurrection? Civil War? Or Stalinist dictatorship?

11. Amin-Khan, *Post-Colonial State*, 134–35. To indicate this, Amin-Khan inserts the tell-tale dismissive quotation marks when referring to 'Indian ... "independence"' (131).

12. Amin-Khan, *Post-Colonial State*, 137–40.

13. As does Alavi himself. He describes the state as one of the 'elements of the super-structure ... in relation to the underlying "structure," i.e. the economic foundations of society (the relations of production)' (Alavi, 'State in Post-Colonial Societies').

14. Although Bardhan contends that:

    > the idea of a centralized powerful state, combining its monopoly of the means of repression with a substantial ownership in the means of production, propel-ling as well as regulating the economy ... is implicit in the writings of Marx and Engels on Asiatic societies [and] has widespread contemporary relevance. (Pranab Bardhan, *The Political Economy of Development in India* (Oxford: Basil Blackwell Ltd, 1984), 36.)

15. See Frederick Engels, 'The Origin of the Family, Private Property and the State', in *Selected Works*, eds. Karl Marx and Frederick Engels (Moscow: Progress Publishers, 1970 [1884]).

16. For an elaboration of this argument, see David Lockwood, 'Historical Materialism and the State', *Critique* 34, no. 2 (June 2006): 163–78.

17. Baldev R. Nayar, *The Modernisation Imperative and Indian Planning* (Delhi: Vikas Publications, 1972), 78.

18. Bipan Chandra, *The Writings of Bipan Chandra: The Making of Modern India from Marx to Gandhi*, ed. Aditya Mukherjee (Hyderabad: Orient Blackswan Private Ltd, 2012), 400, 402. Bardhan makes the same point: '[I]n many newly industrializing countries, the state is today an important part of the economic base itself' (Bardhan, *Political Economy of Development*, 35).Chandra confines his argument in this regard to the colonial state. I would extend it to the state in general.

19. The struggle to overcome imperialist domination required a united struggle by a unified people ... the capitalist class ... strove broadly to relate with the national movement led by the Congress. The programme of national regeneration, establish-ment of democracy and rapid industrialization bequeathed to the Congress by the early nationalists was adopted by the capitalists. (Shashi Joshi, *Struggle for Hegemony in India, 1920–47. The Colonial State, the Left and the National Movement. Volume I: 1920–34* (New Delhi: SAGE Publications, 1992), 27)

20. 'It is one of the tricks of history that when a historical task faces society, and the class that traditionally carries it out is absent, some other group of people, quite often a state power, implements it' [Tony Cliff, *Deflected Permanent Revolution* (London: Socialist Workers Party, 1990 [1963]), 22].

21. The distinction is made by Alex Callinicos, 'Bourgeois Revolutions and Historical Materialism', *International Socialism*, no. 43 (1989), 116.

22. For Marx and Engels, it was 'the product of a long course of development, of a series of revolutions in the modes of production and exchange' (Karl Marx and Frederick

Engels, *Manifesto of the Communist Party* (Moscow: Progress Publishers, 1966 [1848]), 37). Engels describes 'the long fight of the bourgeoisie against feudalism' in Britain as proceeding from the Reformation, through Calvinism and the English Revolution, encompassing the 'Glorious Revolution', inspired by the French Revolution, right up to the 1832 Reform Act—a period of some 300 years (Frederick Engels, 'Socialism: Utopian and Scientific', in *Selected Works*, eds. Karl Marx and Frederick Engels (Moscow: Progress Publishers, 1970), 384–85).

23. Callinicos, 'Bourgeois Revolutions', 124.

24. Robert Brenner, 'The social basis of economic development', in *Analytical Marxism*, ed. John Roemer (Cambridge: Cambridge University Press, 1986), 32.

25. Engels, 'Afterword' in 'Socialism: Utopian and Scientific'.

26. Bhagwan Josh, *Struggle for Hegemony in India, 1920–47. The Colonial State, the Left and the National Movement. Volume II: 1934–41* (New Delhi: SAGE Publications, 1992), 26.

27. See Bipan Chandra on Indian independence as 'a decisive event' which 'removed the overarch of the colonial structure', enabling India to reduce 'the dependence on metropolitan capital and economy and strengthened the drive towards independent capitalist development' (*Writings*, 402, 404).

28. Achin Vanaik, *The Painful Transition: Bourgeois Democracy in India* (London: Verso, 1990), 75.

29. See Sucheta Mahajan, 'British Policy, Nationalist Strategy and Popular National Upsurge, 1945–46', in *Myth and Reality: The Struggle for Freedom in India, 1945–1947*, ed. Amit Kumar Gupta (New Delhi: Manohar, 1987), 57–58. Bhagwan Josh comments:

> [T]he colonial state ... was certainly not of the type of feudal-absolutist state of Czarist Russia. With all its distortions, it was a state closer to the form of the constitutional democracy of the advanced European countries. But simultaneously the state form was colonial which did not express the sovereignty of the Indian people nor was [it] responsible to them. This is one reason we call this state a semi-hegemonic state. (Josh, *Hegemony II*, 43)

See also Joshi, *Hegemony*, 14. Gramsci's note on Gandhi and the nature of civil disobedience can be found in Antonio Gramsci, *Selections from the Prison Notebooks of Antonio Gramsci*, ed. and trans. Quintin Hoare and Geffrey Nowell Smith (New York: International Publishers, 1971), 229–30.

30. Chandra, *Writings*, 21. See also Joshi, *Hegemony*, 13–14.

31. Chandra, *Writings*, 22.

32. Simon Epstein, 'District Officers in Decline: The Erosion of British Authority in the Bombay Countryside, 1919 to 1947', *Modern Asian Studies* 16, no. 3 (1982): 494.

33. 'Preparation for future government was for a large part of the Congress always the necessary obverse to the agitational coin' (Epsten, 'District Officers', 516. See also Chandra, *Writings*, 31, 43, 46); Joshi, *Hegemony*, 15.

34. Munshi cited in Chandra, *Writings*, 35.

35. Desai's memoirs cited by Epstein, 'District Officers', 507.

36. Epstein, 'District Officers', 508. See also Mahajan, 'British Policy', on Congress becoming at this time 'a locus of authority—parallel to the official administration' (60).

37. Cited in David Lockwood, *The Indian Bourgeoisie: A Political History of the Indian Capitalist Class in the Early Twentieth Century* (London: Tauris Academic Studies, 2012), 180.

38. Chandra, *Writings*, 30.

39. Wavell cited in Epstein, 'District Officers', 514. See also Mahajan, 'British Policy', 61.

40. Partha Sarathi Gupta, 'Imperial Strategy and the Transfer of Power, 1939–51,' in *Myth and Reality: The Struggle for Freedom in India, 1945–1947*, ed. Amit Kumar Gupta (New Delhi: Manohar, 1987), 4.

41. Mahajan, 'British Policy', 61.

42. Epstein, 'District Officers', 509; Mahajan, 'British Policy', 60.

43. Epstein, 'District Officers', 509; David C. Potter, 'Manpower Shortage and the End of Colonialism: the Case of the Indian Civil Service', *Modern Asian Studies* 7, no. 1 (1973): 73.

44. Potter, 'Manpower', 68; Mahajan, 'British Policy', 61, 74.

45. Amin-Khan says that it was 'the bourgeoisie in India' who were 'the leadership in the anti-colonial movement' (Amin-Khan, *Post-colonial State*, 131). Kalpana Wilson writes that in the Indian movement, 'the growing indigenous bourgeoisie was able to establish its dominance well before Independence' (Kalpana Wilson, 'Class Alliances and the Nature of Hegemony: The Post-Independence Indian State in Marxist Writing', in *State and Nation in the Context of Social Change*, ed. T. V. Sathyamurthy (Delhi: Oxford India Paperbacks, 1997), 249).

46. The working out of the relationship between the Indian bourgeoisie and the Congress is the subject of my book, *The Indian Bourgeoisie*.

47. Vanaik, *Transition*, 58.

48. Chandra, *Writings*, 401.

49. Ibid., 400.

50. Vanaik, *Transition*, 73.

51. Briton Martin, *New India 1885: British Official Policy and the Emergence of the Indian National Congress* (Berkeley: University of California Press, 1969), 295.

52. Stanley A. Kochanek, *The Congress Party of India: The Dynamics of One-Party Democracy* (Princeton: Princeton University Press, 1968), 364–5.

53. Kochanek, *Congress Party*, 358.

54. Ibid., 380.

55. Nigel Harris, 'India: Part One', *International Socialism* (1st series), no. 17 (Summer, 1964): 4–14 at www.marxists.org/history/etol/writers/harris/1964/xx/india3.htm.

56. For a longer version of this argument, see my 'War, the State and the Bourgeois Revolution', *War & Society* 25, no. 2 (October, 2006): 53–79.

57. J. C. Scott, *Seeing Like a State* (New Haven, CT: Yale University Press, 1998), 98. Scott identifies these social forces with 'High Modernism': 'the ideology par excellence of the bureaucratic intelligentsia, technicians, planners and engineers' for whose influence the Great War was 'the high water mark' (96 and 100).

58. For the enthusiasm of post-colonial elites for these ideas see Cliff, *Deflected Permanent Revolution*.

59. Harris, 'India: Part One'. See also P. C. Joshi on the importance of the intelligentsia, 'the rapidly growing numbers of the skilled personnel and technocrats at various levels' and the bureaucracy, 'as a consequence of the pivotal role assigned to the state in economic development and nation-building' (Puran Chand Joshi, 'Possibilities and Constraints of Intermediate Classes,' *Indian Left Review* 3, no. 3 (May, 1974): 14).

60. See Lockwood, *The Indian Bourgeoisie*, Chapter 6.

61. Note by the Chairman for the 5th National Planning committee session, 30 August 1940. National Planning Committee, *Abstract of Proceedings, Number 4* (Bombay: National Planning Committee, 1940), 5.

62. See Lockwood, *The Indian Bourgeoisie*, 175–77.

63. Lloyd I. Rudolph and Susanne Hoeber Rudolph, *In Pursuit of Lakshmi: The Political Economy of the Indian State* (Hyderabad: Orient Longman, 1987), 77.

64. Writing in 1990, Vanaik tells us: 'There is no major capitalist country in the third world which has a more powerful state than India's or an indigenous bourgeoisie with more autonomy from foreign capital.' (*Transition*, 11). For more on the weakness of foreign capital see Chandra, *Writings*, 404.)

65. Chandra, *Writings*, 402.

66. Nayar, *Modernisation Imperative*, 78. See also Bardhan, *Political Economy of Development*, 34.

67. Nayar, *Modernization Imperative*, 81.

68. Nehru, cited in Nayar, *Modernization Imperative*, 116.

69. Ibid.

70. Nayar, *Modernization Imperative*, 99.

71. Ibid., 85. For the effect on economic policy of India's disputes with Pakistan and China, see 119–28.

72. Atul Kohli, *State-Directed Development: Political Power and Industrialization in the Global Periphery* (Cambridge: Cambridge University Press, 2004), 267; see also Bardhan, *Political Economy of Development*, 38.

73. Vanaik, *Transition*, 28.

74. Bardhan, *Political Economy of Development*, 37–38.

75. Vanaik, *Transition*, 31.

76. Chandra is one of the few who detects the emergence of that difference. Although he noted in 1989 that, under the state's auspices, 'The Indian bourgeoisie has been immensely strengthened', he recognises the deleterious effect of prolonged state domination on the bourgeoisie as a class: 'The licence-quota and control structure put into place by the government has also tended to fracture the class into fractions and groups.' (Chandra, *Writings*, 413–14.)

1

The Communist Party of India from 1947 to 1966

When Indians won their independence in 1947, they were sailing into waters that were virtually uncharted. India was the first colony to be freed in the post-war world. As such, no one really knew what that freedom would mean. Would the British really leave? Or would they seek to maintain their influence through an economic stranglehold and military basis? What about the rising imperialist power, the US—was it a friend or a foe? If the economy were to be free, how would it function and in whose interests? Was the new political system workable? Was the new Congress state?

The answers to these questions were by no means as obvious in 1947 as they may appear today. The nature of the new state, its class structure and its relationship with the former imperial power were matters of debate and speculation rather than certainty.

The CPI was really no clearer on these questions than anyone else. The nature of the Indian state was one of the Party's constant objects of study and analysis. The relationship of the state with the Congress, together with India's economic structure, the nature of the bourgeoisie and the kind of revolution necessary to advance society were constant themes—at times regarded with certainty, at times with sheer bewilderment—in the Party's attempts to situate itself in Indian society. But the Party needed answers on the economy, the state, the bourgeoisie and the Congress in order to assess the new nature of the Indian revolution (the national liberation aspect having been achieved) and its own strategy. The Party leaders wrestled with and argued over these questions for the next 20 years. It is my intention to examine the treatment of these themes by successive post-war Party leaderships.

The Joshi Line: 1946–47

Purand Chand Joshi was appointed general secretary of the Party in 1935. His appointment came in the wake of the Meerut Conspiracy Case, launched by the British against communist activists between 1929 and 1933. By this stage, the communists were disorganised, disunited and dispersed. Further problems arose when, despite the anti-Congress policies of the Communist International's (Comintern's) 'Third Period' being abandoned, the Party had to turn against the Congress once more due to communist support for the British war effort once the Soviet Union entered the conflict.

India and Imperialism

When the war came to an end, Indian communists could cease their support for Britain's struggle against the fascist powers and return to a more recognisable anti-imperialist position. Independence from Britain was regarded as an achievable and positive goal at this point, and also as one that the communists, along with the members of the Congress and the Muslim League, should be striving for. In the Party's manifesto for the 1945 election, Joshi declared that in post-war circumstances both in India and the world, 'the British imperialists dare not directly and openly deny Indian freedom'. But they were preparing the grim prospect of 'three Indias [Hindustan, Pakistan and the Princely States] with the balance of power in British hands'.[1] Unless Indians came to a common agreement on the constitution of a free India, 'the imposition of a British imperialist plan of modified Indian slavery' lay in store.[2] The manifesto exhibited not only a clear appreciation of what the national movement had achieved, but also a real fear that the British would somehow perpetuate their domination. That fear began to fade when it became clear that the British withdrawal—at least in physical and military terms—was genuine.

In June 1947, the CPI declared that the Mountbatten Plan demonstrated that the British had been forced to compromise by the strength of the freedom movement. Independence promised 'new opportunities for national advance'. Further:

> The Communist Party will fully cooperate with the national leadership in the proud task of building the Indian Republic on democratic foundations, thus paving the way to Indian unity.[3]

Due to partition, the truculent Indian princes and the emerging co-operation between British and Indian big business, '[w]e are well ahead on the road but not yet at journey's end'. Nevertheless, 'the Communist Party of India will join the day of national rejoicing' and would fight 'to win complete independence for our country [and] build real democracy'.[4] Thus, the Party's position was that independence was an important gain and based on independence the national revolution (i.e., the bourgeois democratic revolution) could be completed.[5]

The Indian Bourgeoisie

The Party's analysis of the Indian bourgeoisie was neither penetrating nor accurate.[6] Up until 1935, it was considered to be wholly reactionary. After that—being confronted with the industrialists' strong support for the national movement—it was conceded that a 'national bourgeoisie' could support independence. This support, however, was weakened by the fact that the bourgeoisie (even its 'national' component) was more frightened by the prospect of the Indian masses unleashed than by the continuation of British colonial rule. Because of this fear and its own weakness, the Indian bourgeoisie was incapable of completing the bourgeois revolution in India.

According to the CPI, the bourgeoisie exercised hegemony over the Congress. The Indian communists took their authority on this from no less a person than Stalin himself. A national movement, Stalin had written in 1913, 'is always a bourgeois struggle, one that is chiefly advantageous to and suitable for the bourgeoisie'. He asserted, 'The bourgeoisie plays the leading role.'[7] Rajani Palme Dutt, a leading member of the British Party, reiterated the point, telling the CPI, 'While the Congress has a general mass following, the leadership is drawn from the propertied and professional classes, and the big industrialists have a strong influence on it.'[8] Thus, the bourgeoisie's fear of the masses and hesitation in prosecuting the national revolution through to the end were reflected in the Congress leadership, particularly through Gandhi and the Congress Right.[9]

Under Joshi, the CPI did not use this premise (that Congress was a tool of the bourgeoisie) to draw sectarian anti-Congress conclusions. But the premise was fundamentally wrong—and would serve future Party leaders in their sectarian endeavours. The Congress was, in fact, a movement of the Indian people, encompassing all social classes and led (as has been discussed in the Introduction) by elements of the future independent Indian state.[10] The bourgeoisie did not consider the Congress to be its 'class party'.[11] Indeed, even if it had, Shashi Joshi argues:

> [I]n a colonial country the interests of 'bourgeois development' and the perspective of 'national development', and progress and freedom from the imperialist hold on the economy coincide and overlap to a great extent. This coincidence is the basis for the bourgeoisie's opposition to imperialism and its support to national liberation movements. Precisely for this reason in a country like India the bourgeoisie had perforce to support mass movements which often appeared to them as opposed to their own security and interests.[12]

The Indian National Congress

Despite this, the Party supported the Congress. 'The Congress', wrote P. C. Joshi, 'is the greatest national organisation of the country which has grown to its present greatness by uniting within its ranks the various patriotic elements in the country and by serving the people.' He criticised the Congress however, for its 'sectarian arrogance' in denying 'the right of self-determination … to a section of our own countrymen'—the Muslim community. This was encouraging civil war. But in 1944, Joshi expressed confidence that the Congress would get back on the right track: 'After all, how long will the ranks not ask the leadership: How is brother fighting brother [on] the path to the freedom of the country?'[13]

'The National Congress represents the mainstream of the independence movement of the country', wrote Joshi.[14] Within the Congress, the CPI drew a line between the reactionary Right wing of the leadership and the progressive forces led by Nehru—it was to the latter and their mass following that the Party extended its support.[15] Together with them, the Party conceived a rather too neat three-way split:

> The Muslim League has behind it the bulk of the anti-imperialist freedom-loving Muslims. And the Communist Party leads the bulk of the organised workers and peasants.[16]

The Party pleaded for 'a NEW joint front of the Indian people (Congress, Muslim League and Communist Party)' and 'a joint struggle for independence'.[17] It called on 'the great National Congress and the influential Muslim League' to lead the struggle.[18]

> As long as our country remains enslaved, the only path to our national independence lies through a National United Front of all popular forces … With full faith in the patriotism of our Congress and League brothers we will work as unity-crusaders.[19]

The Revolution

As noted earlier, the CPI was convinced that the Indian bourgeoisie could not complete the bourgeois revolution in India, which began with the revolution for independence from Britain.[20] As a result of this proposition, India's communists would spend the next three decades (influenced at times by the international communist movement) oscillating between two propositions: (a) that the bourgeois revolution would be completed by an alliance of workers, peasants and the progressive bourgeoisie, led by the CPI and the progressive elements of Congress, and would result in an advanced form of democracy and (b) that the completion of the bourgeois revolution would be fused with the beginnings of socialism in a 'people's democracy' by the workers and peasants, led by the Communist Party. In fact, I would argue that 1947 etc. represented the *initial stages* of the bourgeois revolution. But it was led by the Congress and the Congress state, not by the bourgeoisie.

As it was, in 1947 the Party concluded that, since the bourgeoisie could not complete its revolution (and since the CPI could not see that the Congress was doing the job), the Indian proletariat would have to step in and take it on. 'Proletarian hegemony'—exercised through the CPI—had to be established over the Indian national movement, or else it would surely fail.[21] It was possible to conclude from this analysis that, without communist leadership, the independence movement could not achieve 'real' independence. That conclusion, however, was avoided for the moment.

Also, for the moment the Party—in line with its acceptance of independence as genuine and its acceptance of Congress leadership—did not advocate an armed insurrection to bring about further gains. The CPI would be 'making every effort to settle industrial and agrarian disputes amicably'.[22] In the villages, where armed revolt was much more likely than in the cities, the Party issued a call for moderation:

> The Communist Party shall not touch the small zamindar or the rich peasant but shall open before them the prospect of becoming the best of the farmers and cattle-breeders, reputed members in their own village.[23]

The Ranadive Line: 1948–50

Immediately following Indian independence, the Soviet leader Andrei Zhdanov, speaking to the Communist Information Bureau (Cominform), revealed a sharpening confrontation in the world between 'the imperialist and anti-democratic camp' led by the USA and the 'anti-imperialist and democratic camp' led by the Soviet Union.[24] The line between the two camps would be drawn not only between countries, but also within them. For India's communists, this meant that the Joshi line on independence, the Congress and the revolution would all be sharply reversed. The new line would be carried by B. T. Ranadive.

There had been Leftist criticism of the Party's positions as early as 1946. The August 1946 Central Committee (CC) meeting produced a compromise position between Joshi and the Leftists.[25] But it was still too conciliatory towards the national bourgeoisie for the Leftists' liking. And Joshi had by no means conceded defeat. 'Immediately after its adoption', according to Ranadive, 'Joshi carried on a persistent fight against it and did his best to sabotage its operation.'[26]

By December 1947, the numbers on the CC were against Joshi.[27] With the added ammunition contained in Zhdanov's Cominform speech, the Joshi line was doomed. Even then:

> Joshi would not move an inch from his reformist line even when the world perspective was put to him … [He] confessed that he had not even read Zhdanov's speech on the international situation.[28]

Not surprisingly, there was some confusion amongst the Party cadre at this point. At the beginning of 1948, the leadership announced that it had discovered 'a deep-rooted reformist trend inside the Party', and declared:

> [T]he C.C. has reviewed the political situation in the country in the context of the international situation and has made a sharp break with our previous faulty understanding.[29]

India and Imperialism

The idea that the independence of August 1947 was an advance for India was unceremoniously dumped.[30] The equation—'no proletarian hegemony (communist leadership)' equals 'no real independence'—was rigorously calculated. This proved that the Indian people had won virtually nothing.

> What the Mountbatten Award has given to the people of our country is not real but fake independence … Britain's domination has not ended, but the form of domination has changed … To parade this new status as national freedom is to shield the imperialist designs and the subservience of the national bourgeoisie.[31]

Party members were, therefore, enjoined to turn out on Independence Day under the slogan '*Yeh Azadi jhuti hai!*' (This Independence is Fake!).

The Indian Bourgeoisie

For the CPI, there was now no section of the bourgeoisie that did not represent reaction: 'the CPI now declared class war on the entire national bourgeoisie, whose leader was Nehru.'[32] Formerly, said the new analysis, some sections of the bourgeoisie needed mass support and, therefore, fell in behind the national movement. This situation had ended since the bourgeoisie as a whole now received support directly from Anglo-American imperialism.[33] One of the 'basic reformist deviations' of the previous line had been the 'failure to identify the bourgeoisie with the Congress leaders'.[34] This mistake was rectified in December 1947: the Government represented 'the class interests of the national bourgeoisie, the industrial bourgeoisie. Gandhi, Nehru and Patel all represent the interests of the Indian capitalist class'.[35]

The Indian National Congress

The Congress, therefore, was attacked root and branch. While Nehru claimed neutrality in the Cold War, for the new CPI leadership, he, his party, his government and all its works were firmly ensconced in the camp of Anglo-American imperialism.[36] Support for the Congress government after 1947 had been 'opportunist and wrong'. In fact, at the time of the Cabinet Mission, the Congress leadership 'representing the interests of the capitalist class ... betrayed the revolutionary movement at a time when it was on the point of overthrowing the imperialist order'.[37] The attempt to draw distinctions within the Congress leadership, between Right and Left, progressive and reactionary, were merely 'opportunist illusions'.[38] Nehru was just as much an enemy as the other Congress leaders. Furthermore, '[i]f the CPI itself suffers from illusions about bourgeois leadership, the revolution will be betrayed'.[39]

The Revolution

The Joshi line had culminated in the proposition of a united front with the Congress in order to further and complete the national revolution. With the new line, no such front was now possible.

> The Communist Party must give up the former conception of national unity ... in which Congress was virtually the main basis of such a unity.[40]

Instead, the Party should strive for a new 'Democratic Front' consisting of the Left parties, and of the Left inside Congress. The core of this front would have to be the CPI itself.[41] The object of the front was no longer national consolidation and the building of a new India on the basis of independence. It was 'an agrarian and democratic revolution'— an attempt to complete the bourgeois revolution and move on to the next stage in one jump.[42] The nature of that jump was indicated at the Party's Second Congress in 1948:

> The post-war revolutionary epoch has brought the colonies to the path
> of armed struggle against the imperialists and their allies. So powerful are
> these struggles ... that the achievement at one stroke of people's democracy
> (as in the countries of Eastern Europe) becomes an immediate obtainable
> objective.[43]

Armed peasant revolt was already underway in Telangana against the
Nizam of Hyderabad who was holding out against a union with India.[44]
The new CPI leadership believed that a rural war, pitching poor peasants
against the rich, could be linked up with insurrectionary general strikes
in the cities. In fact, as it turned out, Ranadive had a tendency to concentrate on the latter rather than the former.[45] Encouraging those who may
have had doubts, the CC declared, 'The strength of the Left forces today
should not be underestimated.'[46]

Attempts to implement the Ranadive line, however, left the Party
in tatters. Rather than planned urban and rural revolts, there occurred
'unorganized and sporadic outbursts of desperate violence', which mixed
guerrilla warfare, individual terrorism and arson together in equal parts.[47]
CPI member Anil Rajimwale recounted later:

> A call for nationwide railway strike was given for March 9, 1949,
> that was supposed to bring the country to a halt and begin armed
> insurrection all over the country. But this strike failed totally. Not a single
> train stopped. The ordinary party members were held responsible for
> this failure and they were labelled 'cowards'. Thousands of them were
> suspended and expelled from the party. Many others left or died or were
> hanged and killed by the police.[48]

The Indian government responded with repression on a state-by-state
basis. Arrests, office closures and newspaper bans rained down on the
communists. The leadership went underground. It has been estimated
that Party membership fell from 90,000 to 9,000 during this period.[49]

The Andhra Line: 1950–51

Discontent with the Ranadive line emerged, most forcefully expressed by
the CPI leadership in Andhra state. Their complaint, however, was not so
much that the Ranadive leadership was pursuing adventurist tactics, but

rather, that it was pursuing the wrong kind of adventurist tactics. In the 'Andhra Letter' of June 1948, they had declared:

> Our revolution in many respects differs from the classical Russian revolution; but to a great extent [is] similar to that of [the] Chinese revolution.

It, therefore, required 'the dogged resistance and prolonged civil war in the form of an agrarian revolution culminating in the capture of political power by [the] democratic front'.[50] This was radically different from Ranadive's vision of socialist revolution through predominantly urban insurrection. The next stage of the revolution, the Andhra leaders said, was 'the new democratic stage', and for this *all* of the peasants, rich and poor, should be united.[51]

Ranadive refuted the Andhra critique in December 1948 with some vigour. He sarcastically summarised their argument: the rich peasants should be fought only when proletarian revolution is on the agenda; proletarian revolution is only on the agenda when the bourgeoisie is in power; since India is still a 'semi-colony', the bourgeoisie is not in power; proletarian revolution is not on the agenda, so the rich peasants should not be fought.[52] For the Andhra leaders, he said, 'only the big bourgeoisie have gone collaborationist'—therefore, the rest of the country could unite against them and imperialism. 'Guerrilla warfare against the Nehru government in cooperation with rich peasants,' he declared, '—can you beat it? … Can anything be more illusory than this?'[53] Ranadive also rejected Andhra's promotion of the Chinese model:

> [T]he CPI has accepted Marx, Engels, Lenin and Stalin as the authoritative sources of Marxism. It has not discovered new sources of Marxism beyond these … some of Mao's formulations are such that no communist party can accept them.[54]

But once again, external forces were to come to the aid of the Indian communist opposition.

The international communist movement was dominated at this point by the twin examples of the successful Soviet state and the recent triumph of the Chinese Communist Party. Given Chinese conditions before 1949, it was believed that the experiences of the Chinese communists would provide useful lessons, if not a model, for communists in the developing countries. At this stage at least, an informal 'division of labour' within the world movement seems to have been agreed upon between the Soviet and

Chinese parties in which communists in the colonies, 'semi-colonies' and ex-colonies would receive their advice from Beijing.

The Chinese seized on the task with a will, beginning at the Asian and Australasian Trade Union Delegates' Meeting in Beijing in November 1949. The opening address was given by Liu Shaoqi, Vice-Chairman of the People's Republic. With little ado, he told the delegates that the Chinese road to liberation was the road 'that the peoples of many colonial and semi-colonial areas should traverse in their struggle for national independence and people's democracy'. It was 'impossible' for them to avoid that road: 'It will be wrong if they do so.'[55] Liu clearly included India in this scheme as he listed it among a number of current national liberation struggles.[56]

According to Liu, the Chinese road had three elements. The first was the unity of all classes (under 'working class hegemony') in a broad united front against imperialism. That front included 'not only workers and peasants but also petty bourgeois elements, the broad masses of intellectuals and members of the national capitalist class'. Despite the latter's weakness as an ally, it was 'opposed to imperialism at [a] certain period and in [a] certain degree'. Liu drew no distinction between rich and poor peasants.[57] The second element was the leadership of the united front by the working class, exercised through the Communist Party. The third element was the armed struggle. There must, he said, 'be a Communist-led, strong and combat-capable national liberation army'. He continued:

> The existence and development of the working class organization and the national united front follow closely the existence and development of armed struggle. This is an unavoidable road that the people of the colonial and semi-colonial areas must take in their fight for independence and liberation.[58]

The armed struggle would be 'the principal form of the fight for liberation' and it would take place in the countryside amongst the peasantry. Legal and illegal struggles could take place in the cities, but the agrarian war would set the pace.[59]

Liu's speech, widely reported in the communist press, with its call for unity against imperialism, armed struggle and an emphasis on rural action, clearly accorded closely with the Andhra line in India. Hot on its heels came a January 1950 editorial in the Cominform paper, *For a Lasting Peace, For a People's Democracy!*, surveying the national liberation movement in the colonial and dependent countries.[60] The editorial reiterated the post-Joshi position that 'sham independence was bestowed on India ... . British imperialism remains, and octopus-like, grips Indian in its bloody tentacles'. Echoing Liu Shaoqi, the editorial advised Indian communists to draw on 'the experience of the National Liberation movement in China' and 'strengthen the alliance of the working class with all the peasantry ... . To unite all classes, parties, groups and organisations willing to defend the national independence and freedom of India'. The formation of 'people's liberation armies under the leadership of the communist party' remained 'A decisive condition', 'when the necessary international conditions allow for it'.[61]

Implicitly attacked by the two pillars of the international communist movement, the Ranadive leadership of the CPI—together with its 'Russian model' of insurrection and its hostility to the rich peasants—could not survive. At a CC meeting in May 1950, Ranadive was removed as General Secretary and replaced by C. Rajeshwara Rao, a leading member of the Andhra group. Other Andhra leaders moved into the Party's positions of authority.

The new leadership encapsulated the new line in a CC letter released on 1 June 1950. It asserted that under the previous regime, the Party was 'sunk in the mire of left-sectarianism, having run its full course in its reckless adventurist actions'. Help, however, had been at hand:

> [T]he entire party wakes up to the ringing calls of the Cominform bureau [editorial] and the Peking [Trade Union] conference to correct the political line and march forward.[62]

In terms of our previous categories—India and Imperialism, the Bourgeoisie and the Congress—there was little new in the Andhra approach. India remained in a 'sham' independence; the national bourgeoisie and the rich peasants were welcomed back into the united front and the Congress was still a dangerous enemy. While much of the old analysis was retained, the emphasis in strategy and tactics was changed. The new leaders endorsed 'the perspective of [the] Chinese path' enthusiastically: 'armed resistance in the rural areas giving rise to liberated areas leading to a final capture of power'.[63] Mohit Sen aptly summarises the Andhra line:

> Looking back on it now, it can only be assessed as a line of continuing the previous disastrous sectarian and adventurist approach but in a new form. The 'Chinese' model was to replace the 'Russian' model. It was Naxalism before the Naxalites.[64]

The 1951 Line: 1951–56

In line with its support for armed rural revolt, the Andhra leadership kept up its support for the Telangana peasant insurgency against the Nizam of Hyderabad. This continued even after the Indian government had ousted the Nizam in a 'police action' in late 1948. After that, the insurgents and the Indian authorities confronted each other face-to-face. A section of the CPI leadership in Andhra, including the insurgent leader Ravi Narayan Reddy, argued that the armed struggle should be called off, the Indian government should be supported and democratic demands should be raised for the erstwhile rebels. They were denounced by the CPI leadership as cowards and collaborators.[65]

Elsewhere, P. C. Joshi kept up his criticism of Party policy from outside its ranks. There was no revolutionary situation in India, he said, certainly not one that was suitable for armed struggle. The Party should return to its policy of an alliance with the Congress.[66] More telling perhaps were criticisms of Party policy by its trade union leaders, especially from Shripad Amrit Dange, an important leader of the All-India Trade Union Congress (AITUC). Together with Ajoy Ghosh and S. V. Ghate, he wrote a critique of Party policy in September 1950. It was officially entitled 'A Note on the Present Situation in Our Party'. But since each of the authors' 'underground [code] names' began with the letter 'P' it was (and is) known as the 'Three Ps Document'.

The Three Ps did not question the Andhra leadership's characterisation of either the nature or method of the revolution in India. That revolution, they agreed, would be a 'people's democratic revolution in a colonial country' against an 'imperialist-feudal regime'. Furthermore, 'the revolution will develop along the path of China'.[67] But that agreement was more for form's sake than for anything else. According to the Three Ps, the 'new' (Andhra) line was just a variant of the old (Ranadive) line which had brought havoc and disaster to the Party:

> The old leadership talked about the 'Russian way', the new leadership talks about [the] 'Chinese way'. The old leadership talked about 'revolutionary upsurge', the new leadership talks about 'civil war' … . Neither bothered to understand and analyse the situation in our own country.[68]

As a result:

> [T]he inner party crisis … remains as deep as ever and is deepening every day. Torn by dissension, threatened with splits, the party stands paralysed.[69]

As might be expected from leaders of the urban trade union movement, the Three Ps called upon the leadership to refocus its attention on India's workers. While not denying 'the decisive role that agrarian struggles will play', they pointed out that 'the working class in India has to play a big role in the development of the liberation struggle'. They also urged the Party to turn its attention to 'winning over the lakhs and lakhs who were getting disillusioned with the Congress but were not prepared to leave it'.[70]

Despite their due acknowledgement of the need for 'partisans', 'liberated areas' and 'the path of China',[71] the most telling point made by the Three Ps against the Andhra leadership was that 'according to the central committee the main and almost exclusive weapon … for every task that faces the party and the movement is the weapon of guerrilla struggle'.[72] The CC believed that a 'civil war' had started in June 1947 (at the time of the Mountbatten Award) and that now 'the situation is ripe for the smashing of the ruling class by armed action of the people'.[73] This, according to the Three Ps, was a grossly distorted assessment of the real Indian situation.

Support from outside India for a review of the CPI's line was not long in coming. The British Party leadership wrote in October 1950 that there was 'paralysis' in the CPI because it had failed to understand the Cominform's advice correctly. Apparently, despite the Cominform's endorsement of the Chinese road for India, and that of 'liberation armies' being a 'decisive condition' for victory, armed struggle in India was not, in fact, an *immediate* prospect. The Party should have instead used all legal avenues of struggle, including elections.[74] Yet another helpful letter from Dutt arrived in December saying the same thing. In fact, Dutt went a little further, stressing 'the positive contribution to world politics of the Nehru government … . The CPI was advised to give qualified support to Nehru'.[75]

Battered from within and without, the hapless CC met shortly after this and declared the existence of 'the gravest crisis in the history of our party, a crisis created by our inability to resolve the sharp political differences that have arisen in our party'. There was, said the CC, only one solution:

> It was realised that only the help of brother parties and the holding of a party congress could lead to the evolution of a unified political line.[76]

On this occasion, the CPI leaders went right to the top. Arrangements were made for direct discussions in Moscow, with the Soviet Party leadership itself.[77] Rajeshwara Rao and Basava Punnaiah (representing the Andhra-line leadership), together with Ajoy Ghosh and S. A. Dange (representing the opposition), went to Moscow in February 1951. The first meetings were conducted with G. M. Malenkov, M. A. Suslov and P. F. Yudin.[78] Rao set out the Indian revolution in three stages: widespread partisan action, creation of liberated areas (e.g., Telangana) and liberation of the whole of India. The agrarian revolution had started. 'It would be wrong', he said, 'to think that we need to first build a party and a democratic front and then begin the armed struggle.' Ghosh, while acknowledging the importance of armed struggle, argued that conditions for it in India 'have not yet matured'. Meanwhile, he said, the leadership was so obsessed with rural warfare that it ignored opportunities in the working class and in the people's disenchantment with the Nehru government. Dange flatly denounced the emphasis on armed struggle as 'political adventurism'. India was neither 'in the grip of fascist style terror', nor were the conditions for civil war present. Rao retorted: 'Dange and Ghosh oppose the armed struggle. This is a reformist path.'

Stalin joined in on 9 February.[79] In line with the CPI leadership and the 'Chinese path', he declared, 'We do not consider that India stands before the socialist revolution.' It was in the midst of 'the bourgeois-democratic revolution or the first stage of the people's democratic revolution'. Thus, the object was to unite with all of the peasantry and with the national bourgeoisie. Neither the rich peasants nor the national bourgeoisie should be expropriated. Stalin then went into a long, rambling and confused speech on what had by then become the main issue of division: the question of armed struggle. He noted that the particular conditions of China's liberation war were forced upon them, and that the Chinese had to have a supportive rear area, in the shape of the USSR.[80] But '[t]he possibility of successful partisan war is lesser for you than in China'. On the other hand: 'Do you need partisan war? Indubitably you do.' So the struggle in Telangana had to be supported. 'It is the first sprouts of civil war. But one does not need to rely on partisan war alone.'

I would suggest that all sides were able to come out of these meetings with a warm feeling of support from the Communist Party of the Soviet Union (CPSU), except perhaps for Dange and his total rejection of armed struggle. This was evident only days later, when Dange and Ghosh wrote on armed struggle, '[D]ifferences continue to exist between the four of us, and we differently understand the formulations of Comrade Stalin.'[81] Any ambiguity from the Soviet side could be assuaged by Stalin's parting remark, 'I have given you no instructions, this is advice.' Nevertheless, that advice appeared to include bringing the Telangana struggle to an end and taking part in elections.[82] A. K. Gopalan, on behalf of the CC, said on 23 October 1951, '[T]he central committee as well as the Andhra committee have decided to advise the Telangana peasantry and the fighting partisans to stop all partisan actions to mobilise the entire people for an effective participation in the ensuing general election to rout the Congress at the polls.'[83]

Returning to India, the CPI leaders drafted new Party documents which attempted to reflect the advice from abroad. In May 1951, these were approved by the CC. Rajeshwara Rao was replaced as the general secretary by Ajoy Ghosh. An All-India Party Conference approved a new programme, statement of policy and tactical line in October.

India and Imperialism

India remained a 'dependent and semi-colonial country'—a 'colonial set-up' dominated by British imperialism. There had been 'no real transfer of power or transition from a colonial state to a sovereign Indian state' in 1947. Likewise, the Indian government was 'tied to the chariot wheel of British capital'. In this situation, India could not advance economically, even to the point of building a capitalist economy. The task therefore remained that of 1947: the fight for national liberation.[84]

The Indian Bourgeoisie

The Indian government was the direct representative of the ruling class—and therefore of the 'big' bourgeoisie, the feudal landlords and of British capital. The 1951 Programme declared, 'Even the industrialists, manufacturers and traders are hit by the policies of this government which is totally in the grip of monopoly financiers, landlords and princes and their British advisers, working behind the screen.'[85]

It did not, however, represent the 'national' bourgeoisie, which was a part of the all-class alliance for the national (or people's) democratic revolution.[86] Stalin had told the CPI leaders in Moscow that the national bourgeoisie had not 'finally joined hands with imperialism'. When asked if the national bourgeoisie would be a part of the united front, Stalin had replied, 'Yes, you are right.'[87] Ghosh declared, 'The Nehru Government cannot be called a government of the national bourgeoisie.'[88]

The Indian National Congress

The Congress represented two forces: one, the big landlords and the princes and the other, the big bourgeoisie, collaborating with British imperialism. The Congress could not promote national development, or strengthen the economy, or defend national independence. Further, to remain in power, the Congress government 'suppresses *all* civil liberties of the people, outlaws political parties and groups, bans trade unions and other people's organisations, imprisons thousands of workers, peasants, students, men and women in prisons and concentration camps'. It presided over 'a police state'.[89] The Party, therefore, approached the 1951–52 election on an anti-Congress platform.[90]

The Revolution

Since nothing much had happened in 1947, the Indian revolution, according to Ghosh, 'is an anti-feudal and anti-imperialist revolution. It is a People's Democratic Revolution of the first stage as in China'.[91] But despite the nod in the direction of the Chinese path, the 1951 line marked the beginning of the abandonment by the CPI of the strategy of armed struggle. While maintaining the fiction that armed struggle was a strategy for the future, the new line admitted that popular discontent was not at such a pitch as to make it a possibility in the present. India was neither on the eve of armed insurrection, nor in the midst of civil war.[92] The Party would, in the future, contest elections.[93]

Elections for India's first Lok Sabha were held from October 1951 to February 1952. The CPI won three and a half million votes and, together with its allies, gained 23 seats in the new assembly, becoming the second largest party. This was a creditable result, given the situation in the Party before the 1951 Congress. The Party's mood, according to Mohit Sen, was 'upbeat' on the basis of these results.[94] However, it is well to remember that the Congress won over 47 million votes, nearly 45 per cent of the electorate and 364 seats.[95] Nevertheless, the CPI convinced itself that the results were a resounding defeat for Congress. The CC believed that before the election 'Disillusionment with the Congress was universal. Hatred against the Congress was mounting … . More and more masses were ranging themselves against the Congress'. In the election itself:

> The Congress has suffered the biggest political and moral defeat in its entire history … its mass base is cracking up—and cracking up rapidly all over the country.[96]

As the next two elections were to show, this simply was not the case. The Party's call for 'all democratic parties, organisations, groups and individuals who are genuinely interested in defeating the Congress Party and its Anglo-American allies' fell on deaf ears.[97]

This was not the only area in which the 1951 line collided with reality. At the Party's Third Congress (December 1953–January 1954), at which the 1951 documents were formally accepted, the position was maintained that Congress was 'controlled by landlords and monopolists collaborating with imperialism'. It was, therefore, opposed to the national bourgeoisie.[98] The First Five Year Plan had been 'prepared in collaboration with imperialism' and from it 'the foreign and Indian monopolists have reaped colossal profits'.[99] Yet by this stage, given the economic initiatives undertaken by the Indian state, it was clear that the Congress leadership was not the pawn of any other social force. It was an independent force, gathered around the state and its interests. As Chandra puts it:

> By no stretch of the imagination could the Nehru Government be said to be opposed to industrialisation or to independent capitalist development or to the protection of the internal market from foreign competition or the creator of a police state or being subservient to British imperialism.[100]

The Party's international stance was confronted by the decline of Britain and the rise of the US on the one hand, and by Nehru's 'progressive' (non-aligned or anti-American) foreign policy on the other. Was India still in the clutches of British imperialism, or was this changing? At the Third

Congress, Ghosh attempted to bestride both positions: 'We hope to win full freedom from the British but we have also to defend our existing freedom from the increasing menace of the United States.'[101] A division arose between those who considered Britain or the US as the greatest danger. This masked a deeper division over strategy. The erstwhile 'Andhra' leaders regarded Britain as the main enemy. Since they continued to believe that the Congress was a puppet of British imperialism, they were able to advocate mass struggle against Congress and all its works. Those who considered the US to be the main enemy (the '1951' leaders and those to their right) really could not portray the Nehru government as subservient to Washington. They were, therefore, on the road to some kind of co-operation with the Congress, against the main imperialist enemy.[102]

From this point, the main division within the CPI revolved around the Party's relationship with the Congress. Everything else—imperialism, the bourgeoisie, the revolution—was refracted through the prism of that relationship. There emerged a broad divide between Leftists, who remained rigorously anti-Congress (a common thread in the Ranadive, Andhra and 1951 lines) and Rightists, who wanted change (even perhaps a return to the Joshi line).

Right Advance: 1956–61

The Rightist position was aided by events in the Soviet Union. The Twentieth Congress of the CPSU had not only accepted a denunciation of the personality cult around Stalin, but had also embraced the possibility of non-capitalist development and a peaceful transition to socialism in the developing countries.[103] This helped the Right in its strategic considerations and enabled it to distance itself from Soviet policy by taking a more critical attitude towards Stalin.[104] However, events in Moscow (and, for that matter, in Beijing) were only one influence on the Indian Party—they were not the cause of its debates.[105] On their side, the Soviet leadership was, in line with their more positive attitude towards Nehru's government, becoming a great deal more circumspect in the aid (both political and material) that they afforded to the CPI. When CPSU Secretary Khrushchev and Premier Bulganin visited India in late 1955, they had little if any contact with the Indian Party. Nehru quizzed them about the extent of Moscow's aid to the CPI (it was, after all, only a few years since the Soviets had been advising the Indian comrades to make armed rural revolution):

> Mr Khrushchev said on his word of honour that they (the Communist Party of the Soviet Union) had no connection with the Indian Communist Party. They knew few Communist leaders in India … . Mr Khrushchev said that the Prime Minister of India had referred to finance coming to the Communist Party from outside. He did not know where it came from.[106]

In these years, there was a steady advance of Rightist ideas in the Party. Many of the debates were inconclusive and produced resolutions that were essentially Left/Right compromises, since there remained considerable support for the Ranadive/Andhra/1951 positions. But the trend was clearly towards a realignment of the Party's attitude towards the Congress.

India and Imperialism

India was no longer a colonial or 'semi-colonial' country. The Fourth Congress in 1956 spoke of 'India's newly won independence and sovereignty'. On this basis, the CC had declared in 1955 that there could be 'a limited advance in the direction of economic development of the country'. To this end, the Party supported the proposals of the Second Five Year Plan (especially in the area of heavy industry). This brought Indian capitalism into conflict with foreign capital.[107]

The Party also discovered very positive elements in the Congress government's foreign policy. Nehru was no longer a puppet of British and/or US imperialism. The government's 'non-alignment' had previously been seen as aiding imperialism: 'Many leaders of the Communist movement suffered from this concept in the past', said a resolution of the Fourth Congress. Now, however, it was regarded 'as a sentinel for peace … Neutrality expresses the sentiment of the masses for maintenance of their national freedom'.[108] The Party now welcomed the government's stand against war and military pacts and the fact that it was 'resisting imperialist pressure and blackmail against India'. At the Fifth Congress in 1958, it was resolved that '[t]he Communist Party supports the foreign policy of the Indian government and consistently works for strengthening it'.[109]

The Indian Bourgeoisie

The Party began to express some support and sympathy for Indian capitalists, 'now faced with fierce competition from imperialist quarters', while at home '[f]eudal remnants in agriculture prevent the expansion of the internal market'. The bourgeoisie had moved away from 'the earlier abject dependence on the British and American imperialists'.[110] According to Ghosh, they were now 'keen to build up an independent capitalist economy and develop India industrially'.[111] The Fourth Congress noted the conflict between imperialism and feudalism on the one hand and 'the entire Indian people, including the national bourgeoisie' on the other. For that reason, the government's foreign policy was also in the interests of the national bourgeoisie.[112] The latter, therefore, favoured 'national democratic tasks' and remained in the 'national democratic front'.[113] But this only applied to those parts of the bourgeoisie 'unconnected with imperialist circles' (Ghosh) or the 'handful of monopolist reactionaries' (Sixth Congress).[114] These elements—about which Ghosh admitted 'there is a lot of confusion in our Party'—were characterised as 'a reactionary force in our economic, social and political life'.[115]

The Indian National Congress

The nature of the Second Five Year Plan and the Indian government's stated intention to create a 'socialist' society further shifted the CPI's attitude towards the Congress. The CC was also coming to terms with the fact that, despite earlier communist predictions, the Congress was not breaking up.[116] While the Fourth Congress still regarded the Congress Government as '[a] government of the bourgeoisie and the landlords, in which the former is the leading force', two years later the Party resolved that:

> The Congress is the organ of the national bourgeoisie *as a whole* ... it would be a big mistake to *equate* the Congress with parties of right reaction. Many of the declared policies of the Congress and some of [its] measures are, in today's context, *progressive*.[117]

There were 'a vast number of democratic [i.e., Leftist] elements ... inside and under the influence of the Congress' who 'are becoming increasingly critical of the anti-people policies of the government'. The CPI would, therefore, 'strive to organise common activity with Congressmen and [the] masses under Congress influence'.[118] The Party's approach had to be one which did not 'repel honest congressmen but draw them towards unity'. Ghosh warned the Sixth Congress against the 'deep-rooted sectarianism' that infected '[m]ost of our cadres and also leaders'. He continued: 'Even when opposing and fighting policies of the Congress and Government concentrate fire wherever possible on the Rightist elements.'[119]

This was not to imply (at least at this stage) that there could be a united front between the CPI and the Congress. The relationship between the two parties would be one of 'unity and struggle'.[120] But this might change—in any case, 'it should not be concluded that the democratic front will be an anticongress front'.[121]

The Revolution

In 1955, the CPI still believed that:

> Allied with landlords and compromising with imperialism, the Indian bourgeoisie cannot complete the bourgeois-democratic tasks that our country has to fulfil in the present stage.[122]

Oblivious to the fact that while the bourgeoisie was not carrying out these tasks (establishment of independence, consolidation of the national economy, construction of infrastructure, construction of democratic institutions), the Congress state certainly was, the CC declared that a 'People's Democratic Revolution' and a 'People's Democracy' were still needed. In the meantime, however, the Party would support '[e]very step that is taken by the government for strengthening national freedom and [the] national economy, against imperialist, feudal and monopoly interests'. The Second Five Year Plan in particular was singled out for support.[123]

Armed insurrection and a war of liberation were explicitly abandoned by the CPI from 1956 onwards. In the Party's comments on the CPSU Twentieth Congress, it was noted that, 'The CPSU Congress also proclaimed the possibility of peaceful transition to socialism.' In countries like India or Indonesia, said the CPI:

[I]n certain circumstances, the transition to the first stage of people's democracy may ... be effected in a peaceful way—without civil war ... . If such [a] transition is a possibility, then the Communist Party in every country strives to turn this into a reality.[124]

The Amritsar Congress, two years later, reaffirmed the possibility of peaceful transition. It also abandoned the 'dictatorship of the proletariat' and guaranteed the existence of civil liberties and political opposition under socialism.[125]

Despite what appeared on the surface to be a smooth move to the Right in its policy outlook, the CPI remained divided, fundamentally around the Party's attitude towards the Congress and its government. A 1961 pamphlet on land reform expressed a conciliatory attitude to the central Congress government on the question, shifting most of the blame for inaction to the states. Congress is accused of 'not faithfully sticking to its own recommendations'.[126] But on the question of its attitude towards India's workers, Dange accused it of being 'a hard-boiled Tory government, covered up with fine phrases about non-violence, peace, welfare of the working people and so on'.[127] The following year, Bupesh Gupta denounced Congress for 'the plethora of concessions which the Congress Government has showered upon foreign monopolies and to which it is ever ready to add more'.[128]

Once again, the divisions within the Indian Party were exacerbated by events outside India, culminating in a full-blown split in 1964.

The first of these events was the border dispute between India and China. This began with a number of skirmishes over territory in the autumn of 1959 and ended up in a short but bloody border war between the two countries in October 1962. Mohit Sen believes that it was this that 'led to a split in the party in 1964'.[129] By and large, the CPI leadership majority (the Right) supported the Indian government in this dispute. The Left minority argued that the government was being pushed into an anti-China direction by the US—and that the Party should stand with China against the Government.[130] The majority position prevailed. Sen comments:

The CPI had at long last taken a stand in support of the nation ... it went against all that the Communists reared in the Stalinist school had been taught to believe.[131]

The Left minority, some of whom had been rounded up by the police for their pro-China views, bided their time.

The second event was the increasingly public split between the Communist Parties of the Soviet Union and China. The leadership majority generally supported the Soviet side in this dispute (perhaps in reaction to many years of being urged to follow 'the Chinese example'). As a result, the CPI was robustly denounced by the Chinese in late 1962, alongside Nehru, the Indian bourgeoisie and the last two Congresses (the Twentieth and Twenty-first) of the CPSU.

While acknowledging the relative importance of these external events, it would not be correct to conclude that the looming split in the CPI simply reflected a division into 'pro-Soviet' and 'pro-Chinese' wings. As E. M. S. Namboodiripad (general secretary after Ghosh's death in January 1962 and—eventually—a protagonist of the Left) put it:

> The government, the bourgeois press—all took a hand in creating the image of the CPI being split into two—'nationalist' vs 'internationalist', 'pro-Chinese' vs 'pro-Soviet', etc. A section of the Party itself began to believe it; what is more a section within the leadership participated in this campaign.[132]

Mohit Sen makes it clear that the divisions between majority and minority had their origins in the divisions between the Ranadive/Andhra/1951 perspective and the views of the Right. The latter considered India to be independent and democratic. Social transformation would come about democratically and the Party's relationship with the Congress should be one of 'unity and struggle'. The Left believed that India was unfree, that the revolution would necessarily involve armed struggle and that the Congress was the chief party of counter-revolution which had to be destroyed.[133]

The split came at a meeting of the Party's National Council (NC) in April 1964 when the minority walked out. In July of that year, they began the process that led to the formation of the Communist Party of India–Marxist (CPI-M).

After the Split

The CPI's attitude to the Congress continued to be somewhat confused for some years after the split. The Congress was now regarded certainly as an *Indian* phenomenon and certainly not the creature of either foreign or 'compradore' imperialism. But it remained dominated by 'the national bourgeoisie as a whole, which upholds and develops capitalist relations of production, distribution and exchange'.[134] Despite this, the desired national democratic front was not an anti-Congress project—in fact, the progressive forces within the Congress would play a vital role in its formation.[135]

The first Party Congress after the split (the Seventh, in Bombay in 1964) declared its intention 'to build the national democratic front and complete the national democratic revolution in India'.[136] The concept of 'people's democracy'—something more like socialism than national democracy—had disappeared. For the national democratic revolution, 'the vast mass following of the Congress and the progressive section of the Congress at various levels [must] take their place'. The Party, therefore, pledged itself to 'make ceaseless efforts' to unite with those forces.[137] The Party Programme that resulted from the December 1964 Congress readjusted the CPI's view of India's post-colonial history. Henceforward, the bourgeoisie was regarded as a whole—though with significant divisions within it. Congress remained the tool of the bourgeoisie. But both Congress and the capitalists—after some early weakness towards British and US imperialism—had pursued a policy of independent capitalist development for India. This had led to policies of state intervention and state control, which were anti-imperialist in their nature.[138] The state sector became 'an instrument of building [an] independent national economy and of weakening the grip of foreign monopoly capital and to a certain extent the Indian monopolies'. This, however, was not socialism. Capitalism remained 'private capitalism in the private sector and state capitalism in the state sector.'[139]

Amarjit Kaur, during the Emergency the general secretary of the All-India Students' Federation in Delhi and today a member of the CPI National Council told the author:

> If you look at the period before Indira Gandhi, of development in heavy industry, in basic industry, mining extraction and the industry building on this, infrastructural development, even the creating of new resource development, you can't call the total economy socialistic. It had both components. The public sector then gave a boost to the private sector, so it became a mixed economy.[140]

But these policies did lead to the major division within the bourgeoisie—between the big monopolists and the rest. The former (which included the Tata and Birla groups, the five largest banks and other 'industrial, banking and marketing companies') were enriching themselves 'at the expense of the people and the broader sections of the national bourgeoisie to the detriment of the county's economic independence'.[141] Therefore, there was division and struggle within the bourgeoisie. This was reflected in the Congress through the manifestation of progressive and reactionary trends.[142] The monopolists 'seek to consolidate the right reactionary forces in the country to bolster up the right-wing in the ruling party'.[143]

The Party's attitude towards the Congress was not a stable one. When Congress governments took pro-business decisions or when they suffered electoral setbacks, 'anti-Congressism' still tended to break out within the Party.[144] The Party then detected a 'rightist consolidation inside the Congress today'.[145] On a more positive note, this was:

> ... accentuating the *political differentiation* within the Congress and the national bourgeoisie, between the reactionary pro-monopoly sections on the one hand and the democratic anti-monopolist sections on the other.[146]

When Indira Gandhi became the prime minister in 1966 and before the Congress split of 1969, the Party's position could be summarised in the following way:

- India was an independent, capitalist economy, struggling in a world dominated by (mostly US) imperialism. It was neither a colony, nor a 'semi-colony', nor (in more contemporary 1960s parlance) a 'neo-colony'. The main enemy now was not foreign imperialism but India's own 'big monopolies'.
- For social advance, India required a national democratic revolution, not a socialist one, which would come later. (Such a revolution could be interpreted as the completion of the bourgeois revolution in India.) This would include: 'complete independence of our country, the emancipation of the peasants from the oppression of the feudals, improvement in the life of all working people ... a major forward stride in our agriculture, a major forward stride in our national industry ... and the cultural advancement of our country.'[147]
- The Indian bourgeoisie controlled both the state and the Congress. It was split between the 'Big Monopolies' and patriotic capitalists. The former supported imperialism. The latter supported India's independence, its progressive foreign policy and the completion of the national democratic revolution.
- The Congress, reflecting the split in the bourgeoisie (which controlled it), was also split. The Right reflected the interests of the

monopolies, while the Left reflected those of the patriotic bourgeoisie. The Congress Left was for the completion of the national democratic revolution—largely manifested in the extension of the state-owned and state-directed economy.

- The national democratic revolution (as will be clear from the above), which began in 1947, had yet to be completed. Only then could the struggle for socialism (as distinct from propaganda for it) commence in earnest.

However, before we proceed, it is well to note once again that no section of the bourgeoisie controlled the Congress. By now, the Congress was well integrated with the Indian state and its prime directive was the defence and extension of the power of that state. The main division within it revolved around how best to do that. The bourgeois revolution (or 'national democratic revolution') in India had indeed begun in 1947. It was led by the Congress and continued by the Congress/State (other examples of states initiating bourgeois revolutions are referred to in the Introduction). It did need to be completed—but, as we shall see, time was running short for it to be completed in the way that the CPI envisaged.

The problem for the CPI—and they were by no means alone on the Left in this respect—was that, by the mid-1960s, the very nature of national states, of bourgeoisies ('national' and otherwise) and of bourgeois and socialist revolutions was (imperceptibly perhaps) beginning to change. Globalisation—the coming into being of an international trading and manufacturing system, forcing aside political ('national') barriers—was beginning to change the very nature of the relationship of capitalists to national states.[148] Since the First World War at least, capital and the national state had been, in most places (and especially in the developing countries), in lockstep on the march to national development. But globalisation, by forcing capital to 'nestle everywhere, settle everywhere, establish connexions everywhere' (as Marx, somewhat prematurely, put it in 1848),[149] was prising their interests apart. What was good for USA (or India) was no longer necessarily good for General Motors (or Tata). The completion of the bourgeois revolution could not now mean simply the consolidation of a national economic unit. Globalisation was making self-contained units of that type obsolete. The bourgeoisie had to free itself, in India as elsewhere, from the integuments of national control and oversight. Only then could the bourgeois revolution be completed. The emerging division within the Indian bourgeoisie was one between the sector that was able and felt forced to 'nestle everywhere' and the sector—whether by inclination, immovable assets or, more often, state ownership or control—that could not. The division within the Congress reflected this—a division between those who saw opportunities for India in a global, export-oriented economy ('neo-liberalism' in modern parlance) and those who preferred to stick with state control. The CPI believed that the latter represented progress, the Left and the national democratic revolution, and lined itself up accordingly.

The way in which these incipient changes on a global scale were manifested in India should become clearer in the next chapter.

Notes

1. Puran Chand Joshi, *A Free Happy India: Election Policy of Indian Communists* (Bombay: People's Publishing House, 1944), 3–4.
2. Joshi, *Free Happy India*, 4.
3. Central Committee CPI, 'Political Resolution: The Mountbatten Award and After', in *Documents of the Communist Movement in India. Volume 5: 1944–1948*, ed. Jyoti Basu et al. (Calcutta: National Book Agency, 1997), 356–59.
4. CPI, 'Onward to Tasks Ahead' (15 August 1947), in *Documents of the Communist Movement in India. Volume 5: 1944–1948*, ed. Jyoti Basu et al. (Calcutta: National Book Agency, 1997), 401–2, 410.
5. See Bipan Chandra, 'A Strategy in Crisis: The CPI Debate 1955–1956', *Studies in History* III no. 1 & 2 (1981): 387–96.
6. Chandra points out that 'at no stage did the Party or its guiding star, R. Palme Dutt [a leader of the Communist Party in Britain and its expert on Indian affairs], make a concrete analysis of the nature or structure of the Indian capitalist class' (Bipan Chandra, 'P. C. Joshi: A Political Journey', *Mainstream* XLVI, no. 1 (2007), www.mainstreamweekly.net/article503.html). According to the CPI leader S. A. Dange, in an interview published in 1992, 'all through the career of the Communist Party they never understood the national bourgeoisie ... they see a class. For them the bourgeoisie everywhere is [the] same' (Bipan Chandra, 'S.A. Dange—An Interview' in *Indian Communism: Life and Work of S.A. Dange*, ed. Mohit Sen [New Delhi: Patriot Publishers, 1992], 58).
7. Joseph Stalin, *Marxism and the National Question* (Moscow: Foreign Languages Publishing House, 1945 [1913]), 21 and 19.
8. R. Palme Dutt, 'A New Chapter in Divide and Rule' (July 1946), in *Documents of the Communist Movement in India. Volume 5: 1944–1948*, ed. Jyoti Basu et al. (Calcutta: National Book Agency, 1997), 246.
9. D. N. Gupta, *Communism and Nationalism in Colonial India, 1939–45* (New Delhi: SAGE Publications India, 2008), 261, 269; Chandra, 'P. C. Joshi'.
10. Shashi Joshi, *Struggle for Hegemony in India, 1920–47. The Colonial State, the Left and the National Movement. Volume I: 1920–34* (New Delhi: SAGE Publications, 1992), 23 and 254.

11. Shashi Joshi, *Struggle for Hegemony*, 251.

12. Ibid., 250.

13. Puran Chand Joshi, *Congress and Communists* (Bombay: People's Publishing House, 1940), 1–2; *A Free Happy India* 19, 22 and 23.

14. Central Committee CPI, Resolution: 'For the Final Assault' (February 1946), in *Documents of the Communist Movement in India. Volume 5: 1944–1948*, ed. Jyoti Basu et al. (Calcutta: National Book Agency, 1997), 116. See also Dutt, 'New Chapter in Divide and Rule', 246.

15. Chandra comments that the CPI's belief that the Congress Right was under direct imperialist influence 'completely misread' the real situation. 'Its Right-wingness lay in its opposition to India adopting radical economic policies after independence . . . Its Right-wingness did not ... lie in its approach to imperialism'—to which it was entirely opposed (Chandra, 'P. C. Joshi').

16. Central Committee CPI, 'For the Final Assault', 116.

17. Ibid., 105 and 110.

18. Central Committee CPI, 'Election Manifesto of the Communist Party of India' in *Documents of the Communist Movement in India. Volume 5: 1944–1948*, ed. Jyoti Basu et al. (Calcutta: National Book Agency, 1997), 200–1.

19. P. C. Joshi, 'For a Free and Happy India (1946)' in *Documents of the Communist Movement in India. Volume 5: 1944–1948*, ed. Jyoti Basu et al. (Calcutta: National Book Agency, 1997), 279–80.

20. 'It is important to remember ... that in the Indian Communist thinking, the belief that in the era of imperialism and the general crisis of world capitalism, etc., capitalism could not be built—that is, the bourgeoisie could not complete the bourgeois democratic revolution—in the ex-colonies played a crucial role.' (Chandra, 'Strategy in Crisis', 389)
See also Gupta, *Communism and Nationalism*, 260.

21. Gupta, *Communism and Nationalism*, 260.

22. CPI, 'Mountbatten Award and After', 366. See also Central Committee CPI, 'For the Final Assault', 122–24.

23. CPI, 'Election Manifesto February', 215. Joshi in fact argued that the notion of an existing agrarian revolt was a myth, designed to cover the suppression of peasant demands by the British. He said 'we ourselves have been guilty of sectarian overglorification of partial struggles' (Joshi cited by B. T. Ranadive, 'Report on Reformist Deviation' (CPI 2nd Congress, 1948), in *Documents of the Communist Movement in India. Volume 5: 1944–1948*, ed. Jyoti Basu et al. [Calcutta: National Book Agency, 1997], 706).

24. A. A. Zhdanov, *The International Situation* (September 1947), n.d., 10. Oddly enough, in view of the attack that the communists were about to open up on the Congress government, Zhdanov described the new government of India as 'sympathetic' to the anti-imperialist camp (11).

25. Ranadive said later 'The August (1946) resolution of the CC was the first successful attempt to break through the shackles of reformism to a revolutionary understanding of the post-war situation. It was preceded by sharp conflict in the P[olit]B[ureau] . . .' (Ranadive, 'Reformist Deviation', 699).

26. Ranadive, Reformist Deviation, 701.

27. As Ranadive put it, 'it was seen that the majority of the CC had independently come to a correct understanding of the present revolutionary situation' (Ranadive, 'Reformist Deviation', 711).

28. Ranadive, 'Reformist Deviation', 711–2.

29. Polit Bureau CPI, 'Introductory Note' (January 1948), in *Documents of the Communist Movement in India. Volume 5: 1944–1948*, ed. Jyoti Basu et al. (Calcutta: National Book Agency, 1997), 533–34. One of the first to feel the full force of this 'break' was Joshi himself. After the 2nd CPI Congress in February 1948, '… [Joshi] was made to carry his own luggage to the railway station after the Party Congress was over. Young comrades were ordered not to help him.' Less pettily, he was suspended from the Party in January 1949 and expelled in December of that year (Chandra, 'P. C. Joshi').

30. According to Ranadive, 'Joshi was a persistent advocate of the theory of advance and was supported by a number of comrades' (Ranadive, 'Reformist Deviation', 708).

31. Central Committee CPI, 'For the Struggle for Full Independence and People's Democracy', in *Documents of the Communist Movement in India. Volume 5: 1944–1948*, ed. Jyoti Basu et al. (Calcutta: National Book Agency, 1997), 524–25. See also Central Committee CPI, 'On the Present Policy and Tasks of the Communist Party of India', in *Documents of the Communist Movement in India. Volume 5: 1944–1948*, ed. Jyoti Basu et al. (Calcutta: National Book Agency, 1997), 537.

32. Bhabani Sen Gupta, *Communism in Indian Politics* (New York: Columbia University Press, 1972), 28.

33. CPI, 'On the Present Policy', 542–43.

34. Ranadive, 'Reformist Deviation', 713.

35. CPI, 'On the Present Policy', 541.

36. CPI, 'For the Struggle for Full Independence', 522.

37. CPI, 'On the Present Policy', 541; CPI, 'Political Thesis of the 2nd Congress of the Communist Party of India' (1948), in *Documents of the Communist Movement in India. Volume 5: 1944–1948*, ed. Jyoti Basu et al. (Calcutta: National Book Agency, 1997), 597.

38. CPI, 'Introductory Note', 533–34.

39. CPI, 'On the Present Policy', 546–47, 562.

40. CPI, 'On the Present Policy', 549.

41. CPI, 'For the Struggle for Full Independence', 529–30; CPI, 'On the Present Policy', 550.

42. CPI, 'On the Present Policy', 554.

43. CPI, 'Political Thesis 2nd Congress', 572.

44. See Arutla Ramachandra Reddy, *Telangana Struggle Memoirs* (New Delhi: People's Publishing House, 1984).

45. See Gene D. Overstreet and Marshall Windmiller, *Communism in India* (Berkeley: University of California Press, 1960), 278.

46. CC On Present Policy December 1947 CPM V 550.

47. Gene D. Overstreet and Marshall Windmiller, *Communism in India* (Berkeley: University of California Press, 1960), 279–80.

48. Anil Rajimwale, *Life and Works of P.C. Joshi* (New Delhi: People's Publishing House, 2007), 23–24.

49. Overstreet and Windmiller, *Communism*, 277–78; Rajimwale, *Life and Works*, 24.

50. Andhra Letter cited by B. T. Ranadive, 'Strategy and Tactics in the Struggle for People's Democratic Revolution in India' (December 1948), in *Documents of the Communist Movement in India. Volume 5: 1944–1948*, ed. Jyoti Basu et al. (Calcutta: National Book Agency, 1997), 894–95.

51. Andhra Letter cited by Ranadive, 'Strategy and Tactics', 880.

52. Ranadive, 'Strategy and Tactics', 872.

53. Ibid., 894.

54. Ranadive, 'Strategy and Tactics', 888. He went on to describe Mao's support for Chinese capitalists (as part of the anti-imperialist united front) as a 'horrifying formulation', a 'reactionary formulation' and 'counter-revolutionary' (890).

55. Liu Shao-Ch'i, 'The Opening Speech at the Asian and Austral[as]ian Trade Union Delegates' Meeting' (November 1949), in *The Collected Works of Liu Shao-Ch'i: 1945–1957* (Hong Kong: Union Research Institute, 19XX), 178, 179.

56. 'Armed struggle for liberation has also broken out in India,' said Liu, probably referring to the Telangana insurgency (Liu Shao-ch'i, 'Opening Address', 177). It should also be remembered that in communist thinking India remained at most a 'semi-colony' after 1947.

57. Liu Shao-ch'i, 'Opening Address', 179–80.

58. Liu Shao-ch'i, 'Opening Address', 179 and 181. Liu's statements here seem quite unambiguous. But in other passages, some ambiguity creeps in. For example, the Chinese path would be followed by 'many'—not all—developing countries. The Chinese road 'may' become 'the fundamental road' for people in the colonies and semi-colonies. And the national liberation army (which 'there must be') should be built 'at places where and times when they can be built'. Liu concludes, 'The question is quite clear.' (Liu Shao-ch'i, 'Opening Address', 179) The Andhra communists adopted an unambiguous interpretation.

59. Liu Shao-ch'i, 'Opening Address', 181. According to Liu, urban workers' demands for better wages, conditions and living standards 'can be solved only after their national liberation war has won victory and imperialism has been driven out' (178).

60. According to his biographer, the editorial was written by Rajani Palme Dutt, a leader of the Communist Party of Great Britain. According to Dutt, it 'released the battle against the sectarian tendencies' in the CPI (John Callaghan, *Rajani Palme Dutt: A Study in British Stalinism* (London: Lawrence & Wishart, 1993), 250).

61. 'Mighty Advance of the National Liberation Movement in the Colonial and Dependent Countries', *For a Lasting Peace, For a People's Democracy!* no. 4, 27 January 1950 at International South Asia Forum. See www.insafbulletin.net/archives/181, last accessed on 3 September 2015.

62. Central Committee CPI, 'Letter of the New Central Committee to All Party Members and Sypathisers' (June 1950), in *Documents of the History of the Communist Party of India. Volume VII: 1948–1950*, ed. M. B. Rao (New Delhi: People's Publishing House, 1976), 620.

63. CPI, 'Letter of the New Central Committee', 631 and 642–44. The new leadership duly apologised for Ranadive's 'slanderous attack in the [Party] press on Mao' (653).

64. It was in fact Mohit Sen who carried the glad tidings of the Andhra line to the Chinese—while on a Party training mission in China (Mohit Sen, *A Traveller and the Road: The Journey of an Indian Communist* [New Delhi: Rupa & Co., 2003], 80).

65. Mohit Sen, *Traveller*, 125.

66. Ibid., 82; Overstreet and Windmiller, *Communism in India*, 301. Joshi was to be readmitted to the CPI in June 1951. He was given positions of responsibility but refused to join the leadership (Chandra, 'P. C. Joshi').

67. Prabodh Chandra (Ajoy Ghosh), Prabhakar (S. A. Dange) and Purushottam (S. V. Ghate), 'A Note on the Present Situation in Our Party' 30 September 1950 (henceforward Three Ps), in *Documents of the History of the Communist Party of India. Volume VII: 1948–1950*, ed. M. B. Rao (New Delhi: People's Publishing House, 1976), 950–51 and 959.

68. Three Ps, 943 and 946.
69. Ibid., 957.
70. Ibid., 964–65 and 972.
71. Ibid., 959 and 972.
72. Ibid., 976.
73. CPI, 'Letter of the New Central Committee' cited by Three Ps, 966–68.
74. Mohan Ram, *Indian Communism: Split within a Split* (Delhi: Vikas Publications, 1969) 45–46.
75. Callaghan, 'Dutt', 251.
76. Central Committee CPI, 'Letter to All Party Members', in *Documents of the History of the Communist Party of India. Volume VII: 1948–1950*, ed. M. B. Rao (New Delhi: People's Publishing House, 1976), 1090, 1092.
77. In those meetings, CPI leaders would portray themselves as virtually helpless without the intervention of the Soviet leadership. According to Dange, 'Our party could never work out its own line without the help of other parties.' ('Record of the Discussions of Comrades G. M. Malenkov and M. A. Suslov with the Representatives of the Central Committee of the Communist Party of India Comrades Rao, Dange, Ghosh and Punnaiah,' comp. Vijay Singh, *Revolutionary Democracy* 12, no. 2 (September 2006), www.revolutionarydemocracy.org/rdv12n2/cpi1.html) Rajeshwara Rao pleaded, 'If we don't get help, the Communist Party of India might fall apart.' Ajoy Ghosh assured the Russians 'the suggestions of the [CPSU] will be acceptable to the whole party' ['Stenographic Record of the Discussion of the Members of the CC A-UCP(B) with the representatives of the CC Communist Party of India on 4th and 6th February 1951'. comp. Vijay Singh *Revolutionary Democracy* 12, no. 2 (September 2006). See www.revolutionarydemocracy.org/rdv12n2/cpi1.htm, last accessed on 03 September 2015]. This was not the first meeting between CPI leaders and Soviet communists. In August 1947, Dange had met with Zhdanov (CPSU second secretary and Cominform luminary). The depth of that encounter (on both sides) can perhaps be gauged from the following exchange:

> Comrade Zhdanov: 'What is Nehru—a capitalist or a landowner?'
> Comrade Dange: 'A bourgeois.'
> Comrade Zhdanov: 'And Jinnah?'
> Comrade Dange: 'Also a bourgeois.'
> ['The Discussions of S. A. Dange with the C.P.S.U. (b) (July–September 1947)', comp. Vijay Singh, *Revolutionary Democracy* 7, no. 1 (April 2001). See www.revolutionarydemocracy.org/rdv7n1/Dange.htm, last accessed on 03 September 2015]

78. Stenographic Record CPSU/CPI Discussions, 4 and 6 February 1951. This is the source of the rest of this paragraph.
79. 'Record of the Discussions of J. V. Stalin with the Representatives of the C.C. of the Communist Party of India Comrades, Rao, Dange, Ghosh and Punnaiah', comp. Vijay Singh, *Revolutionary Democracy* 12, no. 2 (September 2006), www.revolutionarydemocracy.org/rdv12n2/cpi1.htm. This is the source of the rest of this paragraph.
80. Whether the Chinese Communist leaders would have agreed with this assessment seems doubtful.
81. A. K. Ghosh and S. A. Dange, 'Concerning the Question of Partisan Struggle', *Revolutionary Democracy* XVI, no. 1 (April 2010), www.revolutionarydemocracy.org.

82. Reported by Rajeshwara Rao and S. A. Dange to Mohit Sen (Sen, *Traveller*, 81 and 126).

83. 'A. K. Gopalan's Statement' (23 October 1951), in *Documents of the History of the Communist Party of India: Volume VIII: 1951–1956*, ed. Mohit Sen (New Delhi: People's Publishing House, 1977), 60.

84. Chandra, 'Strategy', 264–67 and 277–78.

85. 'Programme of the CPI, 1951' in *Documents of the History of the Communist Party of India, Volume VIII: 1951–1956*, ed. Mohit Sen (New Delhi: People's Publishing House, 1977), 3.

86. Chandra comments that there was 'no clarity' as to who the 'big bourgeoisie' actually was—just that it was not the 'national' bourgeoisie. And there was no clarity about who the latter was either (Chandra, 'Strategy', 266).

87. 'Questions and Answers' appended to the 'Tactical Line, 1951' in *Documents of the History of the Communist Party of India, Volume VIII: 1951–1956*, ed. Mohit Sen (New Delhi: People's Publishing House, 1977), 40.

88. Chandra, 'Strategy', 266 and 384.

89. Chandra, 'Strategy', 269–71.

90. S. Mohan Kumaramangalam, *Communists in Congress: Kumaramangalam's Thesis*, ed. Satindra Singh (Delhi: D.K. Publishing House, 1973 [1964]), 20–23.

91. Ghosh cited in Chandra, 'Strategy', 268.

92. Central Committee CPI, 'Tactical Line' (1951), in *Documents of the History of the Communist Party of India, Volume VIII 1951–1956*, ed. Mohit Sen (New Delhi: People's Publishing House, 1977), 28; Chandra, 'Strategy', 273. The penchant for armed struggle remained in some quarters however. Mohit Sen reports that as late as 1952, all of the leadership still believed that 'sooner or later the Party would have to ignite armed struggle in one part of the country or the other'. As a CPI full-timer, Sen was instructed by Polit Bureau (PB) member Sundarayya in 1953 to build up an underground apparatus in urban centres 'for the time when national insurgency would commence'. Sen refused the task (Sen, *Traveller*, 128 and 130–31).

93. Central Committee CPI, '1951 Statement of Policy', in *Documents of the History of the Communist Party of India, Volume VIII 1951–1956*, ed. Mohit Sen (New Delhi: People's Publishing House, 1977), 51.

94. Sen, *Traveller*, 128.

95. 'The Congress swept the polls … . The elections represented a triumph for the Congress organization, which reached down to the village level, for the ideology of secularism, democracy and national unity, and, above all, for the inspiring leadership of Nehru.' (Bipan Chandra, Mridula Mukherjee and Aditya Mukherjee, *India Since Independence* [New Delhi: Penguin, 2008], 171).

96. Central Committee CPI, 'The results of the General Elections and the Tasks before the Party', in *Documents of the History of the Communist Party of India, Volume VIII: 1951–1956*, ed. Mohit Sen (New Delhi: People's Publishing House, 1977), 87–88.

97. Central Committee CPI, 'Resolution Adopted at the C.C. Meeting of C.P.I. held in March 1952', in *Documents of the Communist Movement in India. Volume 7: 1952–1956*, ed. Jyoti Basu et al. (Calcutta: National Book Agency, 1997), 84.

98. CPI, *Third Congress of the Communist Party of India, Madurai 27 December 1953–4 January 1954: Political Resolution* (Delhi: Communist Party of India, 1954), 10.

99. CPI, *Third Congress*, 12.

100. Chandra, 'Strategy', 281.

101. Ibid., 285.

102.   Democratic Research Service, *Communist Conspiracy in India: An Analysis of the Private Proceedings of the Third Congress of the CPI with Full Text of Secret Documents* (Bombay: Popular Book Depot, 1954), 12–13; Sen, *Traveller*, 133.

103.   For the former see N. S. Khrushchev, *Special Report to the 20th Congress of the Communist Party of the Soviet Union* (New York: New Leader, 1962); for the latter, N. S. Khrushchov, *Report of the Central Committee of the Communist Party of the Soviet Union to the 20th Party Congress* (Moscow: Foreign Languages Publishing House, 1956) 26–27 and 44–45.

104.   Though not too critical. See Ajoy Ghosh, 'On J. V. Stalin' (December 1956), in *Documents of the Communist Movement in India. Volume 7: 1952–1956*, ed. Jyoti Basu et al. (Calcutta: National Book Agency, 1997), 707–12.

105.   Commenting on the differences at the Party's 6th Congress in 1963 at Vijayawada, Mohan Ram writes:

> Neither the Sino-Indian border conflict nor the Sino-Soviet ideological dispute . . . was the principal issue . . . . At best they were peripheral issues because the fight was over a programme and a tactical line for the party . . . there is no reason to believe that the differences in the international communist movement [were] the principal factor in the CPI rift at Vijayawada. (Mohan Ram, *Indian Communism*, 121)

106.   From the account of the meeting on 12 December 1955, in Jawaharlal Nehru, *Selected Works, Volume XXXI: 18 November 1955–31 January 1956* (New Delhi: Jawaharlal Nehru Memorial Fund, 1984–2002), 339–43. The Indians were not entirely abandoned. It is clear that a small amount of material aid (for elections and propaganda) continued (see Ivan A. Benediktov, 'Russian Foreign Ministry Documents on Soviet-Indian Relations', *Cold War International History Project* (www.wilsoncenter.org); Christopher Andrew and Vasili Mitrokhin, *The Mitrokhin Archive II: The KGB and the World* (London: Allen Lane, 2005), 317.

107.   CPI, 'Political Resolution adopted at 4th Congress' (April 1956), in *Documents of the History of the Communist Party of India, Volume VIII 1951–1956*, ed. Mohit Sen (New Delhi: People's Publishing House, 1977), 525; Central Committee CPI, 'Resolution of the Central Committee of the Communist Party of India on National and International issues' (June 1955), in *Documents of the Communist Movement in India, Volume VIII: 1957–1961*, ed. Jyoti Basu et al. (Calcutta: National Book Agency, 1997), 456 and 458; CPI, 'Political Resolution of the Extraordinary Congress of the Communist Party of India' (April 1958), in *Documents of the Communist Movement in India, Volume VIII: 1957–1961*, ed. Jyoti Basu et al. (Calcutta: National Book Agency, 1997), 177; CPI, '4th Congress Resolution', 546.

108.   CPI, 'Resolution and Report on the 20th Congress of the CPSU' (4th Congress, April 1956), *Documents of the Communist Movement in India. Volume 7: 1952–1956*, ed. Jyoti Basu et al. (Calcutta: National Book Agency, 1997), 664.

109.   CPI, '4th Congress Resolution', 526–27; 'Political Resolution of the Extraordinary Congress (April 1958)', 169.

110.   Central Committee, 'Resolution' June 1955, 457.

111.   Ajoy Ghosh, 'New Situation and Our Tasks' (6th Congress April 1961), in *Documents of the Communist Movement in India, Volume VIII: 1957–1961*, ed. Jyoti Basu et al. (Calcutta: National Book Agency, 1997), 753.

112.   CPI, '4th Congress Resolution', 529 and 537–38.

113. CPI, 'National Democratic Front for National Democratic Task' (6th Congress, April 1961), in *Documents of the Communist Movement in India, Volume VIII: 1957–1961*, ed. Jyoti Basu et al. (Calcutta: National Book Agency, 1997), 684; Ghosh, 'New Situation', 764.

114. Ghosh, 'New Situation', 764; CPI, 'National Democratic Front', 684.

115. Ibid., 753. Confusion arose as to where the 'national bourgeoisie' ended and the 'monopolists' began. In a CPI pamphlet published in 1962, Bupesh Gupta equated 'the right-wing of the national bourgeoisie' with 'the big monopolists' (Bupesh Gupta, *The Big Loot: A Brief Study of Foreign Exploitation in India* [New Delhi: Communist Party of India, 1962], 32).

116. 'the Congress is stronger today than it was some years ago' (Central Committee, 'Resolution' June 1955, 463).

117. CPI, '4th Congress Resolution', 535; CPI, 'National Democratic Front', 680.

118. Central Committee, 'Resolution' June 1955, 462 and 464.

119. Centrist as always, Ghosh was also at pains to point to a simultaneous 'tailist and reformist tendency' (Ghosh, 'New Situation', 709, 768).

120. Ghosh, 'New Situation', 765; CPI, 'National Democratic Front', 679.

121. CPI, '4th Congress Resolution', 556. The new CPI policies appeared to have been vindicated when the Party, in a Left coalition, won power in the state of Kerala in 1957. The Party's new attitude to the Congress even survived the dismissal of the Kerala state government in 1959 by the central authorities.

122. Central Committee, 'Resolution' June 1955, 467.

123. CPI, '4th Congress Resolution', 546 and 540–545.

124. CPI, 'On the CPSU 20th Congress', 667 and 671.

125. Sen, *Traveller*, 171.

126. N. Prasada Rao, *Land Reform under Congress Raj* (New Delhi: Communist Party of India, 1961), 20–21.

127. Dange quoted in Raj Bahadur Gour, *Working Class under Congress Raj* (New Delhi: Communist Party Publication, 1961), 25.

128. Bupesh Gupta, *The Big Loot: A Brief Study of Foreign Exploitation in India* (New Delhi: Communist Party of India, 1962), 30.

129. Sen, *Traveller*, 182.

130. Ibid., 201–17.

131. Ibid., 216–17.

132. E. M. S. Namboodiripad, 'Note for the Programme of the CPI' cited in John B. Wood, 'Observations on the Indian Communist Party Split' *Pacific Affairs* 38, no. 1 (Spring 1965): 61; see also 47 and 63. Four years after the split, when Warsaw Pact troops invaded Czechoslovakia, CPI agreement with the Soviet position was by no means automatic. After three days of debate, the NC agreed to support it by only one vote—a majority which, as Dange argued, meant nothing. The question was then put to a full inner-Party discussion, after which it was agreed that the pro-Soviet line had a majority. The point here though was that the Party leadership was not a collection of Soviet acolytes (Sen, *Traveller*, 267).

133. Sen, *Traveller*, 243–44. O. P. Sangal contends that 'the CPM [Communist Party of India (Marxist)] is an authentically Stalinist party while the CPI has broken loose of the Stalinist stranglehold and tries to look at India and the contemporary world through the untinged glasses of Marxism and Leninism.' (O. P. Sangal, 'The Fiftieth Anniversary' [of the CPI], *Indian Left Review* 4, no. 3 (January 1976): 3.

134.   CPI cited in Kalpana Wilson 'Class Alliances and the Nature of Hegemony: The Post-Independence Indian State in Marxist Writing' in *State and Nation in the Context of Social Change*, ed. T. V. Sathyamurthy (Delhi: Oxford India Paperbacks, 1997), 254.

135.   Francine R. Frankel, *India's Political Economy, 1947–1977: The Gradual Revolution* (Princeton: Princeton University Press, 1978), 405.

136.   Victor M. Fic, *Kerala: Yenan of India* (Bombay: Nachiketa Publications, 1970), 171. An interesting early version of the national democratic revolution and the proposition that the communists should work within Congress to achieve it can be found in S. Mohan Kumaramangalam, *Communists in Congress: Kumaramangalam's Thesis*, edited and introduced by Satindra Singh (Delhi: D. K. Publishing House, 1973 [1964]).

137.   Fic, *Kerala*, 176.

138.   Communist Party of India, *The Programme of the Communist Party of India. As adopted by the Seventh Congress of the Communist Party of India, Bombay 13–23 December 1964* (New Delhi: Communist Party of India, 1965), 5–8.

139.   CPI, *7th Congress Programme 1964*, 8 and 10.

140.   Amarjit Kaur, interview with author, 15 January 2014.

141.   CPI, *7th Congress Programme 1964*, 12–13.

142.   Ibid., 12, 14 and 27.

143.   Ibid., 14.

144.   Opposed during those years only by P. C. Joshi and his supporters, O. P. Sangal and R. K. Garg (Sen, *Traveller*, 261).

145.   Communist Party of India, *The Present Political Situation. Resolution of the National Council of the Communist Party of India, Hyderabad 9–15 June 1966* (New Delhi: Communist Party of India, 1966), 1 and 14.

146.   CPI, *Present Political Situation 1966*, 17.

147.   CPI, 'Programme of the Communist Party of India' (1951), in *Documents of the History of the Communist Party of India, Volume VIII: 1951–1956*, ed. Mohit Sen (New Delhi: People's Publishing House, 1977), 18. For a more extensive summary see the 1951 'Election Manifesto of the Communist Party of India', in *Documents of the History of the Communist Party of India, Volume VIII: 1951–1956*, ed. Mohit Sen (New Delhi: People's Publishing House, 1977), 73–75.

148.   For a longer version of this argument see David Lockwood, *The Destruction of the Soviet Union: A Study in Globalization* (Houndmills: Macmillan, 2000)—especially, Chapter 2. There, I described the process as a rise in the level of the development of the productive forces leading to an adjustment of the production relations, with the ongoing power of the national state as the main casualty.

149.   Karl Marx and Frederick Engels, *Manifesto of the Communist Party* (Moscow: Progress Publishers, 1966 [1848]), 45.

2

India: From Liberalisation to Leftism

The capacity of the national state to control its own destiny has been an article of political faith since the increase in the formation of such states in the nineteenth century. It received a new lease of life with the additional states formed in the post-war and post-colonial period. A combination of developments—among them, the Soviet attempt at a planned economy, the ideas of Keynes, the 1930s Depression and the war-economies of 1939–45—produced a widespread belief that the national state could plan, nurture and regulate economic growth within its borders. Provided that the state could keep private capital under control (or abolish it), it could protect its domestic market, marshal its resources and industrialise. National governments, it appeared, could preside over this process and determine the relationship (if any) between the national economy and the rest of the world.

The process of globalisation—the creation of a world market, together with a world trading and manufacturing system—began to eat away the role of the state as a developer from the late 1960s onwards. The trade and investment flows of an emerging global economy began to transgress the historical boundaries between nations. 'National' economies began to dissolve into a global division of labour. The governments of national states, far from controlling this process, were forced to accede to it: 'If the state were to survive, no option was left but to join in the world market economy.'[1]

Paradoxically, attempts to survive (by joining in) weakened state control over economic activities. Once an opening to the world market was made, states found themselves increasingly unable to control the flow of information, technology or capital across their borders.[2] Internally, economic judgements began to be made on the basis of international standards, not those set down or controlled by national governments. Even in Soviet-type economies, incremental moves towards the world market eroded the role of the state: It was no longer the sole economic arbiter. Thus, even before the collapse of Soviet-type economies under these very pressures, 'The world market began to choose those items in the centrally planned economies that it needed, and to bankrupt those it did not.'[3]

By the 1970s, it became clear that in order to maintain economic growth (the foundation of any 'national independence'), an outward economic orientation was required. The alternative, according to *The Economist* in 1989, was 'economic failure on such a scale that it crushes, or threatens to crush, the power of the state. Provided that it does not go too far, reform becomes a matter of self-interest'.[4] But how far was too far? Each step along the path of 'opening up' the national economy, 'restructuring' it according to global requirements and fitting it into a world division of labour was a step away from the autonomy of the state.

States—whether advanced, centrally planned or developing—did not lightly abandon their original project. Some resisted the intrusions of the world market and externally oriented domestic capital on their domain to the extent that they were able to. On the one hand, if the state were capable of resistance, the effects of globalisation were slower. On the other hand, the greater the role of the state in economic development, the more dramatic were the eventual results.[5]

By the 1960s, the Congress state in India had succeeded in creating a state-controlled and regulated economy.[6] It was centrally planned. Industry was dominated by over 200 state-owned enterprises. The private sector—which had, on the eve of independence, strongly endorsed Congress economic plans[7]—was held down by a complex system of regulation, which the state could either rigidly enforce or relax at will. Ostensibly, this was designed to check the rise of monopolies. In fact, it gave the state control over business expansion. Eventually, the state would attempt to bar large business groups from key sectors of the economy.[8] As a leader of the Federation of Indian Chambers of Commerce and Industry (FICCI) wrote later, 'The private sector had been encircled not only by a wide range of legislation but by a variety of countervailing power.'[9]

Vivek Chibber, in *Locked in Place*, argues that there was conflict between the Congress state and the Indian bourgeoisie over economic policy from 1947 onwards. Ostensibly, both were committed to a development strategy of 'import-substituting industrialisation' (ISI):

> [T]he new state would be singularly committed to using public monies as a means of accelerating the development of private industry. This was, of course, directly in the state's interest .... Fostering industrial development was regarded as an essential part of 'nation building'.[10]

Chibber notes that this was the model of choice for '[m]ost developing countries in the aftermath of the Second World War'.[11] In the Indian case, it had a clear ideological motivation, given Congress' Leftism and the prestige of the Soviet model (transmitted by both Congress and Communist leaders) in the interwar period. The Congress version encompassed both the need for independence and the aspiration to self-sufficiency.[12] The strategy was not without its problems. Protectionism, the creation of monopolies and the consequent lack of competition meant that 'firms [were] under no systematic pressure to constantly upgrade their operations'.[13] Chibber maintains that the government wanted to extend 'disciplinary planning' over the economy. Had this happened, India's development strategy would have been transformed into 'export-led industrialisation' (ELI)—similar, for example, to the South Korean model in which 'exports [of manufactured goods, not raw materials] came to occupy the strategic core of the development policy'.[14] On this basis, a strong, disciplinary and developmental state could have been constructed.[15]

This, according to Chibber, was the point of conflict between the Indian state and the bourgeoisie. The reason that ELI and the developmental state did not come into being, despite the government's best efforts, was 'a highly organised and concerted offensive launched by the business class against the idea of disciplinary planning'.[16]

I do not think that this was the case. In fact, I would argue that big business and the Congress remained united around the ISI strategy until the 1980s (despite some short-lived questioning of the strategy under Shastri). This is not to say that there was no conflict between them—simply that the conflict was not over disciplinary planning and ISI.

To take the Congress first. There is little evidence, in my view, that Congress economic strategists were in favour of a concerted turn to exports *à la* South Korea or Taiwan. ELI was not a part of the Left nationalist economic model that they had adopted during the interwar period; it was opposed to it. In terms of independence and self-sufficiency, the ELI approach would not have built the kind of state that they wanted. Chibber's account is long on Congress attempts to extend the economic power of the state, but rather short on the direct link between this and exports.[17] And I think it is fanciful to suggest that an extension of the disciplinary planning would have somehow naturally evolved into an ELI model. The ELI model was the exception rather than the developmental rule—and plenty of 'disciplined' states (the Soviet-type economies, for example) were, for most of their existence, miles away from an export orientation.

As for business, Chibber correctly points out, 'Domestic industrialists rightly saw ISI as a tremendous opportunity for growth and profits, because of the sectors being literally handed over to them free of international competition'—while at the same time, resisting increases in the power of the state over the economy.[18] Indian business tended to be highly concentrated into a number of powerful business houses. This concentration was encouraged by the state-run economy.[19] Thus, 'big business' tended to support ISI and its Congress architects.

So, while there was certainly a good deal of pushing and shoving between the Congress leadership and big business over 'the *scope* of the private sector, or the *terms* on which it would receive its largesse'[20]—there was no confrontation between the Congress and the bourgeoisie over the central importance of ISI. The Congress did not want to introduce ELI and, therefore, big business did not have to oppose it.

The official FICCI history tells us, 'it was not true that industrialists were against all controls, if only because some controls protected industrial demand and were to the producers' interest.'[21] State regulation 'in fact allowed a segment of private capital to monopolise the opportunities for expansion and to erect artificial barriers to the entry of new firms'.[22] Even at the height of the Licence Raj, the system could be used to the advantage of big business. Mrs Gandhi herself told the Congress Parliamentary Party in September 1974:

> I feel that it [the Licensing system] gives greater opportunity to the bigger man than the smaller man … they have competent people, experienced people to advise them. They know how everything works in Government. Because they have the money to do something.[23]

Erdman concludes that 'during the Nehru years, industrialists were not engaged in a life-and-death struggle with the government'.[24] In a recent article on 'crony capitalism', Chandrasekhar contends, '[I]t was clear that policy implementation favoured big business, which was able to garner a disproportionate share of licences, leading to increased industrial concentration and the strengthening of a few industrial houses that competed with each other but kept out new entrants.'[25]

The state-controlled economy was also not without its early successes. This was, after all, the golden age of state intervention. The state-dominated model—from the centrally planned economy of the Soviet Union (despite the destruction of its Italian, German and Japanese versions) to the mixed economies of western Europe—had spread around the world. According to Sumit Majumdar, 'India's planning approaches and economic strategy of the time were, incidentally, fully in step with prevailing fashion. The Marshall Plan's big push for European reindustrialisation was contemporaneous.'[26]

As with both interwar and contemporary examples, the state in India proved to be, at least in part, a successful (if blunt) instrument for the initial transformation of an agrarian to an industrial economy. Beyond that, however, increasingly beset by its own limitations and external pressures, the model ran into serious problems. As AchinVanaik puts it, 'By the end of the third plan (1961–65), import-substituting state capitalism had done its job and come closer to exhausting its possibilities.'[27] Economic growth slowed after 1962. The planners found themselves in a crisis. Domestic savings and the rate of investment both began to fall.[28] Aditya Mukherjee identifies a number of structural features that, by this stage, afflicted the Indian economy. Firstly, 'the excessive protection through import restrictions started leading to inefficiency and technological backwardness in Indian industry'.[29] Secondly, the 'Licence Raj'—the bewildering number of rules, regulations and restrictions that confronted Indian business—stifled entrepreneurship and innovation.[30] The reservation of a growing list of areas of economic activity for small business excluded those areas from advantages of scale and research and development resources. Finally, in the state sector, 'over time, political and bureaucratic pressure on the public sector undertakings led to most of them running at a loss'.[31]

The blame for this sorry state of affairs was consensually sheeted home to the role of the state in India's economy and, specifically, to its attempts to plan, regulate and protect.[32] The Delhi-based journal *Thought* put it harshly:

> Unwittingly, the Government of India is holding back industrial progress just as deplorably as the British rulers did before our Independence.[33]

Liberalisation

Condemnation of India's state-oriented system was not universal—certainly not in the business community. Nevertheless, there was dissatisfaction by the 1960s. The licensing system became a barrier to new entrants to what appeared to be increasingly lucrative markets.[34] As a result, according to Patnaik, the big bourgeoisie

> attempted to break out of the shackles of the constricted home market by setting up projects abroad, by entering the international market from its home base and by entering new avenues … . For many of these options however it needs to collaborate with metropolitan capital and it also needs the lifting of a number of controls in the economy.[35]

Economic liberalisation then seemed to be the order of the day. Chibber argues that this came in two forms: 'internal liberalization, which meant fewer controls on private capital, and external liberalization, which meant a combination of devaluating the rupee and lifting import controls'.[36] Big business, in India, was only really interested in internal liberalisation.[37] For them, the desired liberalisation was limited to a relaxation of state control over the private sector. They were joined in this by managers of the larger state-owned industries.[38]

But big business was no longer alone. New, smaller and potentially more dynamic industrialists had emerged, even during the Licence Raj.[39] These groups had had to either fight state regulation or use it to their own advantage. Either way, they came to regard state control as an obstacle to their advance—both internally and externally. For this reason, they pressed for both forms of liberalisation:

> The more enthusiastic supporters of World Bank-style 'liberalisation' are likely to be found among a number of new houses which are on the rise and which aspire to break the existing monopoly position in the domestic market with the help of metropolitan capital.[40]

It appears then, that by the late 1960s, a division had opened up within the Indian bourgeoisie over the degree of economic liberalisation required to maintain profitability and solve some of the problems of the economy. On the one hand, big business and prominent state managers, content with a mainly domestic orientation, were in favour of internal liberalisation—the relaxation of the Licence Raj. On the other hand, newer industries wanted an end to both state controls and an opening to the world market—and were, therefore, in favour of both internal and external liberalisation. Kochanek identifies this division, describing business reaction to the liberalisation measures initiated by Nehru's successor, Lal Bahadur Shastri.

> Within the [FICCI] committee some members advocated a total abolition
> of controls, some wanted controls modified, and others opposed decon-
> trol because it aided the profitability of their industries. Textiles, coal and
> sugar interests within the committee most strongly opposed decontrol. The
> newer industries, such as engineering, favoured a policy of total freedom
> from control.[41]

The line of division may have been fuzzier than that. Since no one knew
what the effects of globalisation on a state-directed economy would be, it
was unlikely that any representative of the bourgeoisie had a worked-out
response to it in the 1960s, whether that was defending the state economy
or launching an aggressive export drive. Instead, confusion reigned (and
not only in India).[42]

Pressure for some kind of liberalisation was not confined to domestic
business interests. Events, both domestic and foreign, conspired to force
the Indian government towards reform. In 1965, agriculture was stagnant,
industrial growth was slowing down and unemployment was increasing.
Between 1965 and 1966, India was visited by severe droughts, caused by
the failure of the south-west monsoon. These reduced the country's ability
to export. While still recovering from the war with China in 1962, India
was plunged into war with Pakistan in 1965—and, despite (or perhaps
because of) its victory, foreign aid, particularly from the US, was cut off.
A balance of payments crisis now loomed large on the economic horizon.[43] This, in turn, made India more dependent on foreign aid—most
importantly from the World Bank and the US—and, therefore, either more
receptive or more vulnerable to the advice that went with it.[44]

The World Bank's approach was premised on disenchantment with
India's attempts at economic development. A wrong direction, the Bank
felt, had now spilled over into actual mismanagement. It wanted the Indian
government to encourage the private sector—to relax economic controls
and devalue the rupee. The latter was seen as promoting an export orientation by making exports cheaper and imports more expensive.[45] The US
wanted the same things, but the Johnson administration also felt that there
was political and strategic advantage to be extracted from the situation.
The Americans took a dim view of India's non-aligned status—and an
even dimmer one of its friendship with the Soviet Union and criticism of
the US war in Vietnam. National Security Council member Robert Komer
put it bluntly to the President in June 1965:

> Let's tell the Indians we're not very happy with them either, especially their tendency to take our aid for granted without doing enough to help themselves or to recognise that we're fighting their war [against Chinese aggression] in Vietnam.[46]

The US, therefore, decided to keep ongoing food-aid to India on a 'short tether', approved only on a month-to-month basis.[47] The pressure on India increased.

> The Indian case represents perhaps the strongest attempt the [World] Bank has ever made to use its own leverage, and the leverage of consortium associates, to induce changes in aggregative economic policies in a borrowing country.[48]

In 1964, the World Bank dispatched a high-powered mission to India, led by economic consultant Bernard Bell (not, at that time, an employee of the Bank), to study the state of the Indian economy.[49] The mission's report added 14 volumes of grist to the Bank's now-familiar mill.

On economic controls, the report argued that India's licensing system 'has prevented efficient entrepreneurs from expanding … has imposed restraints upon the achievement of economies of scale and … has delayed and hampered investment and production activity. It … has protected and preserved inefficiency'.[50] The Report also criticised the 'comprehensive direct administrative controls over all imports': '[T]he system has effectively blocked virtually all imports of finished consumer goods.' It went on: 'There are other Government controls of economic life which at best serve little purpose, result in delays and foster corruption, and at worst hamper both investment and production and misallocate resources.'[51] Foreign investment was inadequate—and inadequately sought. 'Ambivalence, a lack of consistent and determined effort, and complicated and inordinately time-consuming procedures on the part of the Government of India have limited the extent to which India has attracted foreign private investment.' Finally, the rupee was over-valued and this exacerbated 'a hesitating, and belated, approach to the problem of export stimulation'.[52]

So, the Report demanded the removal of controls, the permission and attraction of foreign investment, the devaluation of the rupee—and, for good measure, 'a massive, energetic and reorganized population control program' plus the reduction of defence expenditure. Without these reforms, growth and progress could not be expected: 'We would expect, in fact, retrogression in all these respects.'[53] Furthermore, a later World Bank study team suggested, 'India should reshape its industrial production, lean away from heavy and capital goods industries and go in for massive export production during the coming decade.'[54]

The Indian government began to move in the direction it was being pushed. Shastri was sceptical of the plethora of economic controls and had made clear his intention to review and reduce them. He told the Lok Sabha that a number of controls were to be reconsidered—and those not serving a useful purpose, terminated. Government ministers began questioning the concept of state intervention. The importance of the Planning Commission was downgraded, economic focus shifted from the Centre to the States and a more open attitude was signalled towards foreign capital. The 1965 Budget was regarded as pro-business.[55]

Shastri's death, in January 1966, did not halt the process. The new prime minister, Indira Gandhi, maintained the momentum for reform. Following the recommendations of the 1965 Swaminathan committee, 42 industries were de-licensed between May and November 1966.[56] Mrs Gandhi told the FICCI annual session in 1966:

> We are reviewing many things, the structure of controls, for instance.... We have weeded out some controls and we will always be ready to eliminate those that outlive their utility.[57]

Negotiations also continued in Washington, though temporarily interrupted by the India–Pakistan war (August–September 1965).[58] The Indian ambassador to the US, B. K. Nehru, visited New Delhi in January 1966, bringing with him the news that devaluation was a condition for further loans. Any increase in aid from the World Bank depended on economic liberalisation.[59] In return, the World Bank would raise the amount of aid to India.[60] Mrs Gandhi visited Washington in March 1966 to agree terms. India promised devaluation and economic reform in return for food aid and more loans. The Johnson administration also extracted a promise of Indian neutrality on US activities in South East Asia.[61] The final touches to the agreement were put in place by India's Minister for Planning, Ashok Mehta, and the World Bank's George Woods. The Minister for Finance, Sachin Chaudhuri, broadcast the decision to devalue the Indian rupee by 36.5 per cent on 6 June 1966.[62] Together with devaluation, there would be a significant reduction in import duties, a liberalisation of import policy and 59 priority industries (responsible for 80 per cent of industrial production) were 'to be granted import licences as and when needed for components, raw materials, and spare parts'.[63]

Leftism

Yet, despite these initial steps towards the liberalisation of India's economy, it is generally agreed that within a few years, the march was abandoned.

Bernard Bell noted somewhat ruefully, '[A]fter the first year, or perhaps two years, on both sides the actions initially implemented sort of dwindled.'[64] Regulation of the economy and of foreign trade was reintroduced from 1968 onwards.[65] J. D. Rockefeller told George Woods in July 1967, 'The devaluation was a flop; India did not make the policy changes we expected.' After that, many of India's aid donors withdrew support.[66]

Various reasons have been advanced to explain this reversal of Indian policy. First, it is argued that Indira Gandhi herself was not a committed proponent of either liberalisation or devaluation.[67] Some significance is attributed to the fact that almost immediately after devaluation, she visited the Soviet Union, signing a joint statement with the Soviet leaders condemning imperialism in South-East Asia and adopted a pronounced anti-American attitude thereafter.[68] Secondly, it appears that the increased aid from the US simply did not materialise.[69] Chibber concludes: 'As a result the Indian state immediately had to re-impose the import controls that the package had targeted for removal by 1969–70.'[70] Thirdly, while Indian business seemed to be solidly behind liberalisation and the continuation of economic reform in public, they were in fact less enthusiastic than their public position made it appear.[71] Mukherji argues that 'if most of the industrial class practices import substitution rather than being export oriented', they would suffer following devaluation. Thus, FICCI 'supported the devaluation overtly, while opposing it behind the scenes'.[72] Finally, political opposition to economic liberalisation in general and devaluation in particular was widespread and loud. We will deal with the communist attitude in the next chapter.[73] But there was also opposition from within the Congress and from the non-communist Left as well.[74] P. N. Dhar (principal secretary to the prime minister during the Emergency) expressed this in a subsequent note to the influential government adviser P. N. Haksar:

> We all but lost our independence in that period … A Plan holiday was imposed on us in the name of consolidation of the economy. Our world image as a progressive non-aligned country suffered … . During the same unfortunate period, the World Bank forced upon us a devaluation of the rupee … . The economy, instead of improving, plunged into a deeper crisis.[75]

All of these features, undoubtedly, had an effect on the Congress government's willingness to proceed with economic reform. But none was as powerful as the translation of political and popular opposition to the policies into electoral losses for the Congress.

In the February 1967 elections, Congress sustained serious losses at both Union and State levels. Its seats in the Lok Sabha were reduced from 361 to 283—though, with support from the communists and others, it remained in government. In several states, it did not. Business was confident that electoral setbacks would make Congress more amenable to its demands. Leading businessman, G. D. Birla, told the Engineering Association of India in early 1967:

> I personally believe from the way in which elections are going that we can reasonably expect a better Cabinet, pragmatic, practical and interested in increasing production.[76]

But his expectations were to be disappointed. According to Dhar, Haksar 'interpreted the electoral reverses of the Congress Party as a rejection of the liberalization trend in the economic policies initiated by Shastri which had climaxed in the devaluation episode'. What was needed was a return to Nehruvian economic principles.[77] Haksar's advice (and that of others) was clearly accepted and there followed a steady resumption of Leftist and statist economic measures.[78] In May 1967, the Congress Working Committee (CWC) was presented with a Ten-Point Programme from Indira Gandhi which included 'social control' of the major banks, nationalisation of the general insurance industry, curbs on business monopolies and the concentration of economic power, rapid implementation of land reform and abolition of the princes' remaining privileges.[79] Despite opposition from the Congress Right and some critique from the Congress Left, the Working Committee adopted the Ten Points.

The Right asserted itself at the 72nd Congress session in late April 1969. The Congress President, Siddavanahalli Nijalingappa, criticised the public sector and the Licence Raj. 'Where there are controls and licensing,' he said, 'there is always corruption and the sooner we do away with licensing and controls the better it [will] be.'[80] Ghose says that the Congress President 'assumed the role of the principal spokesman of the vested interests within the organisation and openly repudiated the socialist objectives which con-stituted the guiding principles of Congress policy'.[81] At this point, for the first time, Indira Gandhi came out with a clearly Leftist position, opposing the President's attack and calling for the defence of a stronger state sector. She followed this up with a 'Note on Economic Policy' to the All-India Congress Committee (AICC) meeting in Bangalore in July. This reiterated the radicalism of the Ten Points. The AICC declared that the aim of the Congress was now 'a Socialist State based on Parliamentary Democracy'.[82]

Following the AICC meeting, the government decided to nationalise 14 major banks—83 per cent of the total banking system. To achieve this, Mrs Gandhi dismissed Morarji Desai, a major force in the Congress Right, as finance minister.[83] She broadcast to the nation on 19 July 1969:

> Control over the commanding heights of the economy is necessary, particularly in a poor country where it is extremely difficult to mobilise adequate resources for development, and to reduce the inequalities between different groups and regions. An institution, such as the banking system, which touches—and should touch—the lives of millions, has necessarily to be inspired by [a] larger social purpose and has to subserve national priorities and objectives.[84]

Later in the year, the government moved to block further expansion of big business houses in many areas of industry through the Monopolies and Restricted Trade Practices Act.[85] These measures produced 'the mobiliza-tion of an extremely wide social support [base] for Mrs Gandhi and her new [that is, post-split] Congress'.[86] Inder Malhotra tells us:

> The effect across the country was electric. In Delhi, rickshaw drivers and other poor people danced in the streets. None of them had ever been inside a bank or was likely to. But they said something was at last being done for the poor and the rich were being put in their place.[87]

At this time, according to Professor C. P. Bhambri, who was carrying out social research in the villages:

> When I asked villages who they would vote for, they said '*Mataji*' [mean-ing Indira Gandhi]. After the 1971 election, Dalits told me 'We feel safe from the Jats because *Mataji* is there'. A cobbler told me, 'If *Mataji* had not

nationalised the banks, my ruffian son would not have become a watch-man for the government![88]

Winning back support for the Congress was clearly her intention. But was it simply an opportunist manoeuvre to preserve the Congress in power? The journal *Thought* had no doubts on this question. Despite conceding that bank nationalisation may have been 'a necessary step towards what to her is Socialism', it was nevertheless 'the product of political calculation, not of a sudden and genuine vision of a Socialist society'. The editor continued: '[E]verything with which she happened to be associated even indirectly is seen as part of her continuing struggle for power and more power.'[89] P. N. Dhar feels that she was trying to establish a 'new image ... to be based on economic radicalism with an anti-American slant in foreign policy'.[90] Dandavate agrees: 'She wanted to create a façade of a radical image around her.'[91] Part of that image-building, according to Rahman, may have been 'to give an ideological turn to the struggle for political supremacy between her and the party bosses'.[92] But Gandhi's alignment with the Congress Left (of whom more below) was based on more than opportunism. Haksar's advice to the prime minister—by which she set considerable store—tells a different story to the versions suggested above. Haksar believed in socialism—state socialism, to be sure—as a way forward out of India's ills. And he addressed Mrs Gandhi as a fellow-believer. In July 1969, he told her:

> I feel that P.M. should reiterate her faith in a socialist society alone being able to solve the problems of our country.

Bank nationalisation in itself was not enough: 'The problem is to convert a system of class banking into banking for the masses.' The influence of industrialists had to be 'reduced and finally eliminated'. The public sector had to be made more efficient. And all these measures had to be accompanied by 'a vast educational programme in favour of socialism'—otherwise, they would just be creating 'state capitalism'.[93]

Sincere, mass-oriented and socialist or not, the government's measures after the 1967 elections represented, at the very least, a reassertion of the Indian state's control over the economy. In the face of the pressures of globalisation, economic decline and popular discontent, the Congress leadership decided that a vigorous bout of renewed statism was required. Vanaik notes on bank nationalisation, '[A]t the time neither the industrial nor agrarian bourgeoisie wanted it … . The existence of state autonomy was the prerequisite for carrying out the measure in the face of class hostility.'[94] The expansion of the state economic power was particularly evident with regard to industry. According to Erdman, the measures 'convinced the industrial community that Mrs Gandhi's government intended slowly to strangle the private sector, ultimately to convert management into paid government functionaries'.[95]

The response of the Congress under Indira Gandhi to the twin pressures of the world market and the Indian electorate was to strengthen the state. In other words, by 1970, India was travelling in precisely the opposite economic direction to that which was becoming virtually *de rigueur* in other developing counties.

The Congress Left

The Congress had declared itself for socialism at the Karachi session in 1931, in the Avadi resolution of 1955 and through various declarations set before the Indian Parliament. 'Congress has officially and explicitly accepted socialism', wrote Gulzari Lal Nanda, in his introduction to a collection of Nehru's writings on the subject in 1965. 'There may be differences in emphasis, there may be differences on minor shades but the broad outlines have already been settled.'[96] There was, however, a considerable body of opinion among Congress members which did not think that these outlines had been settled enough. They wanted policies that were more Left-wing and more explicit. The first attempt, after 1947, to organise this trend was made by S. N. Mishra and K. D. Malaviya in 1957. In that year, they established the Congress Socialist Forum—with the approval of Jawaharlal Nehru. But the grouping proved short-lived.[97]

The next attempt was somewhat more successful. In 1962, Nanda (who was the Union Minister for Labour, Employment and Planning), Lalit Narayan Mishra and Shashi Bhushan founded the Congress Forum for Socialist Action (CFSA) once again with Nehru's approval—and that of the CWC. According to the Forum's biographer, it was established because its leaders wanted to oppose both 'Right reaction' and 'Left adventurism' within the Congress.[98] The Forum had a distinctly anti-communist flavour at this time.[99] The Forum was in favour of an alliance between the

Congress and the Praja Socialist Party (PSP)—uniting the 'national democratic socialist parties'—but not with the CPI.[100] But this was not to last.

Former members of the CPI and the PSP joined Congress after the 1967 election, encouraged by, and encouraging, the Congress turn to Leftism. The ex-communists were led by Mohan Kumaramangalam, a prominent CPI member who had argued within the party (unsuccessfully) that, instead of attacking the Congress for not being socialists, they should either work with, or work within, the Congress to hold the mass organisation to its socialist word.[101] The ex-communists and the ex-socialists (e.g., Chandra Shekhar, Mohan Dharia and Krishan Kant), together with some elements of the existing Congress Left, took over the CFSA, reorganising it from August 1967 onwards.[102] Their aim was 'to consolidate the progressive and radical elements inside the party and weld them into a cohesive organisational force'.[103] From this point, the CFSA looked also to the Left outside Congress.[104]

In order to move Congress further to the Left, the CFSA argued for the immediate implementation of the Ten-Point Programme, which, Dharia complained to the 71st session in January 1968, 'had been put in cold storage'.[105] Chandra Shekhar delivered a thunderous critique of the government's 'socialism' at a Congress Convention to discuss implementing the Ten-Point Programme in 1969:

> The 'ideals' have been thrown to winds one after the other. The net result is that slogans have tended to remain hollow as promises continue to remain unfulfilled.

The planned economy itself, he pointed out, 'contributed to the growth of big companies in Indian industry … the operation of the economic system … tends to support the large and established enterprise against the small and struggling entrepreneur'. This was against the intention of the Five Year Plan to curb the concentration of wealth and economic power. Meanwhile, the Planning Commission had failed: '[I]t has become an instrument of convenience to those very interests against which it was supposed to operate.'[106] The Congress Left was opposed to the interests of the Indian bourgeoisie, which was '[b]asically cowardly, ever afraid to cross swords with the foreign enslavers of our land', according to H. D. Malaviya. He argued for measures 'to not only curb but crush the power of concentrated wealth'. To this end, 'the 20 Large Industrial Houses should be nationalised'. He declared: 'The way out is socialism and yet more of socialism.'[107] This was, as ever, *state* socialism: 'There is no escape in India from economic activity of the State. The State has to intervene and much more effectively than hitherto.'[108] To get more socialism, the Left appeared prepared to split the Congress. Malaviya, Nanda and Chandra Shekhar called for a purge of Congress members who did not support its socialist policies.[109] The CFSA's support, within the Congress, was indicated by the fact that it received the signatures of 118 Congress MPs for a memorandum 'seeking comprehensive socio-economic changes' in late 1967.[110]

The Forum also received the support of Indira Gandhi. At first, this was somewhat lukewarm. While Congress president, from 1959 to 1960, she had signed the earlier Congress Socialist Forum's initial statement; but that was as far as her support would extend.[111] She was more positive towards the CFSA, especially when it went into battle for the Ten-Point Programme.[112] She also appreciated the fact that the Forum lined up with her against the Syndicate (discussed further). Predictably, the CFSA's support for Gandhi remained strong after the 1969 split. Malaviya wrote in 1973:

> The Congress Left is confident that yet bolder and yet more decisive actions by her are in store. The Congress Left had the privilege of enjoying her confidence and she also knows that her most disciplined and trusted supporters are of the Congress Left.[113]

Mrs Gandhi had made it clear that the Congress Left's confidence in a continuation of Leftist policies was not misplaced. It was reported that at the AICC meeting in July 1969:

> Indira Gandhi said [that] mere nationalisation [of the banks] or even removal of industrialists from the Boards of Directors would not make any difference. What was important was to ensure that persons who managed these institutions had a 'commitment to our ideologies and policies'.[114]

The Split

Mrs Gandhi's move towards the Left brought about division in the Congress and eventually a split in the organisation in late 1969. She was opposed by 'the Syndicate'—a grouping of powerful state-level Congress leaders and organisational figures. Ironically, the Syndicate had been instrumental in bringing Mrs Gandhi to the Congress leadership, in the mistaken belief that she would be easily controlled. The battle between them occupied most of 1969 and included a spirited dispute over the preferred Congress candidate for the presidency of India following the death of the incumbent, Zahir Hussain, in May 1969.[115] The Syndicate was also particularly incensed by the nationalisation of the banks. The deposed finance minister, Morarji Desai, joined forces with them over this issue. In October 1969, Gandhi's supporters (407 out of the AICC's 708 members) petitioned the Congress organisation for a 'requisitioned' (i.e., special) meeting of the AICC to pursue and extend their policies. Denied this, they boycotted the CWC meeting on 1 November, met separately and called an AICC meeting for later in the month. On 12 November, 11 of the 21 CWC members met and expelled Indira Gandhi. Each side declared themselves the 'real' Congress—Mrs Gandhi's Congress ('R'—at first for 'Requisionist', sometimes thereafter for 'Reformed') and the Syndicate's Congress ('O'—for 'Organisation', less probably for 'Old'). The former, the Congress (R), with 220 MPs and a solid majority of AICC members was still able to govern at the centre and in the states—with the support of the communists and some regional parties.[116]

What did the Syndicate represent? Mahendra Prasad Singh dates its origin as 'an informal party caucus' of power holders from late 1963. It represented the Congress Right, economic conservatives and those with links to big business, those with ties to the rich farmers and even some 'socialists'.[117] The editor of the Congress *Encyclopaedia* described them as 'city bosses' and a 'fossilised and reactionary leadership', while the (Gandhi-appointed) Congress (R) president told the 75th session that they were 'a group of calculating politicians who used [the Congress] as a tool for grabbing power rather than for rendering service to the people'.[118] H. D. Malaviya, writing for the CFSA in 1965, contended that support for 'the rather conservative wing in the Congress' came from the 'Rajas and businessmen with doubtful records, and others of the careerist and opportunist variety' who had entered the organisation.[119] Singh argues that the Syndicate's support came from new elites—'the big landlords, traders and many other rural communities'—that had joined Congress 'for the chances it offered' at state and local levels after 1947. These people 'naturally had no motivation to jeopardize their positions by radical social change and they therefore exerted an effective moderating influence on the party'.[120] Mrs Gandhi identified them, above all, as an ideological enemy:

the reactionary Right which had to be dealt with, if Congress was to continue its Left trajectory. She told Congress members in November 1969:

> What we witness today is not a mere clash of personalities, and certainly
> not a fight for power … . It is a conflict between two outlooks and attitudes
> in regard to the objectives of the Congress and the methods in which the
> Congress itself should function … . It is a conflict between those who are
> for socialism, for change and for the fullest internal democracy and debate
> in the organisation on the one hand, and those who are for the status quo,
> for conformism and for less than full discussion inside the Congress.[121]

Leftism Resumed

In part, the split was a fulfilment of the desire of the Congress Left for a purge of the Right-wing elements. The 'requisitioned' AICC meeting in October 1969 had expressed the need to 'attune the Congress organisation to this purpose'—that is, the execution of Indira Gandhi's socialist policies. The latter told Congress members that, due to the influence of the Syndicate, the organisation 'has ceased to be a fit instrument of its own aims and is losing its sense of purpose'.[122] Sankar Ghose wrote later that it became increasingly clear that the Congress must rid itself of those elements which belonged to the Syndicate if the Congress wanted to translate into reality it socialist ideal.[123]

Once freed of the Syndicate, the Congress (R) resumed its Leftist course. The new AICC elected three CFSA members to its Working Committee, with Chandra Shekhar and K. D. Malaviya as 'special invitees'.[124] Its president, Jagjivan Ram, told the first session (officially, the 73rd Congress session in December 1969) that 'the Congress must pursue radical policies or disintegrate. It must transform itself into an instrument of revolutionary change'.[125] The Congress (R) voted 'to prevent the evils of concentration of economic power and growth of monopolies' and to expand the public sector.[126] In 1970, a new licensing policy extended controls over the large industrial houses.[127]

The AICC decided at its Bombay meeting in December 1969, 'to build an army of dedicated cadres'—a decision opposed by state Congress leaders, fearful of the emergence of rival centres of power. Despite that, it was planned to hold four 'cadre-building camps' by 1972. At one of these, 'the cadres were taken around the city's slum areas to acquaint them with the real problems of slum dwellers'.[128] The camps continued after 1972, becoming, if anything, more radical in their policy pronouncements. The first *Background Paper* for the camp at Narora in 1974 described the situation in India as:

> a struggle between the vested interests determined to thwart the further progress of our society towards social justice and economic independence and the toiling masses determined to consolidate the social and economic gains that they have made and to move forward on their chosen course.[129]

There was a need for 'a vigorous attack precisely on those elements, such as black-marketeers, tax-evaders, hoarders and smugglers, which had accentuated the political and economic stagnation of the sixties'.[130] In decidedly Marxist terms, the authors of the paper detected a contradiction 'between a highly evolved social and political consciousness of the broad masses and an institutional structure of the economy which thwarts a correspondingly rising level of social and economic development'. The next paper called for 'a determined attack on feudal relationships and indebtedness in rural areas … we must aim for … a rural economy in which the dominant mode of production is peasant proprietorship—an economy of small farmers who cultivate the land mainly with family labour'.[131]

These radical policies were taken to the February 1971 Lok Sabha elections, under the slogan *Garibi Hatao!* (Get Rid of Poverty!). The Congress (R) won a resounding victory—352 out of 518 seats: an absolute majority. The CPI retained its 23 seats. The Congress interpreted these results as a mandate for continued radicalism. Mrs Gandhi told the Leftist magazine, *Link*: 'We are in a revolutionary period. The entire purpose of our elections was to accelerate our social revolution in a constitutional manner.'[132]

Part of that acceleration was a general questioning of the usefulness, motivation and patriotism of the private sector by Congress leaders. H. R. Gokhale for example, the Minister of Law, considered that regarding property as a 'natural right' obstructed the government's plan to restructure society through 'greater and greater State intervention'.[133] The CWC meeting, in October 1972, declared that '[a] planned economy is incompatible with the periodic distortions of the price structure caused by anti-social activities of private trade in commodities'. The Committee recommended the state takeover of the wholesale trade in food grains. It concluded: '[T]he basic question is whether the private sector is conscious of its social responsibility in terms

of strengthening the foundations of the independent national economy.'
D. P. Dhar told the subsequent AICC meeting, 'If the private sector did
not use its surplus and expertise in a patriotic way for the social objectives,
it would pass into history unlamented.' Congress General Secretary and
Minister Chandrajeet Yadav went further, declaring, 'We must completely
eliminate the Private Sector, because the Private Sector is trying to sabotage
the Public Sector.' The AICC demanded 'that the private sector adopt unambiguously criteria imposed by national priorities and discard those of mere
profitability in a sheltered market'.[134] 'Capitalism', remarked Mrs Gandhi on
a tour of eastern India in October 1973, 'is no cure for poverty'.[135]

Consequently, there was a major increase in state economic intervention. Between 1971 and 1974, the coking coal industry, the general
insurance industry, small industries in shipping, gold and copper, a steel
company and a railway construction company were nationalised. The
wholesale trade in wheat and rice was taken over by the state, as were
textile mills and the management of the Indian Iron and Steel Company.
The government declared its intention to intervene in the management of
the Tata Iron and Steel Company. In rural areas, the nationalised banks
were directed to establish branches, cheap food grains were distributed
and an employment scheme undertaken.[136]

Further controls over the private sector appeared. The AICC had
declared in October 1972:

> The Government shall exercise appropriate control over [the] private sector
> so that not only priorities in production are adhered to, but the system of
> distribution is so regulated as not to lead to profiteering or hoarding to
> the detriment of society at large.[137]

The following year, the Government's Industrial Policy Statement made
licensing (government approval for expansion) mandatory for industries
that were above a certain size. It also listed industries in which it was
mandatory, regardless of size.[138] The Foreign Exchange Act imposed
'numerous restrictions on foreign investment and the functioning of foreign
companies in India, making India one of the most difficult destinations
for foreign capital in the world'.[139]

There was also an increase in the power of the state and its leader.
Since Indira Gandhi was seen as the architect both of the Congress (R)'s
Leftism and its election victory, her standing and her power within
the organisation was greatly increased. D. P. Dhar noted in1973, 'It

was her endorsement of a radical and left-oriented programme of socio-economic transformation that gave to the elections the quality of mass movements.' According to Aruna Asaf Ali in *Link*, 'it was not the organisation but the individual leading it who won [the people's] wholehearted support.'[140] The Congress Left was not altogether averse to this trend, since it 'favoured a strong centre because ... it provided the framework to break through the various areas of institutional resistance at the state level'.[141]

But, as power ascended to the leader, the rest of the organisation weakened. The party organisation collapsed into the government.[142] Observing the situation from the CPI, Amarjit Kaur told the author:

> Within Congress collective leadership started dwindling and more power started coming in on one person ... power started centring more and more around Indira Gandhi ... . With the [1969 Congress] split, further power concentration came into her hands and her group.[143]

Mrs Gandhi recognised this; she told *Link* in August 1971, 'The reconstruction of the Congress has been taken up and it is going on. The methods of working which had crept in during the era of bosses [that is, the Syndicate] are being given up. The voice of the rank and file prevails.' The cadre was to be improved through regional camps and campaigns, while a drive to attract youth would be initiated.[144] But atrophy at the base continued. By 1973, Dhar could say, '[W]e [have] become aware of the sickness of this political giant.' Further, '[T]he party ... is fast becoming a dung-heap of defectors.' Congress, according to Dhar, was directionless, its mass support faltering. This was particularly evident in agriculture, where '[w]e have to admit that land reforms have foundered ... . Both politically and socially, the defeat of land reforms is a serious set back'. In an effort to revive the programme, the CWC had called for 'popular Vigilance Committees'—'but the Resolution was not implemented by any State Government'. 'Who was to blame?' asked Dhar. He answered:

> The finger must point unnervingly to the dominant sections of party leadership both in the urban and rural areas, which are strongly linked to the interests of the big traders and the big producers.[145]

Nevertheless, from 1971 to 1974, the progress of the Congress (R) and its leader was generally triumphant. The election victory of 1971 was followed by military victory over Pakistan in the war that created Bangladesh and further successes in the state elections of 1972. Importantly, each step in the Congress advance seemed inextricably entwined with the expansion of state power.

Meanwhile—and not entirely unconnected with that last point—the Congress Left was riding high as well. Following the split, in places where Congress organisations had been controlled by the Syndicate, it was often CFSA supporters who moved to consolidate new Congress (R) structures. Former CPI members continued to join the new Congress and gravitated towards the CFSA. One thousand delegates attended the CFSA's fourth All-India Convention at Madras in October 1970.[146] Leading members of the CFSA were the first to argue for the nationalisation of the wholesale market in wheat and rice.[147] The Congress (R) election manifesto for 1971 was written by Malaviya, Dharia and Yadav of the CFSA. The Forum wanted to establish a formal united front for the elections with other Leftist parties, including the CPI. In this, they were unsuccessful—but they did arrange some electoral adjustments between Congress and CPI candidates.[148] In the new Lok Sabha, some 100 MPs attended meetings of the Forum's Parliamentary Unit and it could rely on the voting support of 60–80 of these.[149] The influence of the Left reached the summit of Congress leadership circles.[150] The CFSA had wider horizons than mere parliamentary ones. It declared in December 1972:

> A State power committed to a socialist society cannot afford to be neutral … . It will have to choose sides, and we have already chosen the side of the overwhelming mass living in poverty amidst plenty.[151]

Following the split in the Congress, the CFSA became increasingly critical of the speed with which Indira Gandhi's government was implementing the party's socialist programme. Chandra Shekhar, Chandrajit Yadav and Mohan Dharia were particularly prominent in these attacks. By 1973, the threat to the Congress leadership no longer came from the Right but from the Left.[152] The CFSA All-India Convention in December 1972 was its biggest, with three thousand delegates attending.[153]

In March–April 1973, the Forum sponsored a two-day seminar on the dangers of 'Right Reaction'. Two leading members of the CPI, Hiren Mukherjee and Mohit Sen, attended. A Forum spokesperson told those present that Right Reaction grouped together '[B]ig Business, property owners in the rural areas, black money economy [and] foreign influence in cultural and educational fields'. A consolidation of socialist forces was needed to combat it. K. R. Ganesh, from the Congress, said:

We (Congressmen) will simultaneously build bridges with the left outside … . In such a consolidation, all patriotic forces and elements committed to a programme of democracy, secularism, non-alignment, world peace, disarmament, planning, primacy of Public Sector and break up of monopolies will have a role to play.[154]

Mohit Sen reported afterwards that 'speaker after speaker insisted that a purge of the Congress was essential so that those undesirable elements could not sabotage from within'.[155] By the time of its demise, the CFSA numbered among its members, 16 ministers, 16 Pradesh Congress general secretaries, 4 Pradesh Congress Committee presidents and 2 members (and 7 invitees) of the CWC. Nevertheless, the Forum's December 1972 Convention, as well as being its biggest, would also be its last.

All was not well within the CFSA. The ex-communists (K. R. Ganesh, K. D.Malaviya, M. Kumaramangalam, Chandrajit Yadav and Vayalar Ravi) were now at some distance from the ex-socialists (Chandra Shekhar, Mohan Dharia, Krishna Kant and Ram Dhan).[156] The latter tended to take a sterner line towards the government than the former. Chandra Shekhar denounced the ex-communists for functioning as a 'clique'. He said that they were attempting to gain personal power to isolate Congress socialists who did not hail from the CPI and to portray themselves alone as enjoying Indira Gandhi's confidence. He and Krishan Kant left the CFSA at this time. Chandra Shekhar accused the former communists of being influenced by 'extraneous considerations' (by which he meant the Soviet model) in which they had 'unquestioned faith'—this ran 'counter to the principle of self-reliance and [was] fraught with many dangerous possibilities'.[157]

Apart from its internal differences, despite the outward appearance of going from strength to strength, the CFSA was fatally undermined by the fact that its erstwhile supporter, the prime minister, no longer needed it. After the Congress election victories in 1971 and 1972, large numbers of former Congress members returned to the organisation. Personally loyal to Mrs Gandhi, they constituted a strong support base for her, within the Congress. The prevailing sentiment was expressed by Bansi Lal, the then chief minister of Haryana, who said in December 1972, 'Haryana has always tried to religiously follow the policies set forth by our Prime Minister.'[158] The Congress Left found itself overwhelmed.

From her position of unchallenged power after 1971, she grew impatient with Leftist criticism of the extent and slowness of her socialist policies. She felt 'well emboldened ... to lay a very heavy hand on the young radicals who were then embarrassing her'.[159]

Before this, in August 1972, what remained of the Congress Right had founded its own 'Nehru Study Forum' (NSF), with the support of some 65 Congress MPs, to counter Left influence. The NSF was especially alarmed at the extent of communist influence in the Congress—particularly in the CFSA. One of its leaders, Panchanan Misra, denounced 'the sectarian activities of the handful of men in the party who were busy importing extraneous ideology into the Congress to subvert its democratic character'. They were intent on making the Congress an 'appendage' of the CPI, he said. Inviting CPI members to the CFSA seminar on Right Reaction, said the NSF, showed 'collusion' between the two organisations. The Congress did not need the help of communists to implement its policies. The war of words between the two Forums continued for some months. The CFSA denounced the NSF as 'a bunch of reactionaries'. The latter accused the former of wanting to drag India into the 'Soviet orbit'.[160]

Haksar replied (in a note to the Prime Minister) that

> The answer ... is not to surrender to anti-communism but boldly defend unity between Congressmen and Communists as historic allies being like-minded parties together pledged to fight the common enemy and realise the common aim ... . The leadership of the CSF[A] either consciously or spontaneously is on friendly terms with the CPI. This friendship needs to be strengthened in a manner acceptable to both sides.[161]

Deaf to this advice, Mrs Gandhi seized the opportunity to curb the more boisterous elements of the Left.

The Congress leadership moved to disband all forums operating within the organisation. Mrs Gandhi told *Blitz*, 'At this moment, there is really no need for a separate Forum.' In the face of prime ministerial opinion, the resistance offered by some CFSA leaders collapsed. The CFSA disbanded on 17 April 1973 and the NSF followed suit.[162] From the CPI, Mohit Sen commented that winding up the CFSA was 'deplorable'. He went on:

> But the Forum had rendered tremendous service and played a sterling role in defeating the Right and pushing Congress to the Left. It represented Left nation-alism at its best and at the point of its evolution into revolutionary democracy ... . The winding up of this body was a concession to the Right ... . The Prime Minister has committed grievous mistake and harmed her own party, to say nothing of the nation, by insisting on the liquidation of the CFSA.[163]

Leftism continued, however—although Congress policy towards Indian business remained somewhat confusing. Leftist policies seemed to convey a fairly straightforward approach: The bourgeoisie was the enemy and countless statements from Congress leaders, great and small, advocated stern regulation—or even threatened complete destruction—if capitalists did not place the interests of the nation ahead of grubby considerations of profit.[164] In reality, it was not quite so simple. Indian capitalists did not generally regard themselves as being part of the 'enemy camp'.[165] Mrs Gandhi herself distinguished between friend and foe amongst industrialists. During her struggle with Morarji Desai, for example, she felt able to appeal for support to the Birla family through her friendship with Krishna Kumar Birla.[166] In fact, sections of Indian business still saw themselves (despite the Congress Left) as being in a kind of nation-building partnership with the Congress government, which dated back to the Freedom Movement.

After the 1971 elections, J. R. D. Tata sought an interview with the Prime Minister in order to discuss 'the main thrust that must be given to economic, particularly industrial, development if we are to set ourselves on the path of self-reliance and self-sufficiency'—an indication of continuing support for ISI.[167] In pursuit of this, Tata wrote a lengthy memorandum on the economic situation, entitled 'Suggestions for Accelerating Industrial Growth', in May 1972. This contained predictable complaints about government restraint on industrial growth and the Licence Raj and the demand for 'a firmer stand … in the matter of labour disputes and indiscipline'.[168] But Tata was also at pains to remain at the side of Mrs Gandhi's Congress:

> We have … sought to recommend only what we think is realistic in the present context and which Government could introduce in modification of their present policies without violating their basic socio-economic policy.

Or, as he wrote to Haksar the following day, 'without any fundamental departure from their basic political and economic philosophy'.[169] Tata suggested that if some of the advice in the memorandum was taken up, then the government could expect the private sector to contribute to the *Garibi Hatao* programme. Erdman describes the relationship between the Congress and big business at this point as one of 'convergence': 'Without arguing that Tata became the de facto minister of industrial development, it is evident that most of his main points found a place in Mrs Gandhi's [Emergency] twenty-point program.'[170] Certainly, there was some speculation that, despite its anti-business rhetoric, Congress was locked in a convenient embrace with big business.[171]

Yet, at the same time, there appeared to be moves afoot to encourage small and medium firms and to restrict the growth of big business. The longest section of complaint in the Tata Memorandum bemoans the 'Curbs on Growth of "Larger Houses"'.[172] Certain areas of the economy were reserved for small-scale industries—and the list kept growing.[173] FICCI's Venkatasubbiah suggests, that at this time:

> Mrs Gandhi began by drawing closer to the younger industrialists, technicians and managers, presumably because the attitude of the older generation had begun to harden … the younger industrialists and the professional managers and technologists were more willing to see the good points of official policy than the older business leaders.

But if the Congress was favouring business (big or small), in line with a policy of self-reliance, how could the Industrial Policy Statement of 1973 (mentioned above)—which, despite its restrictive aspects, opened the door very slightly to the entry of foreign firms into India—be explained? Anil P. Dongre asserts that this started 'the impact of globalization on Indian industry', which rather overstates the case—devaluation and the policy changes of 1974 were much more important.[174] Nevertheless, it is yet another awkwardly shaped piece to fit into a consistent Congress economic jigsaw.

Conclusion

The period from 1966 (when Indira Gandhi became the prime minister) to 1974 (the year before the Emergency) illustrates the two great pressures that bore down on the Congress state. On the one hand, the burgeoning forces of globalisation demanded the entry of world market forces into the economy and, therefore, presaged the weakening of the national state's control over economic mechanisms—'liberalisation' in both its internal and external forms. On the other hand, since India was a democracy, the pressure of the electorate, often manifested through the Congress Left, had also to be taken into consideration. When liberalisation harmed the economic interests of the people—or their perceived interests as manifested in the Congress version of socialism—electoral backlash resulted and the Congress government beat a hasty retreat.

The period began with India's statist economic model, beset by economic crisis, resulting in stern admonition from the World Bank, the IMF and the US administration. In common with many other developing countries, India accepted the advice of these institutions. Orthodox World Bank/IMF policies, including devaluation, were agreed to. Had they continued, these policies may have led (again, in common with developments elsewhere) to a transformation of India's ISI development strategy to one of ELI. This would have required an ideological about-face on the part of India's rulers, but such things were not unheard of.

The process, however, was stopped in its tracks by the reaction of India's voters. And, unlike other countries, where such policies had been implemented (South Korea and Taiwan, for example,—and later, China), India's democracy could not ignore popular opposition to the abandonment of what was seen as the traditional Congress developmental model. A return to statism and Leftism was the result—and Indira Gandhi, most of the Congress and a thumping majority of the electorate were clearly more comfortable with this. Leftism was the overarching theme of the period. And Leftism had important consequences: an increase in the power of the national state; an assertion of the national interest against those of the private sector; and an implementation of national state power through economic controls. Consequently, India under Gandhi was at odds with the direction of powerful world market forces.

A clear picture? Perhaps. But there remained some question marks suspended over it that blurred the picture somewhat. Firstly, what was Congress' relationship with the bourgeoisie? Was the Congress tied to big business—on a path to 'convergence'? And if so, did the Congress and big business converge in a rejection of external liberalisation? Or was it moving in the direction of small and medium business—and an acceptance of the external liberalisation that the latter wanted? Secondly, to what extent was Indira Gandhi's Congress solidly Leftist? In 1966, Leftism had been summarily abandoned in the face of economic difficulties and World Bank/IMF pressure. After devaluation, it had returned. Amidst more difficulties, would it remain in 1975? Dhar wrote later: 'In these circumstances, economic policies hovered between past political commitments and new economic compulsions, between meeting the demands of radical ideologues, on the one hand and a pragmatic response to the realities, on the other.'[175]

Congress approached the new year with a confused economic policy outlook and such questions as these hanging over it. It was, of course, entirely possible that there were different answers to the questions circulating, even within such a centralised leadership as that of Mrs Gandhi. That possibility will be taken up once we have re-joined the CPI and examined its evolution up to 1975.

Notes

1. Susan Strange, 'New World Order: Conflict and Co-operation', *Marxism Today* (January 1991): 31. In *States and Markets*, Strange concluded: 'Change in the production structures changes the very nature of the state. Its capabilities are changed and so are its responsibilities' (Susan Strange, *States and Markets* [London: Pinter, 1994], 89).
2. 'By the last decade of the twentieth century, governments could successfully block at their national borders few things other than tangible objects weighing more than three hundred pounds' (Robert Reich, *The Work of Nations* [New York: Knopf, 1991], 111).
3. Nigel Harris, *Of Bread and Guns: The World Economy in Crisis* (Harmondsworth: Penguin, 1983), 194.
4. *The Economist*, 'Third World Survey', 23 September 1989, 58.
5. For an examination of the process in the Soviet (and related) contexts, see: David Lockwood, *The Destruction of the Soviet Union: A Study in Globalization* (Houndmills: Macmillan, 2000).
6. On the evolution of Congress economic policy see: David Lockwood, *The Indian Bourgeoisie* (London: IB Tauris, 2009), especially Chapter 5.
7. See David Lockwood, 'Was the Bombay Plan a Capitalist Plot?' *Studies in History* 28, no. 1 (2012): 99–116.
8. Stanley A. Kochanek, 'Briefcase Politics in India: the Congress Party and the Business Elite', *Asian Survey* 27, no. 12 (December 1987): 1280–83.
9. H. Venkatasubbiah, *Enterprise and Economic Change: 50 Years of FICCI* (New Delhi: Vikas Publishing House, 1977), 149. An example of the state's economic power and consequent micro-management can be found in the papers of Indira Gandhi's principal secretary and Deputy Chairman of the Planning Commission, P. N. Haksar. In October 1976, Haksar submitted a two-page typed memo to the Prime Minister outlining why the British-owned Brooke Bond India Ltd should not be allowed to manufacture its own tin boxes. Haksar argued that this would be 'a thin end of the wedge for others to demand licence to set up captive tin can manufacturing plants' (P. N. Haksar, 'Note to PM on Brooke Bond', 26 October 1976. Nehru Memorial Museum and Library [henceforward NMML]: P. N. Haksar papers. Instalment III. Subject Files: O. Deputy Chairman, Planning Commission).
10. Vivek Chibber, *Locked in Place: State-building and Late Industrialization in India* (Princeton: Princeton University Press, 2006), 131.
11. Chibber, *Locked*, 35. For an account of its origins in the First World War, see David Lockwood, 'War, the State and the Bourgeois Revolution', *War & Society* 25, no. 2 (October 2006): 53–79.

12. See Lockwood, Chapter 6 in *The Indian Bourgeoisie*.
13. Chibber, *Locked*, 35.
14. Ibid.
15. Ibid., 200.
16. Ibid., 29, 43 and 193.
17. Ibid., 127–28.
18. Chibber, *Locked*, 34.
19. Nigel Harris, 'India: Part One', *International Socialism* (1st series), no. 17 (Summer 1964): 4–14 at www.marxists.org/history/etol/writers/harris/1964/xx/india3.htm (last accessed on 03 September 2015). Chibber notes that 'the small size of the market meant that it was easy for the first entrant to secure a dominant position' (Chibber, *Locked*, 33).
20. Chibber, *Locked*, 131.
21. Venkatasubbiah, *Enterprise*, 138.
22. Surajit Mazumdar, 'The State, Industrialisation and Competition: A Reassessment of India's Leading Business Enterprises under Dirigisme', *Economic History of Developing Regions* 26, no. 2 (2011): 34.
23. Indira Gandhi to the Congress Parliamentary Party, 11 September 1974 in Moin A. Zaidi, *Full Circle 1972–1975: The Dynamics of A Social Revolution: The National Emergency* (New Delhi: Michiko & Panjathan, 1975), 206. H. K. Vyas (from the CPI) says that between 1969 and 1971, out of 457 industrial licenses issued, 209 went to big business (H. K. Vyas, *Communist Reply to Tata Memorandum* (New Delhi: Communist Party Publication, September 1972), 26–27.
24. Francine R. Frankel, *India's Political Economy, 1947–1977: The Gradual Revolution* (Princeton: Princeton University Press, 1978), 334; David B. H. Denoon, 'Cycles in Indian Economic Liberalization, 1966–1996', *Comparative Politics* 31, no. 1 (October 1998): 46; Chibber, *Locked*, 252; Howard L. Erdman, 'The Industrialists', in *Indira Gandhi's India: A Political System Reappraised*, ed. Henry C. Hart (Boulder: Westview Press, 1976), 132. Business was apparently encouraged to take a positive attitude towards Congress economic policy by no less a person than J. P. Lewis, the Director of the US Aid Mission in March 1964. He warned FICCI against 'a monotonous monologue of protest and complaint' (Quoted in Harsh Dev Malaviya, *The Danger of Right Reaction* (New Delhi: Socialist Congressman Publications, 1965), 239).
25. C. P. Chandrasekhar, 'Crony Capitalism and State Capture', *Frontline*, 21 March 2014: 36. See also Frankel, *India's Political Economy*, 439.
26. Sumit K. Majumdar, *India's Late, Late Industrial Revolution: Democratizing Entrepreneurship* (Cambridge: Cambridge University Press, 2012), 159.
27. Achin Vanaik, *The Painful Transition: Bourgeois Democracy in India* (London: Verso, 1990), 28.
28. Bipan Chandra, Mridula Mukherjee and Aditya Mukherjee, *India Since Independence* (New Delhi: Penguin, 2008), 294.
29. As K. B. Lall told FICCI's 43rd annual session in 1970: 'Through the kindness of our Government, through the imposition of customs duties and import controls, you are deprived of the criteria for judging your efficiency and comparing it with the rest of the world' (Venkatasubbiah, *Enterprise*, 148).
30. Mukherjee argues that these regulations, despite their 'socialist' pretensions 'actually ended up building a distorted, backward capitalism, as they went against the basic laws of capitalism such as the need for continuous expansion on the basis of innovation and efficient investment' (Aditya Mukherjee, 'Indian Economy 1965–1991' in Chandra, Mukherjee and Mukherjee, *Since Independence*, 467).

31. Mukherjee, 'Indian Economy 1965–1991', 465–6.

32. Atul Kohli, 'Politics of Economic Liberalization in India', *World Development* 17, no. 3 (1989), 307.

33. *Thought*, 12 April 1974, 6. Indira Gandhi's adviser, P. N. Dhar states: 'India's rigid controls and licensing needed to be loosened to increase production and promote exports… . Large business houses had to be permitted to expand production' (P. N. Dhar, *Indira Gandhi, the 'Emergency', and Indian Democracy* [New Delhi: Oxford India Paperbacks, 2001], 234).

34. Chibber, *Locked*, 252.

35. Prabhat Patnaik, 'On the Political Economy of Economic "Liberalisation"', *Social Scientist* XIII, no. 146–47 (July–August 1985): 12. McDonald adds: 'In the India of economic plans and government control of the "commanding heights" that had developed by the 1960s, a lot of grovelling was required for businessmen to get the clearances they needed. Inevitably, the bureaucratic signature needed to move a file from desk to desk came to have a price on it as well' (Hamish McDonald, *The Polyester Prince: The Rise of Dhirubhai Ambani* (St Leonards: Allen & Unwin, 1998), 36.

36. Chibber, *Locked*, 217.

37. It 'was clear that it was quite naïve to expect the industrialists, who had been conditioned over a long period to the comfortable situation of a totally sheltered market, to agree to a switchover to an efficient system involving international competition and competitiveness as a price of survival'. (Jagdish N. Bhagwati and Padma Desai, *India: Planning for Industrialization* (London: OECD & Oxford University Press, 1970), 486. See also Jorgen Dige Pedersen, 'Explaining Economic Liberalization in India: State and Society Perspectives', *World Development* 28, no. 2 (2000): 266; Patnaik, 'Political Economy', 13.

38. Denoon, 'Cycles', 46; Chibber, *Locked*, 217–8. Chibber points out that when external liberalisation started in 1989, it was opposed by big industrialists in the 'Bombay Club' and the Confederation of Indian Industries (*Locked*, 253).

39. Dwijendra Tripathi and Jyoti Jumani, *The Concise Oxford History of Indian Business* (New Delhi: Oxford University Press, 2008), 167–76 and 192–94.

40. Patnaik, 'Political Economy', 13.

41. Stanley A. Kochanek, *Business and Politics in India* (Berkeley, CA: University of California Press, 1974), 190. Answering the question, 'Why did the [1966 to 1968] Liberalization Stall?', Denoon replies: 'Split in the business community: protectionists vs. those wanting more open trade.' (Denoon, 'Cycles', 56.)

42. Prime Minister Shastri asked the FICCI committee for recommendations as to which controls should be abolished on no less than four occasions between May and December 1965. The committee was unable to agree on specific suggestions (Kochanek, *Business and Politics*, 190).

43. Rahul Mukherji, 'India's Aborted Liberalization—1966', *Pacific Affairs* 73, no. 3 (Autumn 2000): 379–80; Medha M. Kudaisya, '"Reforms by Stealth": Indian Economic Policy, Big Business and the Promise of the Shastri Years, 1964–1966', *South Asia: Journal of South Asian Studies* 25, no. 2 (2002): 210; Mary C. Carras, *Indira Gandhi: In the Crucible of Leadership* (Bombay: Jaico Press Private Ltd, 1980), 109; P. N. Dhar, *Indira Gandhi*, 139.

44. Kudaisya, 'Reforms by Stealth', 217; Denoon, 'Cycles', 48; Chibber, *Locked*, 219.

45. Denoon, 'Cycles', 49; Kudaisya, 'Reforms by Stealth', 217; Edward S. Mason and Robert E. Asher, *The World Bank since Bretton Woods* (Washington: Brookings Institution,

1973), 680; Chandra, Mukherjee and Mukherjee, *Since Independence*, 458; Mukherji, 'Aborted', 377.

46. Praveen K. Chaudhry, Vijay L. Kelkar and Vikash Yadav, 'The Evolution of "Homegrown Conditionality" in India/IMF Relations', *Journal of Development Studies* 40, no. 6 (August, 2004): 61.

47. Chaudhry, Kelkar and Yadav say that this forced India to succumb to US demands ('Evolution', 61); Sengupta says the US policy pushed India 'into near-famine conditions' (Mitu Sengupta, 'Making the State Change Its Mind—the IMF, the World Bank and the Politics of India's Market Reforms', *New Political Economy* 14, no. 2 (June, 2009): 86).

48. Mason and Asher, *World Bank*, 455.

49. See Bell's account of the mission and its Report: Bernard R. Bell, *A Conversation with Bernard Bell, Part 1*, interviewed by Robert W. Oliver (Washington D.C.: California Institute of Technology, 1985), http://go.worldbank.org/ASNT3Q5DE0 (last accessed on 3 September 2015). When the Bank informed the Government of India of its intention, it initially refused. The government finally accepted on the condition that the Report would be available *only* to India's Finance Minister (T. T. Krishnamachari) and to World Bank Governor Woods. As we shall see, this condition did not last long (Bell, *Conversation*).

50. Bernard R. Bell (ed.), *Report to the President of the International Bank for Reconstruction and Development and the International Development Association on India's Economic Development Effort, Volume 1. Main Report*, 1 October 1965. At www-wds.worldbank. org, 25. When the mission put the case for the reduction of controls to leading government economist I. G. Patel: 'He said "But those entrepreneurs might make mistakes," which was characteristic of the attitude and the views … of the government of India: bureaucrats, the civil service could make all economic judgements far better than anyone in the private sector.' (Bell, *Conversation*, 6.)

51. Bell, *Report*, 17 and 24.

52. Ibid., 13, 16 and 23.

53. Ibid., 34–36, 30. According to Mason and Asher, the Bank said that without reform, 'no increase in assistance for the Fourth Plan could be expected, and possible a reduction should be anticipated.' (Mason and Asher, *World Bank*, 196.)

54. Report in *The Eastern Economist* cited in Ahok Bhargava and Gopalan Balachandaran, 'Economic Changes during the Indian Emergency', *Bulletin of Concerned Asian Scholars*, 9, no. 4 (October–December, 1977): 51.

55. Kudaisya, 'Reform by Stealth', 210–14. See also Bhagwati, *Planning for Industrialization*, 480. All this despite the fact that 'Prime Minister Shastri said in a press interview that the Congress was irrevocably committed to democratic socialism' (reported by H. D. Malaviya to the Congress 64th session, 7 January 1957. Harsh Dev Malaviya, *Socialist Ideology of Congress: A Study in its Evolution* (New Delhi: Socialist Congressman Publications, 1966, 61).

56. Bhagwati, *Planning for Industrialization*, 477–79. The first group of these included iron and steel castings and forgings, electric motors, pulp, glue and gelatin, glass, power alcohol, gypsum and timber products (Kudaisya, 'Reform by Stealth', 220).

57. In Kudaisya, 'Reform by Stealth', 220.

58. Bell, *Conversation*, 14.

59. Francine R. Frankel, *India's Political Economy, 1947–1977: The Gradual Revolution* (Princeton: Princeton University Press, 1978), 296–97; Sengupta, 'Making the State', 185–86. When asked about devaluation, L. K. Jah, one of the prime minister's

secretaries at the time, replied, 'Oh that … that was what [World Bank director] George Woods told us we had to do to get aid' (Mukherji, 'Aborted', 385).

60. Sengupta says, to US$900 million (Sengupta, 'Making the State', 185); Denoon says, to $1.6 billion (Denoon, 'Cycles', 49).

61. Chaudhry, Kelkar and Yadav, 'Evolution', 62. See also Mason and Asher, *World Bank*, 516.

62. According to Bell, 'They [the Indian government] agreed on a 35 percent devaluation of the rupee, which we, in fact, thought was not quite big enough, but accepted' (Bell, *Conversation*, 4).

63. Frankel, *India's Political Economy*, 298–99. See also, Bhagwati, *Planning for Industrialisation*, 477.

64. Bell, *Conversation*, 11.

65. Mukherji, 'Aborted', 375–78; Chibber, *Locked*, 221; Chandra, Mukherjee and Mukherjee, *Since Independence*, 469; Atul Kohli, *State-directed Development: Political Power and Industrialization in the Global Periphery* (Cambridge: Cambridge University Press, 2004), 272; Bhagwati, *Planning for Industrialisation*, 492.

66. Rockefeller in Mukherji, 'Aborted', 378. See also Sengupta, 'Making the State', 186—who attributes the 'flop' remark to Woods himself; Chaudhry, Kelkar and Yadav, 'Evolution', 63.

67. Mukherji points out that 'domestic executive orientation is essential for charting out a development trajectory' ('Aborted', 376; see also 379 and 385).

68. Frankel, *India's Political Economy*, 393; Denoon, 'Cycles', 50.

69. Frankel, *India's Political Economy*, 394; Chaudhry, Kelkar and Yadav, 'Evolution', 63; Dhar, *Indira Gandhi*, 141. The American attitude can perhaps be gauged from Bell's account of the discussion on raising the level of aid:

> 'BELL: Although I won't mention his name, there was one very prominent individual in the U.S. government who said, "It's throwing money down a rat hole." I can mention his name if you like.
> INTERVIEWER: Sure.
> BELL: His name was Johnson.' (Bell, *Conversation*, 13)

70. Chibber, *Locked*, 221. It should be noted that, despite the hostile attitude of the US state, the World Bank (for which, according to Patnaik, 'the institution of a "liberal" economic regime of its liking was not insisted upon') (Prabhat Patnaik, 'On the Political Economy of Economic "Liberalisation",' *Social Scientist*, XIII (146–47) July-August 1985: 6) kept up a low-profile engagement with the Indian government through the 1970s (Sengupta, 'Making the State', 187; William B. Gilmartin, *A Conversation with William Gilmartin*, conducted by Robert W. Oliver, Washington D.C., November 14 1985. World Bank Archives, Oral History: web.worldbank.org: 21–22). This illustrates the different agendas of the US state and the World Bank. The former was primarily interested in questions of Cold War strategy, while the latter was concerned with the smooth running of the world economy.

71. For FICCI's public position, see Venkatasubbiah, *Enterprise*, 139.

72. Mukherji, 'Aborted', 377.

73. The Bell Report—meant for the eyes of Woods and Mitra only (note 47)—was leaked to the CPI. The CPI's *New Age* and the pro-Congress Left *Blitz* then appeared with four-inch headlines declaring 'TO HELL WITH BELL'. Bell comments: 'my

impression, perhaps mistaken, is that the intent in making [the Report] available was to arouse opposition to the recommendations which the Bank was making' (*Conversation*, 8–9).

74. Denoon, 'Cycles', 50; Chandra, Mukherjee and Mukherjee, *Since Independence*, 458; Kudaisya, 'Stealth', 224.

75. P. N. Dhar, 'A note on economic situation and remedies to correct the economic difficulties,' (n.d.). NMML: P. N. Haksar papers. Instalment III. Subject File 248, 1973.

76. G. D. Birla, speaking on 2 January 1967 in Frankel, *India's Political Economy*, 306.

77. Dhar, *Indira Gandhi*, 143.

78. Tripathi and Jumani, *History*, 201; Kudaisya, 'Stealth', 228–29; Ramachandra Guha, *India after Gandhi* (London: Picador, 2007), 435–36.

79. Chandra, Mukherjee and Mukherjee, *Since Independence*, 296; Frankel, *India's Political Economy*, 397–99; Guha, *India after Gandhi*, 436. Ram Singh Awana maintains that the Ten Points were 'implicitly drafted' by the CFSA—on which, see further (Ram Singh Awana, *Pressure Politics in Congress Party: A Study of the Congress Forum for Socialist Action* [New Delhi: Northern Book Centre, 1988], 54).

80. Carras, *Indira Gandhi*, 137–38.

81. Sukhomoy Sen Gupta, 'The Task Ahead', in *The March towards Socialism* (souvenir of the 74th Congress Session, 26–29 December 1972, Calcutta) ed. Sankar Ghose (Calcutta: H. Chakravorty, 1972), 77. According to Ghose, Indira Gandhi told Nijalingappa later that his speech at the Congress session 'was regarded by many as more appropriate to a leader of the Swatantra Party which was hostile to socialism' (Ghose, 'The Congress and Democratic Socialism', in *March towards Socialism*, 116).

82. Frankel, *India's Political Economy*, 403–4; Mohammed Mahafoozur Rahman, *The Congress Crisis* (New Delhi: Associated Publishing House, 1970), 77–80,149. Sukhomoy Sen Gupta argues that Gandhi's Note 'vindicated the nation's unfailing faith in socialism. The note was more than a testament of faith—it was a positive call to action to redeem the pledges which the Congress had made to the people' (Gupta, 'The Task Ahead', in Ghose, *March*, 76).

83. According to Madhu Dandavate, P. N. Haksar was the major proponent of bank nationalisation (NMML Oral History Project: Madhu Dandavate, 2000: 221–22).

84. Indira Gandhi, 'Broadcast on Bank Nationalisation, 19 July 1969', in *The Encyclopaedia of the Indian National Congress. Volume Twenty, 1968–1969: Facing the City Bosses*, ed. Moin A. Zaidi (New Delhi: S. Chand and Company Ltd. 1983), 572. McDonald however points to trouble in store: 'the government takeover led to a steady bureaucratisation of management and lending directed by political connections rather than commercial viability' (*Polyester Prince*, 41).

85. Medha M. Kudaisya, *The Life and Times of G.D. Birla* (New Delhi: Oxford University Press, 2003), 368–69.

86. Michelguglielmo Torri, 'Factional Politics and Economic Policy: The Case of India's Bank Nationalization,' *Asian Survey*, 15 (12) December 1975: 1095. Torri contends that the measures 'were bound to convince large strata of the population that a real change had occurred in New Delhi and, at long last, the Prime Minister and her followers, defying powerful vested interests, were seriously trying to cope with the problems of the common people.' (1096)

87. Inder Malhotra, 'Indira Gandhi: An Overview' in *A Centenary History of the Indian National Congress. Volume V: 1964–1984*, ed. Aditya Mukherjee (New Delhi: Academic Foundation, 2011), 45.

88.   C. P. Bhambri, interview with the author 4 November 2014.

89.   *Thought*, 14 February 1970, 3; 21 March 1970, 4. In October, the editor warned darkly: 'She would not even mind disregarding the Constitution if she found it was an obstacle in her path to establish herself as the sole repository of political virtue and wisdom' (10 October 1970, 3).

90.   Dhar, *Indira Gandhi*, 143.

91.   NMML Oral History, Madhu Dandavate, 220.

92.   Rahman, *Congress Crisis*, 19.

93.   Haksar, 'Note to Prime Minister', 9 July 1969; 'Note to Prime Minister,' 25 July 1969. NMML: P. N. Haksar papers. Instalments I & II. Subject File 42, July 1969. That education had to start with the Congress itself: 'the Congress Party has been so long in power that it has forgotten the most elementary principles of politics, namely, to help the people in fighting injustice.' Haksar, 'Note to Prime Minister', 14 December 1970. NMML: P. N. Haksar papers. Instalments I & II. Subject File 213, 1970–71.

94.   Vanaik, *Transition*, 29. The 'Correspondent' of the *Bulletin of Concerned Asian Scholars* noted, 'These could be called movements in the direction of "state capitalism" and "anti-feudalism"' ('Correspondent', 'The Emergency in India', *Bulletin of Concerned Asian Scholars* 7, no. 4 [October–December, 1975]: 12).

95.   Erdman, 'Industrialists', 134. See also Kohli, *State-directed*, 273.

96.   Gulzari Lal Nanda, 'Introduction', in *Congressman's Primer for Socialism* by Jawaharlal Nehru, compiled by H. D. Malaviya (New Delhi: A Socialist Congressman Publication, 1965), n.p.

97.   Awana, *Pressure Politics*, 4 and 6; Frankel, *India's Political Economy*, 212.

98.   Awana, *Pressure Politics*, 24–43 and 81.

99.   Frankel, *India's Political Economy*, 214–15. Frankel suggests that the Forum's influence was weakened by war with communist China in 1962. If this were the case, it proved to be a temporary setback.

100. Awana, *Pressure Politics*, 14.

101. See S. Mohan Kumaramangalam, *Communists in Congress: Kumaramangalam's Thesis*, edited and introduced by Satindra Singh (Delhi: D. K. Publishing House, 1973 [1964]). See also Frankel, *India's Political Economy*, 407–08.

102. Awana, *Pressure Politics*, 54 and 67; Frankel, *India's Political Economy*, 410; Christopher Andrew and Vasili Mitrokhin, *The Mitrokhin Archive II: The KGB and the World* (London: Allen Lane, 2005), 318. Vasudev names the prominent members of the Congress Left and the ex-PSP as Chandra Shekhar, Krishan Kant, Mohan Dharia, K. D. Malaviya, Dev Kant Barooah, K. P. Unnikrishnan, Chintamani Panigrahi and Shashi Bushan. The most prominent ex-CPI members were Nandini Sat Pathy, Inder Kumal Gujral, Chandrjit Yadav, K. V. Raghathana Reddy, K. R. Ganesh, Nurul Hasan, D. P. Dhar, Mohan Kumaramangalam, Rajni Patel and Amrit Nahata (Uma Vasudev, *Two Faces of Indira Gandhi* [New Delhi: Vikas Publishing House, 1977], 47–48, 50).

103. Awana, *Pressure Politics*, 54.

104. See K. R. Ganesh on building 'bridges with the left outside' in Awana, *Pressure Politics*, 197. Chandra Shekhar said, 'The Indian National Congress being the largest political force in the country should start a dialogue with democratic socialist forces' (Chandra Shekhar, *Presidential Address: Congressmen's National Convention for Implementation of 10 Point Programme* [New Delhi: Congress Forum for Socialist Action, 1969], 19).

105. Congress Encyclopaedia, Volume 20, 71st session Hyderabad, 10–11 January 1968, 37. See also S. N. Mishra to the AICC 2–4 June 1968, Congress Encyclopaedia, Volume 20, 92.

106. Chandra Shekhar, *Presidential Address*, 5, 7–9, 15. Before this, Chandra Shekhar had submitted three memoranda to the government denouncing the Birla business group for circumventing the licensing system, profiteering, evading tax and breaching the foreign exchange regulations. In a letter to Mrs Gandhi in July 1967, he said, 'They [the Birlas] have amassed money at the cost of the suffering, the anguish, the starvation and degradation of out people … . Under the circumstances, a vigorous onslaught on their infinite crimes is essential' (Chandra Shekhar, *A Peep into Birla House* [New Delhi: Shashi Bushan, M.P., April 1969], 4–5).

107. Harsh Dev Malaviya, *The Danger of Right Reaction* (New Delhi: Socialist Congressman Publications, 1965), 240, 342, 356; 'Nationalisation for Economic Advance,' *Indian Left Review* 2, no. 11 (January 1974), 29.

108. Malaviya, *Danger*, 243. Malaviya explicitly endorsed the Soviet model in his book *Ours is the Right Path: A Study of 20 Years of the GDR* (New Delhi: Socialist Congressman Publication, 1969) and in his 'Note on Land Situation in India and the Korean example' in Kim Il Sung, *Theses on the Socialist Agrarian Question in Korea* (New Delhi: Socialist Congressman Publication, 1970).

109. Awana, *Pressure Politics*, 245–46; Frankel, *India's Political Economy*, 214. More broadly (and perhaps more darkly) Ghose stated: 'Everything that stands in the way of the establishment of a free, democratic and socialistic society would have to be removed peacefully, if possible, and through the coercive machinery of the democratic state, if necessary' (Sankar Ghose, 'Editorial', in *The March towards Socialism* (souvenir of the 74th Congress Session, 26–29 December 1972, Calcutta), ed. Sankar Ghose (Calcutta: H. Chakravorty, 1972, 1).

110. Awana, *Pressure Politics*, 55.

111. Ibid., 7.

112. At times, however, she was wary of the Forum's grasp of strategy. In a note to Chandra Shekhar, who was campaigning for state intervention in the import/export trade, the establishment of a Monopolies Commission and the abolition of the princes' privileges, she said, 'I would request you to apply your mind to making bank nationalisation a success' first (Indira Gandhi to Chandra Shekhar (n.d.—probably July 1969). NMML: P. N. Haksar papers. Instalments I & II, Subject File Number 42.)

113. Harsh Dev Malaviya, 'Congress Left is Alive and Kicking', *Indian Left Review*, 2, no. 7 (September 1973): 20.

114. Congress Encyclopaedia, Volume 20, 363.

115. In the presidential election, according to Malhotra, 'The task of Indira's adversaries was simple: to choose one of themselves as the future President and once in Rashtrapati Bhavan he would do the rest'—that is, dismiss the Prime Minister (Inder Malhotra, 'Indira Gandhi: An Overview', in *A Centenary History of the Indian National Congress. Volume V: 1964–1984*, ed. Aditya Mukherjee (New Delhi: Academic Foundation, 2011), 44). Arjun Dev, a CPI student activist at the time, told the author that there was 'mass rejoicing' when Mrs Gandhi's favoured presidential candidate was elected (Arjun Dev, interview with the author, 15 January 2014).

116. Rahman, *Crisis*, 59–69; Bipan Chandra, Mridula Mukherjee and Aditya Mukherjee, *India since Independence* (New Delhi: Penguin, 2008), 299; Guha, *India after Gandhi*, 439.

117. Mahendra Prasad Singh, *Split in a Predominant Party: the Indian National Congress in 1969* (New Delhi: Abhinav Publications, 1981), 43.

118. 'Editor's Note', Congress Encyclopaedia, Volume 20, 15; Barooah to 75th session, 31 December 1975 in *The Encyclopaedia of the Indian National Congress. Volume Twenty Three, 1974–1975: The Lengthening Shadows*, ed. Moin A. Zaidi (New Delhi: S. Chand

and Company Ltd. 1984), 414. The editor of *Thought* pointed out that the Syndicate leaders 'grew in power and influence precisely during the long years of Nehru's reign. Jawaharlal relied on them each to run his province, and was not above utilizing them for some bloodless political liquidation ...' (*Thought*, 3 January 1970, 5).

119. Malaviya, *Danger*, 335.
120. Singh, *Split*, 43–45.
121. Indira Gandhi, 'Letter to Congressmen', 8 November 1969 in Rahman, *Crisis*, 143.
122. Ibid., 147.
123. Sankar Ghose, 'Editorial', in Ghose, *March*, 1.
124. Awana, *Pressure Politics*, 300.
125. Congress Encyclopaedia, Volume 20, 281. At the same session, Y. B. Chavan from Maharashtra said that 'the capitalists not only controlled the economy but also tried to control the Governments as well ... . But now the workers had woken up and there was no going back' (282).
126. Resolution on Economic Policy—Industry, 73rd Session, 28–29 December 1969. Congress Encyclopaedia, Volume 20, 340–1. The expansion was to include elements of worker participation in management.
127. Ila Patnaik, 'Turn the Clock Back'. See http://openlib.org/home/ila/MEDIA/2005/turn_clock.html (last accessed on 2 November 2015; Frankel, *India's Political Economy*, 437.
128. Carras, *Indira Gandhi*, 159–60.
129. 'The Present Political Situation and the Tasks Before the Congress', *Background Paper Number 1* for the AICC Central Training Camp, Narora, 22–24 November 1974 in P. C. Joshi Archives (JNU), Communism in India 1974, File 74, 4.
130. *Background Paper Number 1*: 9.
131. 'Economic Outlook,' *Background Paper Number 2* for the AICC Central Training Camp, Narora, 22–24 November 1974 in P. C. Joshi Archives (JNU), Communism in India 1974, File 74, 26–27.
132. 'Interview with Indira Gandhi,' *Link*, 15 August 1971, 16. In March 1971, D. P. Dhar (at that time, the ambassador to the Soviet Union) had advised Haksar that 'Our [CPSU] Central Committee friend' had suggested that the election victory provided an opportunity for a 'progressive re-orientation of Indian politics.' But, according to Dhar, the unnamed CPSU representative had warned that speed was essential due to differences within the Congress: 'These differences will surface soon and they may even present difficulties in the path of radical measures.' (Letter from D. P. Dhar to P. N. Haksar, 25 March 1971. NMML: P. N. Haksar papers. Instalments I & II, Subject File Number 213, 1970–71.)
133. Cited in Guha, *India after Gandhi*, 473.
134. CWC motion for the AICC, 4 October 1972 in *Congress Marches Ahead* VII: 8–9; D. P. Dhar to the AICC meeting, 9–10 October 1972 in *Congress Marches Ahead* VII: 75; Chandrajeet Yadav, 'On Socialism', in *The March towards Socialism* (souvenir of the 74th Congress Session, 26–29 December 1972, Calcutta) ed. Sankar Ghose (Calcutta: H. Chakravorty, 1972), 53; AICC Resolution, 9–10 October 1972 in *The Encyclopaedia of the Indian National Congress. Volume Twenty-Two, 1972–1973: At War with Poverty*, ed. Moin A. Zaidi (New Delhi: S. Chand and Company Ltd. 1984), 296.
135. Reported in *Thought*, 5 January 1974, 4.
136. Chandra, Mukherjee and Mukherjee, *Since Independence*, 309; Carras, *Indira Gandhi*, 147–50. Carras comments: 'The intent was to establish a public-distribution system that would make food available to the poorer section of the population at fair prices' (150).

137. AICC Resolution on Economic Policy, 9–10 October 1972 in Moin A. Zaidi, *Full Circle 1972–1975: The Dynamics of a Social Revolution: The National Emergency* (New Delhi: Michiko & Panjathan, 1975), 62.

138. Jagadeesh Sivadasan, 'Regulatory Regime in India: 1947 to 1998'. See webuser.bus. umich.edu/jagadees/other/indmfg_data/Reg_history_india.pdf (last accessed on 04 September 2015).

139. Chandra, Mukherjee and Mukherjee, *Since Independence*, 460. The act required that multinationals 'dilute their holdings in their Indian subsidiaries to 40%' and was 'intended to restrict the inflow of foreign capital into the country', according to Tripathi and Jumani (*History*, 199). See also Patnaik, 'Turn the Clock Back'.

140. P. N. Dhar, 'A note on economic situation and remedies to correct the economic difficulties' (n.d.). NMML: P. N. Haksar papers, Instalment III Subject File 248, 1973; Aruna Asaf Ali, 'Vigilant Leadership for a Vigilant People, *Link*, 15 August 1971, 40. The *Thought* editor was characteristically critical: 'She was the symbol of Socialism; she was the assurance of abolition of poverty tomorrow ...' (*Thought*, 27 March 1971, 3).

141. Vernon Hewitt, *Political Mobilisation and Democracy in India: States of Emergency* (New York: Routledge, 2008), 97. Shortly before the split, in August 1969, the CFSA had agreed with its allies in the Congress on the need to strengthen the hand of the Prime Minister (Hewitt, *Political Mobilisation*, 277).

142. Hewitt, *Political Mobilisation*, 93. Hewitt argues that this was not just an accumulation of power. There were 'ideological motives behind her attempts to restructure the Congress and through it a state able to implement meaningful social reforms' (Hewitt, *Political Mobilisation*, 97).

143. Amarji Kaur, interview with author, 15 January 2014.

144. 'Interview with Indira Gandhi,' *Link*, 15 August 1971, 16.

145. Dhar, 'A note on economic situation'.

146. Frankel, *India's Political Economy*, 433, 462–63.

147. Hewitt, *Political Mobilisation*, 103.

148. Awana, *Pressure Politics*, 201; Frankel, *India's Political Economy*, 443, 451.

149. Ibid., 302; Christopher Andrew and Vasili Mitrokhin, *The Mitrokhin Archive II: The KGB and the World* (London: Allen Lane, 2005), 319. Some of the new members were very Left-wing indeed. Priya Raijan Das Munshi was one of the new, young Congress MPs from Bengal. *Link* reported: '"There is no difference in objectives between us and the Naxalites," Das Munshi said. The difference was only in methods, he emphasised' ('Youth Restive, Old Guard Warned,' *Link* 15 August 1971, 49).

150. See, for example, R. K. Dhawan (an 'insider') on Haksar's Leftist role (Vasudev, *Two Faces*, 53).

151. CFSA statement cited by Arjun Arora (CFSA chairman), 'Planning Without Direction', *Indian Left Review* 2, no. 1 (March 1973): 45.

152. Awana, *Pressure Politics*, 317–22.

153. Malaviya, 'Congress Left', 18.

154. Awana, *Pressure Politics*, 196–97. Hiren Mukherjee from the CPI upset things at the seminar somewhat by criticising the outsourcing of the Maruti small car project to Sanjay Gandhi. Both the Maruti and the vehicle industry as a whole, he said, should be nationalised. He went on: 'any young person with talent engaged in such an enterprise—be he the Prime Minister's son, should be given the opportunity to serve the Public Sector.' CFSA leaders apologised for this breach of political etiquette the following day (Awana, *Pressure Politics*, 313).

155.   Mohit Sen, 'Anti-Rightist Counter-attack,' *Indian Left Review*, 2, no. 2 (April 1973): 7.

156.   Stanley A. Kochanek, 'Mrs Gandhi's Pyramid: The New Congress', in Indira Gandhi's India: A Political System Reappraised, ed. Henry C. Hart (Boulder: Westview Press, 1976), 103.

157.   Awana, *Pressure Politics*, 322–6.

158.   Bansi Lal, 'Haryana Enters its Seventh Year', in *The March towards Socialism* (souvenir of the 74th Congress Session, 26–29 December 1972, Calcutta) ed. Sankar Ghose (Calcutta: H. Chakravorty), 1972, 71.

159.   Awana, *Pressure Politics*, 317–21. See also Kochanek, 'Pyramid', 103.

160.   Awana, *Pressure Politics*, 304–14.

161.   NMML: P. N. Haksar papers, Instalment III Subject File IV, 29 March 1973, 4 and 8.

162.   Awana, *Pressure Politics*, 327–33. Those that considered resistance were H. D. Malaviya, Arjun Arora, Mohan Dharia and K. V. Raghunathan Reddy.

163.   Mohit Sen, 'Skirmishes and Confrontations', *Indian Left Review* 2, no. 3 (May 1973): 5.

164.   See, for example, Indira Gandhi to the Indian Merchants' Chamber, 28 December 1974 in Indira Gandhi, *Selected Speeches and Writings of Indira Gandhi. Volume III: September 1972–March 1977* (New Delhi: Ministry of Information and Broadcasting, Government of India, 1984), 347.

165.   See Erdman, 'The Industrialists', 125–26.

166.   Kudaisya, *Birla*, 354.

167.   J. R. D. Tata, letter to Haksar, 1 March 1972. NMML: P. N. Haksar papers. Instalment III, Subject file 225. The reasons for Tata, as a representative of big business, advocating 'self-reliance and self-sufficiency' (the watchwords of 'import-substituting industrialisation') have been discussed earlier in this chapter.

168.   J. R. D. Tata, 'Suggestions for Accelerating Industrial Growth', 17 May 1972. NMML: P. N. Haksar papers, Instalment III, Subject file 225 (henceforward, Tata Memorandum).

169.   Tata Memorandum, 17 May 1972.

170.   Erdman, 'Industrialists', 137.

171.   See Primila Lewis, *Reason Wounded: An Experience of India's Emergency* (London: George Allen & Unwin Ltd., 1978), 22–23; Frankel, *India's Political Economy*, 438. Such speculation was aboard not only on the Left. The *Thought* editor suggested in April 1974 'we have the spectacle of the Government talking tough on Leftist lines but in practice letting favoured firms go ahead' (*Thought*, 13 April 1974, 5).

172.   Sections 3.23–3.41, Tata Memorandum, 17 May 1972.

173.   Aditya Mukherjee, 'Indian Economy 1965–1991', 465; Patnaik, 'Turn the Clock Back'.

174.   Anil P. Dongre, 'Policy Changes in the Wake of Globalization and Its Impact on Indian Industries', *Journal of Policy Modelling*, 34, no. 3 (2012): 481.

175.   Dhar, *Indira Gandhi*, 236.

3

The Communist Party of India and the Congress: Crisis Years

We left India's communists on the eve of Indira Gandhi's prime minister-ship. The CPI saw the ensuing years—from devaluation in 1966, through Congress split and economic crisis, to the mass anti-Congress agitations of the mid-1970s—as years of crisis for India. 'Right reaction' and external interference were ever-present dangers—and the Party spent most of its time considering how these threats were to be defeated, rather than in any quest for power in its own right. Its activities remained punctuated by familiar questions as to the process of the Indian revolution, the nature of the Congress and its relationship to the Indian bourgeoisie. The purpose of this chapter is to examine the CPI's attitude to the Indian state and the Congress during this time of troubles, and to establish how it found itself so firmly on the government's side, come 1975. The communist attitude towards Congress changed dramatically after 1969 due to what the Party regarded as the emergence, after the 1969 split, of the most progressive Congress leadership since Nehru. Its initial enthusiasm waned in the fol-lowing years leading it to eventually adopt a sharply critical attitude to the Congress (R) government. But in 1974, external and internal developments caused the CPI to return to a position of support.

Before the 1969 split, the Party's attitude towards the Congress remained somewhat changeable, leaning to the side of a basic mistrust. This seemed to be borne out during the Shastri years when, as we have seen, steps were taken in the direction of economic liberalisation. When Indira Gandhi became the prime minister, the CPI remained hostile.[1] Sensing potential Congress losses in the 1967 elections, the CPI called on its supporters to vote against 'this intolerable Congress misrule' and to replace it with coalition governments 'of all democratic and left parties'.[2] At these times, the Party position was interpreted as one that wished to split the Congress between its progressive and reactionary wings—so that the National Democratic Front (NDF), led by the CPI, would be 'taking in tow a Congress, weakened and divided, if at all it continued to exist'.[3]

The communists interpreted the election result as 'a mighty blow to the Rightists, especially within the Congress whose monopoly of power was now broken and strength in Parliament greatly reduced'.[4]

The decision to devalue the Indian rupee in June 1966 was seen as the justification of the Party's attitude. This was 'the blackest act of treachery since independence. Carried out at the dictates of US imperialism, acting through the World Bank, by a clique in Delhi'.[5] The Party's NC demanded the government's resignation since 'it has proved itself wholly unworthy of any national trust and thereby forfeited its moral and political right to be placed at the helm of the national affairs'. Nevertheless, the same resolution called for 'a friendly dialogue with … progressive Congressmen at all levels'.[6] In a trenchant critique of devaluation published by the Party in 1966, Srinivas Sardesai accused the government of opening up India to predatory foreign capital and indiscriminate imports. This would 'cripple hundreds of our industrial units which we have built since independence'. A 'staggering list' of industries would now be allowed to import raw materials and accessories. Devaluation, wrote Sardesai, 'put all that was healthy and progressive in Indian life into the melting pot'. It was 'an immediate and dire threat to popular living standards and to our economy, democracy and national independence'.[7] Furthermore, Mohit Sen argued some years later that the 'economic coup' of devaluation laid the basis for a projected Rightist takeover in 1969.[8]

Unity and Struggle

As we know, Mrs Gandhi did not continue with the Shastri economic liberalisation for very long. Electoral reversals for the Congress in February 1967 necessitated a turn to the Left and Mrs Gandhi appeared willing to lead that turn. The CPI believed that the difficulties the Congress was now facing were widening the divisions within the leadership—and that these, in turn, reflected the division between India's 'monopoly' and 'non-monopoly' bourgeoisie.[9] The former was represented by the Syndicate. According to the CPI, the Syndicate represented 'the most reactionary forces', who were 'always trying to resist any progressive trend in [the Congress] or progressive changes in government policies'. They wanted 'to turn the entire Congress organisation into an instrument of money interests'. To this end, their aim was 'to establish a rightist coalition government at the centre'.[10] Amarjit Kaur told the author:

> All those people who were opposed to Nehru on the self-reliant economy opposed Indira Gandhi. Firstly, on the foreign policy issue, those who were pro-US, they were with the Syndicate. And those who were with [the princes], they were with the Syndicate. And those who were opposed to subsidies to benefit poor people and others (as a welfare state might have) they were with the Syndicate.[11]

Ranged against the Syndicate was that section of Congress representing the 'non-monopoly' bourgeoisie. Led by Indira Gandhi, it wanted 'to stop the drift to the right, initiate some democratic reforms, implement some of the pledges of the Congress and maintain the line of independent capitalist development'. It represented the non-monopoly bourgeoisie and the rich peasants, whose 'class interests are in contradiction with the imperialists, landlords and monopolists'. This section was a part of the Left.[12] Accordingly, the Party aligned itself with the Indira wing of the Congress and called on its supporters to 'defeat the conspiracy of the Syndicate and its reactionary allies'. The Syndicate's attempts to oust Mrs Gandhi around the presidential election in 1969 were denounced by Bupesh Gupta as, 'The most criminal plot in post-independence India against the masses, against democracy and against the nation.' He continued: 'The election of Sanjiva Reddy [the Syndicate presidential candidate] is to be [the] first step in the process of preparing for a right-reactionary take-over of power at the centre.' The election of V. V. Giri, Mrs Gandhi's preferred candidate, however, would be 'the first step in the building up of all-India left and democratic unity in order to thwart the plans of Reaction and give it a crushing rebuff'.[13] The Gandhi government's economic measures in 1969 (including bank nationalisation) and its defiance of the Syndicate bosses caused the communists to move closer to it.[14]

After the Congress split, the CPI extended its support to what was now the Congress (R). Amarjit Kaur comments:

> It was at that stage that Indira Gandhi contacted the communists—the CPM and the CPI. The CPI said our support can't be unconditional. We are ready to support you and save you but we want certain steps to be taken by you. It was at that stage that we asked for [the privy purses] to

be removed. It was at that stage [we asked for] the wholesale trade to be taken over so that you can begin a system in India where some kind of welfare measures could ensure that that food or rations reach the people. If you really want to expand the base and tackle unemployment then you nationalise the banks, nationalise insurance, have money in your hand so that you can do social sector spending. The communists also asked that land reforms should be pursued.[15]

Dange told the delegates to the Ninth CPI Congress in October 1971:

> The split in the Congress, which was led by Indira Gandhi ... barred the road for the return of right reaction to power and it promises to make room for new alignments in the further development of the left and democratic fronts.[16]

The communists knew that cooperation with the Congress (R) would not be smooth sailing and recognised that, having defeated the Syndicate and regained (by 1971) its electoral popularity, the move to the Left could well slow down.[17] Communist support was critical in its nature. Rajimwale wrote later:

> The CPI, while extending its support to Congress government, opposed every measure against the people and the country. The Party thus followed a policy of 'unity and struggle'.... The CPI consistently opposed any non-Congressism or anti-Congressism. Simultaneously, it also opposed the negative policies of the Congress.[18]

The Congress split caused the CPI to review its analysis of the Indian bourgeoisie. Before proceeding, a note on terminology is required here. Party analysts pointed out that the Indian bourgeoisie contained 'big business' or 'the monopolies', on the one hand, and 'non-monopoly' sections on the other. In communist writing, the term 'national bourgeoisie' at times means exactly that—the bourgeoisie of India as a whole. But, confusingly, at other times it is used to refer to the 'non-monopoly' sections alone—the 'national' section of the bourgeoisie (as opposed to the monopolies and their friends, the foreign investors) which has an interest in prosecuting the national democratic revolution. Further, the bourgeoisie is often simply identified with the Congress (see below). The actions of the Congress government are traced directly to the Indian capitalist class, with few, if any, stops on the way.[19] This writer will use the term 'national bourgeoisie' to refer to the CPI's 'non-monopoly' sections. And, for reasons explained earlier, I will maintain a respectful distance between the Indian bourgeoisie (all sections) and the Congress.

In the CPI's view, the Gandhi government was more strongly influenced by the national bourgeoisie: 'They also want profit and prosperity, they also want to exploit the workers. But they want the economic development of the country. They are also against the monopolies and the foreign imperialists.'[20] This brought them into conflict with the monopoly bourgeoisie over economic, social and foreign policies.[21] Differentiation between the monopolies and the national bourgeoisie was proceeding apace, producing conflict between the two wings of the capitalist class. The Ninth Congress declared that 'these elements [the "small and medium bourgeoisie"] are now coming more and more in open conflict with the monopoly sections', while the Tenth was told, 'The economic situation has sharpened the differentiation among the Indian bourgeoisie.'[22] The national bourgeoisie ('which is now in power', according to Reddy) was, therefore, potentially on the side of the national democratic revolution—'[They were] objectively interested in carrying through the national-democratic programme.'[23] What exactly the role of the national bourgeoisie in that revolution was remained a point of some confusion. While it was generally agreed that the national bourgeoisie was incapable of completing it, Reddy believed that they were in favour of doing this.[24] The *Party Education Series* (Grade 1), however, indicated that 'even before the exclusive leadership of the working class is established in the N[ational]D[emocratic]F[ront], the national democratic revolution can be completed'.[25] This would seem to imply that it might be completed under the leadership of the national bourgeoisie—an important indicator for later events when we remember that, for the communists, the national bourgeoisie translated politically into Indira Gandhi's Congress. The equation of the bourgeoisie with Congress—and the Congress (R) with the national bourgeoisie—was maintained throughout. Sardesai wrote in 1973 that 'the Indian bourgeoisie . . . led our freedom movement and have subsequently become the ruling class of the country'.[26] In fact, since they identified the Indian bourgeoisie with the Congress, India's communists read the 1969 Congress split *back into* the bourgeoisie.[27] The split between the Syndicate and the Congress (R) was a political manifestation of the division between the monopolies and the national bourgeoisie. The Congress (R) election victory of February 1971 was described by the CPI as 'a shift in favour of the national bourgeoisie', which now had 'its party in power'. Sen said that the Congress (R) was 'the political expression of the non-monopoly strata of the Indian bourgeoisie, or the national bourgeoisie properly so called'.[28]

Positive developments seemed on the horizon. There was, said the CPI after Congress victory in the 1971 *Garibi Hatao* elections, 'a very real possibility for wresting significant concessions from the national bourgeoisie and the government in the interests of the working people'.[29] The prospect of 'a great move forward in the direction of the completion of the national democratic revolution' had 'immensely brightened up', according to the Ninth Congress in October of that year.[30]

Nevertheless, significant shadows remained. Despite identifying the Congress (R) with the national bourgeoisie, the CPI realised that it still contained strong Right-wing elements.[31] Dange wrote that even after 1969, 'the new Congress in power failed to change itself into a new party with a revolutionary make-up and most of its leading elements stuck to the same old groove of bourgeois thinking and bourgeois aggrandisement'.[32] But the triumphal Congress campaign in the 1971 elections seemed to indicate that, under Indira Gandhi's leadership, the Congress was on a Leftward course. During that campaign, 'the CPI and some other left and democratic forces in the opposition joined with the Congress led by Indira Gandhi in meeting the challenge from the extreme right'.[33] The Congress victory meant that '[a] monstrous threat to the nation's future has been averted and those constituting that threat have been delivered a smashing blow'. It meant that the Indian people had been radicalised.[34] Within the Congress, wherein resided the majority of India's 'anti-Rightist' forces, the leadership was moving Leftwards, while the Congress Left was resurgent. Arjun Dev, then a CPI student activist, told the author:

> We should not lose sight of the fact that Congress had a fairly strong left wing group, the CFSA ... they were a very good group of people who were also demanding the things that eventually the communists were demanding ... these people were not anti-communist and they were in general considered to be pro-communist. Some of them had been communists in the past ... . [So] there was a left within the Congress and a left outside the Congress ... . Indira Gandhi had the support within the Congress of a very strong leftist group.[35]

The Left and democratic forces could now unite and, thus, advance the national democratic revolution.[36]

Positive feelings between communists and the Congress were not one-sided. Haksar had told H. N. Bahaguna (AICC General Secretary) in December 1969 that, 'The CPI has been a partner in the freedom struggle, was with us during the Chinese aggression and it is honestly trying to experiment with the Parliamentary system in India.'[37] P. N. Dhar advised Haksar in 1973 that understanding with the CPI should be strengthened: 'There should be greater cooperation and coordination in organising mass campaigns. There should be more active liaison between the two parties.'[38] He continued:

> The Congress does not have to develop as a simple appendage of the CPI, though towards the CPI we have to develop greater understanding and greater forbearance.[39]

According to Mohit Sen, Indira Gandhi regularly despatched D. P. Dhar and Sukhamoy Chakravarty, on behalf of the government, to consult with the CPI general secretary.[40]

For the CPI, from 1971 onwards, the national democratic revolution required the unity of 'the left and democratic forces', drawing in 'not only the masses following the Congress but also its progressive sections' (which now included its leadership).[41] The notion of 'anti-Congressism'—'taking the Congress as the main obstacle that would have to be removed if the country was to progress and the revolution was to advance'—was cast aside.[42] The Ninth Congress declared, 'The old concept of anticongressism has proved a barren and reactionary concept' which was now 'a weapon of sabotage of left and democratic unity'. The CPI would henceforth concentrate on holding the Congress to its progressive word.[43] Winning over Congress progressives, wrote Rajeshwara Rao, would not be achieved by the 'blind anticongressism or noncongressism of some of the left parties'—but only by 'patient work', drawing them into mass struggles.[44]

Congress and the communists moved into a series of electoral pacts with each other at the state level. This had begun in Kerala, as early as 1967, but developed more strongly in that state during and after the 1969 Congress split. From September 1970, Kerala was ruled by a coalition government of the United Front (which included the CPI) and the Congress. Electoral arrangements were made between the two parties for elections in Punjab (1972), Uttar Pradesh, Orissa (1974) and Manipur.[45]

The state and its machinery, however, remained a stumbling block to the national democratic revolution. According to the *Party Education Series*, 'It has without exception been used by the ruling Congress party to maintain the domination of the Indian capitalist class as a whole.'[46] But if, given its 'monopoly' and 'national' manifestations, the Indian capitalist class no longer had interests 'as a whole' and if the ruling Congress (R) only represented one section of it, this position was not tenable. The solution was to draw a distinction between the Congress (R) and the state bureaucracy. Gupta saw 'the hand of the Indian Civil Service and the top bureaucracy behind the rise of Right-reaction and its bid for power'. The top civil servants were the 'fifth column of Right-Reaction' and had to be 'disbanded and weeded out'.[47] 'After all,' wrote Mohit Sen, 'the enemies of the Indian people are not all in the opposition. They are also stationed at key levels of the political and administrative branches of state power.'[48] Defending and strengthening parliamentary democracy was also necessary to combat this danger.[49]

Despite the political bonhomie, economic policy became a source of tension between the CPI and the Congress in the early 1970s. As we have seen, the government periodically veered to the Right economically when crisis loomed. Workers took action against the privations imposed upon them, with CPI support. The government's refusal to grant concessions exacerbated the sense of crisis. Over 20 million worker-days were lost in strikes and lockouts in 1972. In the first half of 1973, over 11 million were lost. In 1974, mass strikes broke out among Bombay textile workers. Mass demonstrations of workers, unemployed and students became increasingly violent. Universities were shut down. In May 1973, the Uttar Pradesh Provincial Armed Constabulary mutinied, leading to 35 deaths.[50] A government supporter wrote later (in support of the Emergency), '[A]n appalling situation came to prevail, a situation of utter laxity, alarming flabbiness, near-complete erosion of the ethos of work and impermissible disregard of the financial disciplines necessary for a country like India.' He complained of 'irresponsible demands', 'agitations and demonstrations … violence' and 'competitive radicalism' and concluded, 'It was a situation which could only have culminated in disaster and disintegration.'[51]

The economic crisis culminated in the Railway Strike of 1974, the political one in the anti-Congress movements in Gujarat and Bihar—all of which, we will examine further.

While welcoming the government's shift to the Left in economic policy after 1969, the CPI felt that in the aftermath 'a kind of stalemate in government policies has come to stay'.[52] Dange believed that after the 1971 election, 'quite an influential set of ministers and leaders want to call a halt to that [Leftist] line and [implement] a changeover to accommodating the demands of monopoly capital'.[53] The Party detected a 'slide to the Right' in early 1972 and an even bigger 'shift to the Right' in 1974.[54] Evidence for the latter included the abandonment of the wholesale trade in wheat, the opening of previously closed areas of the economy to the monopolies and a 'desperate search' for US loans and multinational investment.[55] By giving concessions to 'the monopolists and landlords', the government had contributed to the rise in prices: '[I]t is this that the National Council of the CPI has condemned as a slideback on the part of the government.'[56] The CPI sourced this backsliding to the division in the Congress over economic policy, 'between the radical, progressive wing in the Congress Party and the spokesmen for the interests of monopolies, big landowners and the village rich'.[57] The former, according to Dange, were 'being slowly manoeuvred into a stand in relation to the working masses and the national economy that plays into the hands of monopoly capital, which is the source of right reaction and neo-colonialism'.[58] The influence of the latter could be seen in the reluctance to press forward with nationalisation (or to allow the government in Kerala to do so), relaxing the licensing system and passing legislation to curb the monopolies that was 'little more than eye-wash'.[59] Vyas however pointed out:

> The slideback is neither complete nor is it a complete retreat. Forces inside the Congress too are perturbed about this situation .... The rank-and-file of the Congress in many places is restive.[60]

On the question of land reform too, Congress was in retreat. Despite having introduced 'comparatively progressive laws and adopted comparatively radical positions' on the question, 'the ruling Congress leadership has sought all means of excuses to postpone and even sabotage their implementation'.[61] The Tenth CPI Congress accused the Congress of 'calculated sabotage of land ceilings ... at the centre and the states'.[62] The communists realised, however, that 'in most parts of the country the Congress retains the loyalty and faith of the majority of the rural toilers, including the agricultural workers and poor peasants'.[63] Holding the Congress to its radical promises was an effective method of 'drawing broad sections of the Congress masses' into a movement for 'the speedy implementation of radical agrarian laws'.[64] The Party advocated the formation of people's committees to agitate for and institutionalise radical land reforms.

The height of economic unrest came with the massive railway strike in May 1974.[65] The railway workers took action in protest against low wages and long hours in appalling working conditions. They demanded higher wages and bonuses, and the provision of subsidised food grains and other economic concessions. They were organised into a large number of trade union organisations, only two of which were recognised by the employer: the All-India Railwaymen's Federation (AIRF) that had links with the socialists and the National Federation of Indian Railwaymen (NFIR) that was Congress-affiliated. In February 1974, all of the railway trade union organisations and a number of non-Congress political parties formed a National Co-ordinating Committee for Railwaymen's Struggle that proceeded to plan for a strike from 8 May. A few days beforehand, the government invoked emergency legislation, declared the planned strike illegal and arrested large numbers of railway workers and their trade union leaders. The strike went ahead and thousands more railway workers were arrested as well as being evicted from railway housing estates. On 28 May, the strike was called off. Mrs Gandhi told the Lok Sabha at the beginning of the strike that the government had thus far been too lenient in its dealings with the workers. This would stop—and was to serve as a warning to others.

> The country's interests come first and they are above the interests of any one section. Today we cannot afford the exorbitant demands that have been made, or the others that are being hinted [at] on behalf of other sections.

The CPI and its union organisation in the railways supported the strike.[66] Mohit Sen wrote at its outbreak of 'the magnificent class conscious solidarity of India's railway workers'. He went on, 'Whatever may be the final outcome, what has taken place is imperishable.'[67] The Tenth Party Congress in the following year 'hails the all-India railway strike of May 1974, an outstanding event in the working class movement'. Through its own organisation of railway workers and other AITUC-affiliated unions, the Party pursued 'a just and honourable negotiated settlement'. But even though this appeared possible, 'the blow was struck against the whole thing by the arrest of George Fernandes [the strike leader] and others, and the breaking off of negotiations'. The CPI blamed the prime minister directly for this, accusing her of wanting to defeat the railway workers 'as the first step towards extending this "tough" line to the entire trade-union front'.[68] The Party condemned the central government, the Government of West Bengal and the central bureaucracy for their suppression of the strike.[69] The strike was defeated, according to the communists, through a combination of 'leonine repression' and 'the left-opportunist tactics and disruptive approach of the Socialist Party and the CPM'.[70]

The complicating factor for the Party in this was that the strike came in the midst of the movement for Total Revolution—the main aim of which was the ejection of the Congress government—led by Jayaprakash Narayan (JP). We will deal with this in detail later, but for the moment it will suffice to say that as far as the CPI was concerned, JP's movement was a reactionary one, backed by Right-wing, communal and semi-fascist organisations, which endangered democracy. George Fernandes, as well as being the leader of the railway strike, was also an enthusiastic warrior for the JP Movement and linked the strike to the campaign for the destruction of the government. He said in March 1974 that 'railwaymen could unseat the present Central Government through a general strike'.[71] In October, he declared:

> Seven days' strike of the India railways—every thermal station in the country would close down. A ten days' strike of the Indian railways—every steel mill in India would close down and the industries in the country will come to a halt for the next twelve months .... [O]nce the steel mill furnace is switched off, it takes nine months to refire. A fifteen days' strike in the Indian railway—the country will starve.[72]

This was clearly not the aim of India's communists in their support of the strike—no matter how critical they were of the government's economic policies. But it placed them in something of a dilemma. According to Sen's account, while the mainstream leadership dithered on the issue, the Party's venerable trade union leader, S. A. Dange, 'was determined to have the strike ended but on the best possible and most honourable terms for the railwaymen'.[73] Despite only 'lukewarm support' from the CPI leadership, Dange negotiated with the then railway minister, L. N. Misra—negotiations which eventually brought the strike to an end.[74]

The CPI encapsulated its relationship with the Congress at this time as one of 'unity and struggle'. This did not mean, according to O. P. Sangal, 'that the CPI ... had reduced itself to a B team of the ruling party and had practically liquidated its mass base'.[75] The Party remained convinced that the national bourgeoisie was still part of the bourgeoisie. It maintained that the Congress government should be replaced 'by a government of left and democratic forces'.[76] Clearly, overestimating the pro-Congress atmosphere in the Party at that time, *Party Life* reader Pranab Banerjee wrote to the 'Question & Answer' section asking whether the CPI should 'put forward only such programmes and propose such forms of struggle as are accept-able to the Congress?' Comrade Banerjee may have regretted this. Mohit Sen swiftly replied that this was 'absolutely incorrect'. It represented 'the abandonment of the most fundamental viewpoint of Marxism–Leninism', it 'negates ... the independent role, initiative and struggle of the CPI' and it 'betrays a revisionist and tailist attitude'.[77]

Contrary to some accounts, the CPI was not attempting to 'take over' the Congress at that time.[78] Nor was it acting as a cat's paw for the Soviet Union.[79] Sahgal suggests that during Leonid Brezhnev's visit to India in 1973, 'the party [CPI] had been told to back Mrs Gandhi regardless of her policies'.[80] As we have seen, the Party needed no such injunction from Moscow. Even in the friendliest Indo-Soviet atmosphere (for example, at the time of the Joint Treaty of Peace, Friendship and Co-operation in August 1971), the Party's backing for the Gandhi government was by no means unequivocal.[81]

By this stage, it was clear that the Congress had disappointed those who had supported it in 1971 and 1972. According to Sen, Indians expected that:

> ... a radical improvement in their lives and a radical change in the society in which they live would be brought about by the Prime Minister at the head of a rejuvenated Congress. This belief has now largely evaporated.

They had lost faith not in the Congress project, but in the ability of that party to implement it.[82] The communists again pointed at the division between progressive and reactionary wings of the ruling party. The 1969 split, said Sen, 'does not represent the completion of the polarisation process'.[83] The Congress might have to split again. Sangal declared, '[I]t would appear that the only possible way out of the crisis is for a challenge to develop inside the Congress party itself and a repetition of the events of 1969 in the context of 1974.'[84] Thus, in terms of 'unity and struggle', the communist emphasis from 1971 to 1974 was more on struggle than on unity—while avoiding the pitfalls of 'antiCongressism'.[85] The Party warned that after the 1971 elections the future would 'not be one of calm or relative stability', but rather one of 'sharp confrontation and struggle' in order to hold the Congress to its election promises.[86] The Congress Left was criticised for its lack of courage in refusing 'to come out boldly against the wrong policies of the Congress leadership and lead the masses in struggle against them'.[87] Rajeshwara Rao commented: 'Left congressmen ... do not come into mass struggles. This is their biggest weakness ... . It is necessary that they are drawn into mass movements along with other left and democratic parties.'[88] This meant that the independent role of the CPI was that much more important.[89]

The relationship of the Party to the Congress was still a matter of considerable debate within the CPI. At the Tenth Congress, Party members (especially from West Bengal) tried to put a more militant spin on the leadership's Political Resolution. Rabi Mitra declared that:

> It will also be a wrong tactic to view unity with Congress or that with democrats within Congress as a lever for building left unity ... . The real lever to left and democratic unity is the independent militant class role.[90]

Gopal Chandra wanted the Party Congress to reject the 'Congress–CPI alliance as the main plank of our basic tactical line.' He urged delegates to reject the 'new image of the national bourgeoisie as anti-capitalist and as builders of socialism' which was designed 'to ideologically disarm and cripple the working class'. Other delegates from West Bengal warned:

> ... It is extremely urgent to bear in mind that uncompromising struggle against the anti-people policies of the Govt and its tendencies to compromise with the Right constitutes an urgent task and any hesitation [about] the same may lead to serious right deviations.[91]

P. C. Joshi, on the other hand, had put forward a position which, even a few years before, might have been accepted, but was now too moderate in its assessment of the Congress. Urging 'a warmly fraternal but duly critical attitude towards the Indian National Congress and the policies of its leadership', he stressed the need for the CPI 'to fraternally unite with all the anti-imperialist and democratic forces inside the country including those under the banner of the Indian National Congress'. The purpose of unity was to implement the Congress' *Garibi Hatao* programme of 1971.[92]

Steering its way through these competing ideas, the Party leadership tacked away from unity and towards struggle. The Ninth Congress had declared in late 1971 that 'the demarcation between the CPI and the Congress has got blurred.'[93] Bringing it into sharper focus in the next few years, the CPI conducted a campaign to make the Congress 'implement the mandate' in mid-1972, organised a half-million protest march in Delhi, in March 1973, and conducted two campaigns against hoarding in 1973 and 1974. It played a role in the 40-day Bombay textile workers strike and the 33-day West Bengal jute workers' strike. Its role in the 1974 railway workers' strike has been dealt with. It was also active in strikes by coal workers, port and dock workers and agrarian workers.[94]

The CPI's preferred solution to the crisis was an extension of state economic power. 'State capitalism', wrote Mohit Sen, 'is the most progressive form of capitalist development in newly independent countries and creates the highest degree of the socialisation of production as well as the material basis for the noncapitalist transformation to socialism'.[95] Chandavarkar points out, 'They [the CPI] invested the strong centralized state with progressive potential and so could scarcely develop a critique of the unitary powers of the Indian constitution.'[96] This would cause problems for the Party as it tended to identify a stronger state with a move to the Left.

At that time, however, while endorsing further state economic intervention, the Party rejected the strengthening of the state's political power. It seems that, as one of the conditions for communist support in 1969–70, the Congress (R) had undertaken to scrap plans for the introduction of preventive detention legislation.[97] Despite this, in May 1971 the government introduced the Maintenance of Internal Security Act (MISA), which provided for detention—without trial—for up to a year for those acting against the defence of India, the security of the state or the maintenance of public order. The CPI led a hard battle against the legislation. *Link* reported in June 1971:

> Bhupesh Gupta (CPI) called it 'treachery and fraud on the nation'. He said the Congress was talking about socialism because it was the fashion and gave it respectability. In fact, it was a body of capitalists anxious to preserve capitalist rule in the country.[98]

Gupta led a walkout from the Lok Sabha in protest against the Bill.[99] The Tenth CPI Congress protested against 'Illtreatment of Political

Prisoners' and condemned 'the frequent misuse of government powers under DIR [Defence of India Regulations] and MISA in order to suppress trade union, kisan and other democratic mass movements'.[100]

As the crisis continued, elements in the Congress began to press for an increase in state political power. Shashi Bhushan, a one-time leader of the CFSA and a prominent member of the Congress Left, began speaking of a 'limited dictatorship' to bring things under control. He wrote in *Indian Left Review*:

> Democracy has become a double-edged weapon which often gives unbridled power to a few sophisticated people of our society to amass wealth and continue to exploit the teeming millions … . Having this state of affairs in view, I have suggested a 'limited dictatorship' for a limited period to solve the economic malaise facing our country.[101]

The CPI leaders reacted sharply to this. Srinivas Sardesai and Satyapal Dang rejected any such idea. Mohit Sen warned that, 'Any toying with this idea would be the height of folly and would be a menace not only for the nation but in the first place for the Prime Minister herself.'[102]

Imperialist Threat and the JP Movement

In a number of fields—economic policy, the character of the Congress leadership, the political power of the state—the CPI was not quiescent during this period. For much of the time, 'struggle' overshadowed 'unity'.

There then occurred two events (or two series of events) that would reverse the Party's position. The first was what was perceived to be a threatening international situation for India and the Congress government. The second was the mass anti-Congress movement led by Jayaprakash Narayan.

A Hostile World

By the early 1970s, the Congress government—with, in this instance, CPI support—was convinced that India was surrounded by a hostile Western world, which was directed by the imperialism of the USA. As we saw in the last chapter, relations between Washington and the Gandhi government cooled considerably in the aftermath of the devaluation debacle and amidst India's criticism of the US policy in Southeast Asia. The CPI's Sardesai had declared then that devaluation (in which he detected a conspiracy by 'the World Bank, the IMF and the American and West German Chambers of Commerce and Industry') 'poses the question of whether we are going to survive as a politically independent and democratic country or become a despotic, servile appendage of American imperialism'.[103] This attitude towards US interests was echoed at the highest levels of government. A note in Haksar's papers (unsigned, but probably by him; undated, but almost certainly from 1972) points to an active American campaign to create a pro-US lobby in India—particularly with regard to US policy in Vietnam.[104] Dhar wrote to Haksar in the same year, 'the USA remains our most powerful enemy.' The links that the Americans had established with the administration, trade, industry and political parties had to be broken.[105] There is a little doubt that the Johnson and Nixon administrations were generally hostile to the Congress government and that this hostility was exacerbated by a number of international crises.

The collapse of East Pakistan and the war to liberate Bangladesh (March–December 1971) was one of these. The USA felt that the interests of its ally in the region, Pakistan, were being undermined (as indeed they were) and took up a hostile attitude to the new nation and to its liberator, India. During crisis and war, the CPI strongly supported the Congress government and played some role in gaining Soviet support for the Indian position.[106] In the years after liberation, Bangladesh faced political crisis and, in 1974, a deadly famine. Its leader, Mujibur Rahman, turned to authoritarian solutions—a state of emergency, the declaration of a one-party state and repression of the opposition. The communists saw an American (and a Chinese) hand: '[T]he CIA and the Maoists are behind the treason', declared the Central News Service in January 1975.[107] Indira Gandhi herself 'had become appreciative of what she called "the foreign hand". Intelligence reports about plots to overthrow Mujib[ur]'s government in Bangladesh added to her fears', P. N. Dhar tells us.[108] She later told the Seventy-fifth Congress session, 'All that happened in a neighbouring country about that time [of the Emergency] was not a mere coincidence. It was all part of a pattern.'[109] In 1975 (just after the Allahabad judgement), Petr V. Kutsobin, representing the Central Committee of the Soviet Communist Party, turned up with a letter from the Soviet leadership (one copy to be read and destroyed). It told of 'a ramified conspiracy ... to damage and destroy all the leaders in the subcontinent who were responsible for the establishment of Bangladesh' (i.e, Indira Gandhi, Mujibur Rahman and Zulfikar Ali Bhutto).[110]

Another warning seemed to come from Chile. In September 1973, the mildly socialist government of Salvador Allende was overthrown in a military coup which had the backing of the USA through the CIA. Harsh Dev Malaviya of the Congress Left told the International Conference against Fascism in 1975, '[I]t was ITT [a powerful US transnational company] and CIA who stage-managed the military coup in Chile which resulted in the murder of President Allende and massacre of democracy.'[111] V. P. Sathe (also of the Congress Left) wrote that the events in Chile 'should serve as an eye-opener to India ... because we have seen the same pattern working recently in Gujarat and Bihar.'[112] The CPI hastened to agree, also comparing the crisis in India to events in Chile.[113] The Party brought out the Chilean Communist Party leader, Orlando Milas, for the Tenth Party Congress and Allende's widow and daughter—who had a long meeting with Indira Gandhi—for the Anti-Fascist Conference to illustrate the case.[114] Both the Party and Mrs Gandhi went considerably further in their forebodings in private. Mohit Sen relates:

> Some years later Indira Gandhi told me that Fidel Castro had warned her on the basis of his own and Soviet intelligence reports, the US administration was planning a similar fate [to that of Allende] for her. She had become far too much of an obstacle to the realisation of their plans especially in the developing world.[115]

Further indications of the aggressive intent of the USA were found in its decision to set up a military base at Diego Garcia in 1973 and its chagrin at defeat in Indochina in 1975.[116]

From all of this, the CPI, as well as the Congress Left, had concluded by 1975 that a well-planned conspiracy was afoot, which had its origins in Washington and extended its tentacles into India—the most important of which were the anti-Congress movements in Gujarat and Bihar. It was aimed at bringing down Indira Gandhi and the Congress, and locking India into the Western camp. From the communist point of view, such a conspiracy endangered India's democracy, its independence and its state-planned economy. At the Tenth Party Congress in January/February 1975, there was talk of a crisis situation in India, with the country caught between the twin pincers of external imperialism and internal Right-reaction. 'Civil war' and the need to train volunteers were discussed. In the face of such a severe threat, the Party's line tipped back towards unity with Congress.

The JP Movement

What became known as the JP Movement had its beginnings in Gujarat—although at this stage Jayaprakash Narayan (JP) was not involved.[117] In the beginning of 1974, students at Gujarat's universities were protesting against rising charges for food on university campuses. In what would become a pattern of state overreaction, riot police stormed the errant institutions and carried out mass arrests. Students then went on strike. They now also demanded the arrest of hoarders and profiteers—whom they held responsible for the price rises. Gujarat's middle class rallied to the students' cause, as did white-collar trade unions, including that of the university teachers. But 'urban workers and the rural landless and the poor' appeared to keep their distance.[118]

In an article published in late 1975, just after the Emergency was proclaimed, the *Bulletin of Concerned Asian Scholars*' unnamed 'Correspondent' argued that the JP Movement represented two things to the Indian bourgeoisie (and it is important to note here that s/he included here the rural bourgeoisie—rich farmers and the declining feudal interests).[119] Firstly, for the bourgeoisie as a whole, it represented a possible alternative to Indira Gandhi and her Congress—an alternative that was sought, particularly after 1969, because Congress held out the possibility of more intrusive state economic intervention and even control. Secondly, it represented the interests of a particular section of the bourgeoisie against the rest. Politically, the conflict between these two sections was manifested in 'the pro-American political parties ... and the pro-American, anti-Soviet section of the Congress Party versus the CPI and the pro-Soviet Congress Party'. Economically, it meant 'the interests of the rural elite ... versus the industrial bourgeoisie ... and the state'.

This was, in my view, a prescient analysis—but with the benefit of several decades' hindsight, we might adjust the terms somewhat. Forty years on, the 'American' or Cold War factor would not now seem to have had as much importance as it did in 1975. We have already explored the fact that what bore down on the Indian economy from the late 1960s onwards was not a US conspiracy, but the forces of the world market and globalisation—albeit represented by the World Bank, the IMF and (on occasion but not always) the USA. What stood against them in India were not 'pro-Soviet' forces but the Indian State, represented by the Congress and defended by the CPI. Nevertheless, our Correspondent's analysis still seems to work. The bourgeoisie as a whole was undoubtedly disenchanted with Congress' turn to Leftism after 1969—though not, I think, fatally so. In terms of 'a section ... in opposition to the rest', the rural bourgeoisie was more viscerally hostile to Congress—and with good reason. Chandra points out that the Congress 'could not satisfy rich peasant demands without alienating the rural poor or endangering the path of economic development that had been adopted'.[120] Mutual hostility, therefore, was locked in. The rural elites supported the JP Movement, and it drew much of its initial street support from the sons and daughters of those elites.[121] The rich farmers wanted protection from further land reform, less state intervention and easier agricultural exports. They, therefore, represented a 'pro-globalisation' force which eventually lined up against big business and, most important of all, against the state.

Correspondent goes on to argue that for most of 1974, the first aspect of the conflict (the bourgeoisie as a whole against Congress) predominated. But by the end of the year, the movement was faltering. JP had failed to create an all-India movement: 'In his visits elsewhere in India [outside Bihar] he could get nothing going.' All that was promised for the following year was further chaos: '[I]t was at this point that the big bourgeoisie took alarm and switched their support to Indira Gandhi.'[122] After that, the second aspect came to the fore: a conflict between the rural bourgeoisie on the one hand and the industrial bourgeoisie and the state on the other.[123]

The Jan Sangh (JS) and the Congress (O) expressed support for the protest movement—which now moved on to demand the resignation of the chief minister (Chimanbhai Patel) and the dissolution of the state assembly. Riots, bloodshed and the imposition of curfew followed. Police action (and overreaction) led to at least one hundred deaths, thousands of injuries and over eight thousand arrests. On 9 February, the state assembly was suspended (but not dissolved) and president's rule imposed. Morarji Desai—formerly of the Congress Right, now of the Congress (O)—commenced a hunger strike in March 1974 for dissolution while the movement continued to rage around him. While the Congress accused the movement (and particularly the political organisations involved in it) of representing 'vested interests' and paving the way for fascism, the opposition accused the Indian government of repression and preparing a Left-wing dictatorship. Four days into Desai's hunger strike, however, Mrs Gandhi agreed to the dissolution of the Gujarat Assembly, opening the road to state elections. Round One, it must be said, went to the opposition.

Round Two took place in Bihar, in March. Taking their cue from Gujarat, students began mass protests against high prices, shortages of essential commodities, graduate unemployment and educational methods.[124] They too demanded the resignation of the state government and dissolution of the state assembly. Plans were laid for a mass *gherao* (encirclement) of the assembly building. Once again, anti-Congress political forces entered the field—the Congress (O), the JS and its student organisation (the ABVP) and its ally, the Rashtriya Swayamsevak Sangh (RSS). Accusations of police violence, arbitrary arrests and even shootings flowed thick and fast.[125] Mrs Gandhi, fearing replication of the movement all over India, refused to dissolve the assembly. But when it sat on 18 March, the violence, looting and arson spread.

In early April, several student organisations requested Jayaprakash Narayan—veteran Congress socialist and freedom fighter, who had been in political retirement for some years—to assume leadership of their movement. JP accepted. He believed that 'a revolutionary situation had arisen in Bihar and was building up in India as a whole, that only a spark was needed to ignite it, and that the student movement in Bihar would provide this'.[126] Clearly, as far as JP was concerned, this revolution encompassed a good deal more than student canteen prices, or commodity shortages or even dissolution of assemblies. He described it as a 'Total Revolution'—but what that meant remained unclear.

The tactics of the movement did not change [127]—but its politics moved clearly to the Right. This was, perhaps, not surprising for a movement that wanted to see the results of democratic processes (no matter how mistaken or corrupt these may have turned out to be) swept aside in a whirlwind of 'extra-constitutional mass agitation mainly confined to urban areas'. The Bulletin Correspondent described the movement by this stage as 'amorphous, populist [and] anti-working class'.[128]

JP professed an aversion to ideology both for himself and for the movement in general.[129] Others were not so circumspect. We have already noted the interest and the increasing participation of the JS and the RSS (Right-wing, communalist and, in the latter case, semi-fascist organisations) in the Gujarat and Bihar movements. When JP's leadership was in full swing, the movement was no longer controlled by students—and student organisations were no longer capable of controlling it.[130] The experienced and well-trained grassroots cadre of the JS and the RSS stepped up to take on the job.[131] Since they were rapidly becoming the backbone of the movement for 'Total Revolution', it was not surprising that JP moved closer to them. He addressed the twentieth plenary session of the JS saying that, '[H]e wished to communicate the conclusion that after a year's work with the JS and the RSS he had found them neither reactionary nor fascist.' Later he said, '[I]f the Jan Sangh is fascist, then I too am a fascist.' The RSS, he said was simply 'an organisation of volunteers rendering social service'.[132]

Having taken up the leadership of the movement, JP was anxious to spread it across the nation and to widen it into a movement against corruption, the Congress and the Indira Gandhi government. He toured the country to this end. But the movement did not gain the support of the urban and rural poor and, after a tumultuous eight months, it began to slow down in November 1974. At this point, Mrs Gandhi met with JP and challenged him to test his support against hers in the forthcoming election in February/March 1976—a challenge he readily accepted.[133]

From the Congress point of view, the JP Movement was an attempt at 'overthrowing a legitimate government that had dared to identify with the poor'.[134] Further, the AICC told its cadre at a training camp in November 1974 that the movement aimed 'to destroy the democratic political institutions in the country'. It castigated JP's 'Total Revolution' and his schemes of 'partyless democracy':

> Behind the façade of partyless democracy lurk the dark and sinister forces of Indian fascism, well organised and well poised to destroy the democratic institutions and impose their reign of terror.[135]

However, the JP Movement had its sympathisers inside the Congress. Chandra Shekhar, Mohan Dharia and Krishna Kant (all formerly of the ex-socialist grouping in the CFSA) criticised the treatment of the movement and tried, unsuccessfully, to arrange a compromise between JP and Mrs Gandhi.[136] But the majority of Congress was hostile to the movement and set out to beat it back.[137] The role of the Congress, according to the leadership, was vital in this. The AICC told the Narora camp, '[T]he main burden of beating back the anti-democratic tide has fallen on the Congress organisation.' To this end, Congress workers had to be mobilised, 'hundreds' of rallies and meetings had to be held—and 'personal and factional differences have to be submerged'.[138]

Initially however (and after some hesitation), it was the communists who took the lead in mobilising against the Right-ward trajectory of the JP Movement. To begin with, the CPI sympathised with the issues that the student movements in Gujarat and Bihar had taken up. Sangal wrote, '[T]he urban petty bourgeoisie is, by and large, just sick of the present government. It has no hope whatsoever that this government will ever learn from its own experience and make any serious effort to fulfil its many promises and pledges to the people.'[139] At the first outbreak of violence in Gujarat, *Link* wrote of an 'almost spontaneous' upsurge against 'government ineptitude, widespread corruption, colossal indifference on the part of the rulers towards the miseries of the people and the disgusting and continuing internecine warfare in the ruling party'. The article also noted that:

> Left parties and democratic elements have been in a quandary. The people's wrath against the [Gujarat] Ministry was so intense that they have been duty-bound to associate with it and try to channelise it. They also know that reaction, which is organisationally strong, will take advantage of the situation.[140]

Sen warned that 'it is the height of folly to put it all down to the disruptive machinations of Jana Sangh or the CIA ... basically, the Gujarat movement is a shining example of popular initiative and mass valour'.[141] In a pamphlet written in April 1974, Srinivas Sardesai objected to the movement's 'indulgence in wanton loot and arson and the resort to forcible, coercive methods for securing the resignation of legislators', pointing out that this would not lower prices, release scarce commodities, end corruption or admit more students into schools and colleges. A contemporary observer, C. P. Bhambri—a JNU History Professor and non-Party Marxist—comments, 'If you want parliamentary reform, you cannot compel the parliamentary representative—blacken his face, seat him on a donkey and say "Resign." You have to be able to put forward an alternative elected government.'[142] Sardesai also said that the attempt to keep political parties out of the Gujarat movement allowed 'backseat driving' by the JS, RSS and the Congress (O).[143]

At the same time, the Party placed the movement in an international context of imperialist offensive—in which it was 'drawing strength from the imperialist powers … which are annoyed at the foreign policy of the Indira Government'.[144] The movement was based on the monopolist bourgeoisie and the landlords. It had also attracted sections of the traders, students, middle class intelligentsia and the peasantry.[145] But its leadership (JP notwithstanding) came from the extreme Right, spearheaded by the JS and the RSS.[146]

> [JP] thinks he is utilising their support for advancing his movement which he hopes to 'radicalise' in due course. But they [Jan Sangh and RSS] think they are exploiting his prestige and personality for developing their own counter-revolutionary agitation.[147]

These organisations, with their communal and fascist origins, posed a real threat to democracy and the imposition of a 'party-less' dictatorship; 'the dark forces behind Jayaprakash Narayan, though they vow fidelity to democracy, are working for a counter-revolutionary dictatorship of the most reactionary sections of the bourgeoisie and the landlords', wrote Rajeshwara Rao.[148] From 1974 to 1975, the threat of fascism within the JP Movement seemed to increase. P. C. Joshi wrote in May 1975:

> Jayaprakash Narayan's movement resting mainly on the support of the most communal and reactionary sections of Indian politics and aiming only at replacing the present set of rulers by another has greater identity with fascism. Of course it is too weak to be a serious threat at least for the time being.[149]

Other party writers were not so sanguine, and the assassination of the Congress Union Minister for Railways, L. N. Mishra, by bombing on 4 January 1975, made them even less so. Dange wrote:

> This murder is the inevitable outcome of the politics that is being let loose in the country by Jayaprakash Narayan and his followers. This is the line of settling politics by the politics of murder. Therefore the Communist Party was not wrong in warning that Jayaprakash Narayan's politics is the politics of fascism. We did not think that we would be proved so correct so soon.[150]

To the fascist colouration of the JP Movement for the CPI was now added the possibility of a military coup 'to restore stability'. According to Sinha, '[T]he idea of a military dictatorship runs like a thread through all the theoretical concoctions of Jayaprakash Narayan.'[151] Supporters of the JP Movement in Bihar were apparently in the habit of chanting 'Manekshaw Zindabad!'—in reference to Field-Marshal Sam Manekshaw, a senior army commander and the victor of the war for Bangladesh.[152] Sen wrote later:

> I am still of the view that something sinister with enormous destructive potential was brewing in the summer of 1975 and that a section of the top army personnel was, at least considering involvement in whatever course of action was being planned.[153]

Fear of military action was almost certainly the reason behind the curious case of CPI's pamphlet, *The Political Role of the Army*, published in 1974. This brought together an article from *World Marxist Review*, plus two articles by Soviet writers, all of them concerned with the role of the army and taking their examples from Egypt, Chile, Portugal, Iraq, Pakistan, Burma and Syria.[154] In her hostile biography of Indira Gandhi, Nayantara Sahgal makes enormous play of the sinister connotations of this publication, claiming that the CPI was 'setting forth the thesis that armies, properly infiltrated, can be used to overthrow governments'—as if the Party was advocating this as a strategy.[155] Mrs Gandhi is condemned for remaining silent on this shocking development. Surely, it is beyond belief that the CPI issued this publication with a view to either infiltrating the armed forces or bringing about a military coup (if that was the case, would they really have declared it in print?). Rather more likely is the idea that the pamphlet was a gentle warning against the military aspirations of the JP Movement itself.

Once its political trajectory was located, a powerful section of the CPI leadership wanted the Party to fight the JP Movement by out-doing it in its opposition to the Congress.[156] Sinha reflects this approach when he blames the success of the JP Movement on 'the failure of the left and democratic forces to provide leadership to the angry and discontented masses'.[157] But when the implications of the JP Movement became clear, the communist position changed—from opposition to the JP Movement *and* Congress in equal parts, to opposition to the JP Movement *in alliance* with Congress. The General Secretary himself enunciated the change. 'The alternatives are', he wrote, 'the unity of the left and democratic forces, including the progressive sections of the Congress … or siding with the reactionary and chauvinist forces led by Jayaprakash Narayan.'[158]

Despite its message to the AICC cadre camp in late 1974 (as mentioned earlier), the Congress was at first rather timid in its commitment to mass mobilisation to combat the JP Movement, fearful that such moves might unleash a greater social upheaval than the Congress leadership was prepared to countenance. Sinha detected a 'paralysis that has seized the Congress Party and its government in face of the reactionary assault'.[159] The Congress circles were also divided on whether such a mobilisation should include the only political force that was attempting to oppose the movement—the CPI. Within the Bihar Congress, L. N. Mishra advocated cooperation with the CPI, while Jagjivan Ram opposed it.[160] It was apparently Dange and Bhupesh Gupta from the CPI who convinced Indira Gandhi that mobilisation and cooperation with the CPI were vital for the struggle.[161] In January 1975, the CPI was able to note that 'officially the Congress leadership has taken the stand in favour of resistance to right reaction and Prime Minister Indira Gandhi and others are showing a greater awareness of the threat posed by it and JP's movement'.[162] The Party's NC also made the point that the Gandhi leadership had taken a firm stand against those within the Congress calling for a dialogue with JP.[163] Bhupesh Gupta concluded with some relief:

> It is always to be welcomed when some sections of the bourgeoisie come out in resistance against the forces of [the] extreme right and fascism, all the more when those sections are in control of state power.[164]

The pattern of the CPI opposition to the JP Movement can be illustrated by events in Bihar. There, as elsewhere, the party had some sympathy for the movement's initial aims. But on 23 April 1974, the movement took up the demand that the state assembly should be dissolved. At this point, the CPI (along with the CPM and the trade unions under communist control) withdrew. The CPI began organising against it.[165] The Congress turned to the CPI for help. A communist delegation was invited to a meeting with the Bihar state cabinet where '[i]t was decided to take hard lines against JP as he was destabilising the democratic set up'.[166] The Congress had a little choice in the matter, according to Henry C. Hart:

> To enlist thousands of people to march on behalf of the government in power it had to turn to its junior ally, the Communist Party of India ... . To counter a mass agitation like that in Bihar Mrs Gandhi had no option: the CPI's members were the only disciplined party activists available to her. Her own party's field men were contented office holders, often mistrusted by those hungry enough to march.[167]

The CPI organised its first mass demonstration on 3 June in Patna, the state capital, which brought in some 100,000 protesters. The demonstration opposed the demand for the dissolution of the state assembly—as well as high prices, black marketeering, hoarding and corruption. It called for the government takeover of the wholesale trade in essential commodities and for the increased wages.[168] Following this, together with the Congress, the Party organised joint rallies against the JP Movement in towns outside Patna, while the youth wings of the two parties jointly campaigned against the movement and against rising prices, hoarding and black marketeering.[169] In October, a 'World Anti-Fascist Conference' was held in Patna. Organised largely by the CPI, it was inaugurated by the Bihar Chief Minister and addressed by D. K. Barooah, the Congress President.[170] The CPI organised another mass march—'against fascism' and to 'defeat the rightist plot'—in November, which was followed by a Congress rally. The size of these events was sufficient for *The Indian Nation* to declare:

> ... if the strength of a procession is the measure of popular support, certainly the CPI demonstration and the Congress rally have weakened the claim of the [JP Movement] agitationists that all people are with them on the demand for the dissolution of the Assembly.[171]

The Party itself, however, was more critical of its own performance. It noted in early 1975 that in Bihar, it 'did succeed to a certain extent in moving the working class in state-wide actions, [but] it could not move the peasants, students, and the middle classes with sufficient striking power'.[172] It also suffered losses: some six or seven CPI members were killed in Bihar during 1974.[173] Nevertheless, the Party's membership was growing—from 49,000 in 1971 to 88,000 by the end of 1974. In the following year, it would rise to over 100,000.[174]

This was where the CPI stood in 1975. Following the Congress split, the communist programme of struggle and unity with the Congress had not translated into political quiescence on its part. Its role in opposing Congress economic policy, in strikes and in continuing battles for land reform stood witness to that. But what was interpreted as Western hostility and the rise of the JP Movement caused the CPI to move back to the side of the Congress, in what the Party considered was an escalating political, economic and social crises. It took up that position with an agenda of its own. The CPI's preferred solution to the crises was mass mobilisation coupled with an increase in the power of the state, especially in economic terms. Both of these things would come, in a certain sense, in the year that followed. Thus the Communist Party was prepared for the events of 1975.

Notes

1. Sen notes that, among the leadership only, Dange 'tentatively advanced the view that there was a possibility for the Congress moving to the left.' CPI General Secretary, Rajeshwara Rao adopted this position later (Mohit Sen, *A Traveller and the Road: The Journey of an Indian Communist* (New Delhi: Rupa & Co., 2003), 270 and 274).

2. CPI, *The Present Political Situation. Resolution of the National Council of the Communist Party of India, Hyderabad 9–15 June 1966* (New Delhi: Communist Party of India, 1966), 2 and 5. These positions were substantially reiterated by the 8th Party Congress in February 1968 (see CPI, *Political Resolutions Adopted by Eighth Congress of the Communist Party of India, Patna 7–15 February 1968* (New Delhi: Communist Party of India, 1968). See also Anil Rajimwale, *Glimpses of CPI History through Party Congresses* (New Delhi: People's Publishing House, 2005), 94–96; Victor M. Fic, *Kerala: Yenan of India* (Bombay: Nachiketa Publications, 1970), 339.

3. Sen, *Traveller*, 252.

4. Bupesh Gupta, *Right-Reaction Bids for Power* (New Delhi: Communist Party Publication, 1971), 8.

5. CPI, *Party Education Series: Grade 1 Course* (New Delhi: Communist Party of India, 1972), 32. See also Gupta, *Right Reaction*, 7.

6. Cited in Fic, *Kerala*, 341 and 344.

7. Srinivas Sardesai, *Devaluation: The Great Betrayal* (New Delhi: Communist Party Publication, 1966), 2, 4, 47–8.

8. Mohit Sen in 'Left Round Table', *Indian Left Review* I, no. 1 (February 1971): 64.

9. See CPI, *Party Education Series Grade 1*, 37; S. A. Dange, *Defeat Government—Monopolist Offensive with United Struggles* (New Delhi: AITUC Publication, 1972), 8; Gupta, *Right Reaction*, 8–10.

10. Gupta, *Right Reaction*, 5 and 26; CPI, *Party Education Grade 1*, 36.

11. Amarjit Kaur, interview with the author, 15 January 2014.

12. CPI, *Party Education Grade 1*, 37; Mohit Sen, 'Question and Answer: CPI and the United-Front Tactics', *Party Life* (Inner-party Journal of the Organization Department), 1971 (no other date provided), 15–16. For 'left' see Sen, 'Left Round Table', 64; Rajimwale, *CPI Congresses*, 98.

13. Gupta, *Right Reaction*, 11–12.

14. Mohit Sen points out that this was unexpected: 'the CPI leadership had not expected her to take such radical measures. Nor did it expect her to take [the] battle against the Syndicate to the point of contesting the official Congress candidate for the presidentship' (Sen, *Traveller*, 291). The split in Congress, when it came at the end of 1969, 'was certainly not foreseen' by the Party (CPI, *Documents of the 9th Congress of the Communist Party of India, Cochin 3–10 October 1971* (New Delhi: Communist Party of India, 1972), 123).

15. Amarjit Kaur, interview with the author, 15 January 2014.

16. CPI, *Documents of the 9th Congress of the Communist Party of India*, 9.

17. Ibid., 130.

18. Rajimwale, *CPI Congresses*, 98. The 10th Congress elaborated on 'unity and struggle': 'Both aspects are an integral part of the party's tactical line, though in the matter of concrete application one or the other aspect may seem more pronounced, depending on the specific situation or on issues involved' (CPI, *Documents of the 10th Congress of the Communist Party of India, Bhowanisennagar, 27 January to 2 February 1975* [New Delhi: Communist Party Publication, 1975], 188).

19.   An example. On the 1971 election, the CPI declared: '[The] national bourgeoisie [by which is clearly meant the 'non-monopoly' sections], having taken a limited radical stance ... this time seized new initiatives to lead the masses in the election battles' [by which is clearly meant the Congress]' (CPI, *On the General Election of March 1971. Resolutions and Review report of the National Council of the Communist Party of India, New Delhi 23–28 April 1971* [New Delhi: Communist Party of India, 1971], 51).

20.   CPI, *Party Education Series: Preliminary Course* (New Delhi: Communist Party of India, 1972), 15.

21.   Jagannath Sarkar (Bihar State Council, CPI), 'Bankruptcy of Centrism,' *Indian Left Review* 2, no. 7 (September 1973): 11; O. P. Sangal, 'A Permanent Contradiction,' *Indian Left Review* 3, no. 3 (May 1974): 7; CPI, *Party Education Series Grade 1*, 39.

22.   CPI, Political Report, *Documents of the 9th*, 105; CPI, National Council, *Draft Political Resolution for Tenth Party Congress* (New Delhi: New Age Printing Press, 1974), 14. See also Mohit Sen, *The Indian Revolution: Review and Perspectives* (New Delhi: People's Publishing House, 1970), 53.

23.   N. Rajsekhar Reddy, *What Is CPI's Programme?* (New Delhi: Communist Party Publication, 1975), 24 and 26. See also Mohit Sen, 'Revolutionary Process in India,' *Indian Left Review* 2, no. 4 (June 1973): 13; Sen, *The Indian Revolution*, 71–72.

24.   Sen, *The Indian Revolution*, 78; Reddy, *What Is CPI's Programme?* 25–26.

25.   CPI, *Party Education Series Grade 1*, 49. Sen also wrote that communists must not insist on Party leadership of the national democratic revolution (Sen, *The Indian Revolution*, 80–81).

26.   Srinivas Sardesai, 'The Future of the Congress Left,' *Indian Left Review* 2, no. 7 (September 1973): 29. For a prolonged argument seeking to prove that they did nothing of the sort see David Lockwood, *The Indian Bourgeoisie: A Political History of the Indian Capitalist Class in the Early Twentieth Century* (London: Tauris Academic Studies, 2012).

27.   Krishnan wrote of 'the split within the bourgeoisie and its main political party, the Indian National Congress'—the order of precedence here is significant (N. K. Krishnan, 'The Initiative is in the Hands of the Left and Democratic Forces,' *World Marxist Review*, XVI, no. 4 (April 1973): 19). Bhowani Sen said that 'a section of the bourgeoisie and landlords—the right reactionaries—have been thrown out of the government, while the leadership of the state power is assumed by the other section of the national [that is, Indian] bourgeoisie' (Bhowani Sen, *The Truth About CPM: A Critique of the Ideological-Political Line of the Communist Party of India (Marxist)* (New Delhi: Communist Party of India, 1972), 90.

28.   CPI, *On the General Election March 1971*, 52 and 84; Sen, 'Revolutionary Process', 13. India's communists were not alone in this characterisation. Bhabani Sen Gupta described the conflict between Mrs Gandhi's government and the opposition as 'a grim polarization in the national bourgeoisie' (Bhabani Sen Gupta, 'Communism Further Divided,' *Indira Gandhi's India: A Political System Reappraised*, ed. Henry C. Hart (Boulder: Westview Press, 1976), 153). Taking identification of class with party one step further, the CPI's Gangadhar Adhikari declared, 'The relation of the Communist Party with the Indian National Congress is thus part of the larger question of the relation of [the] proletariat with the national bourgeoisie' ('The Communist Party and the Indian National Congress,' *Party Life* [an internal CPI publication] XI, no. 2 (22 January 1975): 30 cited in P. C. Joshi Archive (JNU), Communism in India, File 1975/43).

29.   CPI, *On the General Election March 1971*, 84.

30. CPI, *Documents of the 9th*, 196.

31. Gupta, *Right Reaction*, 46; N. K. Krishnan, 'The Situation in India and the Tasks of the CPI,' *World Marxist Review* XV, no. 8 (August 1972): 34.

32. Dange, *Defeat Government*, 8–9.

33. CPI, *On the General Election March 1971*, 32.

34. Ibid., 40.

35. Arjun Dev, Interview with the author, 15 January 2015.

36. CPI, *On the General Election March 1971*; CPI, National Council, *Draft for the 10th*; Krishnan, 'Situation and Tasks', 33–34; Rajimwale, *CPI Congresses*, 100–01.

37. Nehru Memorial Museum and Library (NMML), P. N. Haksar Papers. Instalments I & II, Subject File Number 213: Interview with H. N. Bahaguna (General Secretary, AICC), 7 December 1969.

38. NMML, Haksar Papers. Instalment III, Subject File Number 248: P. N. Dhar, 'Summary of Recommendations (Political),' 1973.

39. NMML, Haksar Papers. Instalment III, Subject File Number 248: P. N. Dhar, 'A Note on Economic Situation and Remedies to Correct the Economic Difficulties,' 1973.

40. Sen, *Traveller*, 334.

41. Reddy, CPI Programme, 27. See also CPI, Political Resolution, *Documents of the 9th*, 218; Krishnan, Initiative, 19; 'CPI Steps into the Future', *New Age*, 2 February 1975; 'Bihar: Party Looks Confidently to the Future', *New Age*, 2 February 1975.

42. Sen, *Traveller*, 313.

43. CPI, Political Resolution, *Documents of the 9th*, 201 and 218. See also CPI, *Review of Elections to State Assemblies (1972) and Resolutions adopted by the National Council, New Delhi 14–18 April 1972* (New Delhi: Communist Party of India, 1972), 40; Mohit Sen, 'Our Wonderful People', *Indian Left Review* 2, no. 6 (August 1973): 3–4.

44. C. Rajeshwara Rao, *Lenin's Teachings and Our Tactics* (New Delhi: Communist Party Publication, November 1974), 4, 31–32.

45. See CPI, *Resolutions of the National Council of the Communist Party of India* (New Delhi: Communist Party of India, 1970), 6–8; CPI, *On the General Election March 1971*, 33; CPI, *Review and Resolutions April 1972*, 36; 'CPI As A Force', *Link*, 9 February 1975, 13; N. E. Balaram, *Three Years of UF Government Headed by C. Achutha Menon* (New Delhi: Communist Party Publication, 1973), 1–4 and 48; Joseph Varkey, 'The CPI—Congress Alliance in India,' *Asian Survey*, 19, no. 9 (September 1979): 882; Francine R. Frankel, *India's Political Economy, 1947–1977: The Gradual Revolution* (Princeton: Princeton University Press, 1978), 519–20. As it will now appear frequently in these notes, it is worth explaining that *Link* was a Left-wing weekly news magazine, edited by Edatata Narayanan. According to Ajoy Bose, Narayanan was 'an eccentric genius who obsessively combatted the forces of American capitalism and its minions in India. The newspaper's editorial policy was unabashedly partisan, supporting the CPI and Left Congress … .' ('Resident Alien', *Seminar*, 24 August 2002, www.india-seminar.com). While not an official Party publication, *Link* was a reliable purveyor of the Party's views.

46. CPI, *Party Education Series Grade 1*, 34. Dange lamented that 'the state machinery was not cleaned up of all those civil service bosses whom we had inherited from the colonial regime and who still continue to follow their old ideology and policies as well as the policies of the newly arisen Indian monopoly capital.' (Dange, *Defeat Government*, 8.)

47. Gupta, *Right Reaction*, 45.

48. Mohit Sen, 'New Confrontation,' *Indian Left Review* 3, no. 3 (May 1974): 4.

49. CPI, National Council, *Draft for the 10th*, 20–21.

50.   *Thought*, 12 January 1974, 4; Bipan Chandra, Mridula Mukherjee and Aditya Mukherjee, *India since Independence* (New Delhi: Penguin, 2008), 312.

51.   V. P. Dutt, 'The Emergency in India: Background and Rationale,' *Asian Survey* 16, no. 12 (December 1976): 1125.

52.   CPI, On left policies, *Documents of the 9th*, 102; CPI, *Resolutions of the National Council*, 40–42; Mohit Sen, 'Forward from Plan Approach', *Indian Left Review* 2, no. 1 (March 1973), 99–106. The *Party Education Series* pointed out to newer members, 'Not to see these changes, not to acknowledge them for fear that this acknowledgement would bring grist to the mill of the Congress is to violate the most basic tenet of Marxist science'—and reminded older ones that this was a fault of 'the CPI as a whole in the first eight years after independence' and of the CP (Marxist) today (CPI, *Party Education Series Grade 1*, 26). On stalemate: CPI, *On the General Election March 1971*, 32.

53.   Dange, *Defeat Government*, 11.

54.   Sen, 'Revolutionary Process', 12; Rajimwale, *CPI Congresses*, 101.

55.   Sen, 'New Confrontation', 4.

56.   Panly V. Parakal, *Prices, Monopolies and Government Policies* (New Delhi: Communist Party Publication, September 1972), 21.

57.   Krishnan, 'Situation and Tasks', 35.

58.   S. A. Dange, Opening speech in *Documents of the 9th*, 10.

59.   CPI, *On the General Election March 1971*, 33; Balaram, *Three years of UF Government*, 51; H. K. Vyas, *Communist Reply to Tata Memorandum* (New Delhi: Communist Party Publication, 1972), 23–28; CPI, *Documents of the 9th*, 104 and 197; Draft Resolution 'On Prices' for 10th Party Congress, Party Circular Number 48, Joshi Archives (JNU) File Number 1975/19. On licensing, the Party did concede, 'It is true that licensing procedures are too intricate, overlapping and time-consuming … . But all the same it is necessary to recognize that in a developing country like India, licensing system with rigorous check is absolutely essential to determine priorities from the point of view of needs of national economy' (Vyas, *Reply to Tata*, 10).

60.   Vyas, *Reply to Tata*, 33.

61.   CPI, National Council, *Some Problems Concerning the Agrarian Movement and Our Tasks* (New Delhi: Communist Party Publication, 1975), 11.

62.   'On Land Ceilings,' Draft Resolution for the 10th Congress, Party Circular Number 50, P. C. Joshi Archives (JNU), Communism in India, File Number 1975/19.

63.   O. P. Sangal, 'People's Mood,' *Indian Left Review* 3, no. 6 (August–September 1974): 3–5.

64.   CPI, National Council, *Some Problems Concerning the Agrarian Movement*, 11.

65.   For a comprehensive account see Stephen Sherlock, *The Indian Railways Strike of 1974*, (New Delhi: Rupa & Co, 2001). See also, P. N. Dhar, *Indira Gandhi, the 'Emergency', and Indian Democracy* (New Delhi: Oxford India Paperbacks, 2001), 239–44; Mary C. Carras, *Indira Gandhi: In the Crucible of Leadership* (Bombay: Jaico Press Private Ltd, 1980), 172; Frankel, *India's Political Economy*, 529–530.

66.   Sunil Chakravartty (then a *Patriot* correspondent, today the editor of *Mainstream*), told the author, '[T]he other railway unions, including those of the CPI participated … . So, as far as the working class movement was concerned, the CPI was part of it.' (Interview with the author, 8 November 2014.)

67.   Sen, 'New Confrontation', 3.

68.   CPI, Political Report, *Documents of the 10th*, 114.

69.   'Against Victimisation of Railmen,' *New Age*, 16 February 1975, 8–9.

70.   CPI, Political Report, *Documents of the 10th*, 115.

71. Dutt, 'Emergency', 1128.
72. Cited in Uma Vasudev, *Two Faces of Indira Gandhi* (New Delhi, Vikas Publishing House, 1977), 71.
73. Sen, *Traveller*, 339. This was why *Thought* was able to claim that 'the CPI-controlled unions were only half-heartedly for the strike … torn as the party is between … cooperation with the ruling party and the need to oppose it as an ostensible Opposition party' (*Thought*, 1 June 1974, 3).
74. Given the arrests and evictions during the strike and the subsequent events of 1974–75, one could question Sen's conclusion that 'Dange helped them [the railway workers] to return honourably and helped the nation to avoid chaos' (Sen, *Traveller*, 339).
75. O. P. Sangal, 'The March to Delhi—and What Next?' *Indian Left Review* 2, no. 2 (April 1973): 3.
76. CPI, *On the General Election March 1971*, 84; CPI, National Council, *Draft for the 10th*, 14.
77. All that in the first paragraph—with a further five pages that follow in similar tone. It is perhaps little wonder that the 'Question & Answer' section appeared infrequently in *Party Life* (Mohit Sen, 'Question and Answer: CPI and the United-Front Tactics,' *Party Life*: Inner-Party Journal of the Organization Department, 1971 [no other date provided], 15).
78. Jayaprakash Narayan made much of this accusation—see Bipan Chandra, *In the Name of Democracy: JP Movement and the Emergency* (New Delhi: Penguin Books, 2003), 63; JP quoted in *Thought*, 25 January 1975, 3. This was a favourite theme of *Thought* itself, which, in the same issue, referred to 'the Communist contamination of the Congress' (3). Three months later, the same journal noted, somewhat contradictorily, 'the CPI, even though its nominee heads the Government, is a virtual prisoner of Mrs Gandhi's party' (26 April 1975, 3).
79. See Vasudev, *Two Faces*, 87; *Thought* 26 October 1974, 5 and 5 April 1975, 4–5.
80. Nayantara Sahgal, *Indira Gandhi: Her Road to Power* (New York: Frederick Ungar Publishing Co. 1982), 130.
81. The CPI, in fact, complained to Moscow about funds that the Kremlin was contributing to the INC on the grounds that the Communist Party deserved a share of the financial largesse (Oleg Kalugin, *Spymaster* (London: Smith Gryphon Ltd, 1994), 126–27; Christopher Andrew and Vasili Mitrokhin, *The Mitrokhin Archive II: The KGB and the World* (London: Allen Lane, 2005), 323). Some financial redress towards election campaigns was made to smooth ruffled CPI feathers through an 'import–export business'.
82. Sen, 'Revolutionary Process', 12.
83. Sen, *The Indian Revolution*, 80.
84. Sangal, 'People's Mood', 5. He added: '[S]he [Indira Gandhi] is more likely to change when there is a real challenge to her authority in the party.'
85. The Party castigated the rest of the Left (the CPM and the Socialists) for its 'sectarian and disruptive line' towards Congress—which led to 'a debacle' for the non-Congress, non-CPI Left in the March 1972 state assembly elections (CPI, *On the General Elections March 1971*, 9; CPI, *Review of Elections*, 36–37).
86. CPI, *On the General Election March 1971*, 8 and 83.
87. O. P. Sangal, 'The Left's Dilemma', *Indian Left Review* 3, no. 2 (April 1974): 5.
88. Rao, *Lenin's Teachings*, 31–32.
89. It is worth noting here that at the 9th Congress in October 1971, the CPI had 134,662 members; at the 10th Congress in January–February 1975 it had 355,663 (reported in *New Age*, 2 February 1975, 2).

90. '10th Congress: Amendments to Political Resolution', *Party Circular*, Number 41, 30 January 1975 in P.C. Joshi Archive (JNU) File Number 1975/46.

91. All from '10th Congress: Amendments to Political Resolution' in Party Circular Number 41, 30 January 1975 in P. C. Joshi Archive (JNU) File Number 1975/46. None of the amendments was accepted by the Commission on the Draft Political Resolution (P. C. Joshi Archive [JNU], Pamphlets Collection 843).

92. '10th Congress: Amendments to Political Resolution' in Party Circular Number 41, 30 January 1975 in P. C. Joshi Archives (JNU), Communism in India, File Number 1975/46. These sentiments also fell by the wayside at the hands of the Commission on the Draft Political Resolution (P. C. Joshi Archive [JNU], Pamphlets Collection 843).

93. CPI, Political Report, *Documents of the 9th*, 193.

94. *Central News Service* (CNS), 22 January 1975. The CNS was a daily news summary issued from CPI headquarters in Delhi starting in 1974: 'Edited, cyclostyled and published by Sadham Mukherjee on behalf of the Communist Party of India.' See also Mohit Sen, *The People's March to Delhi* (New Delhi: Communist Party Publication, January 1973); Parakal, *Prices, Monopolies and Government Policies*; Frankel, *India's Political Economy*, 519.

95. Sen, *The Indian Revolution*, 48.

96. Rajnarayan Chandavarkar, 'From Communism to Social Democracy: The Rise and Resilience of Communist Parties in India, 1920–1995', *Science and Society* 61, no. 1 (Spring 1997).

97. Vernon Hewitt, *Political Mobilisation and Democracy in India: States of Emergency* (New York: Routledge, 2008), 100.

98. *Link*, 27 June 1971, 10.

99. *Link*, 4 July 1971, 11.

100. 'On Illtreatment of Political Prisoners and Their Release,' Draft Resolution for the 10th, Party Circular Number 64 in P. C. Joshi Archives (JNU), Communism in India, File Number 1975/19.

101. Shashi Bhushan, 'The Only Answer', *Indian Left Review* 3, no. 1 (March 1974): 8–9. Such views were not limited to Bhushan or to 1974. In January 1975, Shankar Ray, Rajni Patel and D. K. Barooah wrote to Indira Gandhi, suggesting the Emergency (Vasudev, *Two Faces*, 58).

102. Srinivas Sardesai, 'Positive Mass Action, Not Search for a Saviour', *Indian Left Review* 3, no. 1 (March 1974); Satyapal Dang, 'Not Dictatorship But a Revolutionary Government', *Indian Left Review* 3, no. 1 (March 1974); Mohit Sen, 'Radical Turn Not Limited Dictatorship', *Indian Left Review* 3, no. 1 (March 1974).

103. Sardesai, Devaluation, 1 and 7. The danger was not confined to economic policy. Imperialism was also infiltrating the Indian education system (39–40).

104. NMML, Haksar Papers. Instalment III, Subject File Number 225, 'A Note on Overt and Covert Activities of the Americans in Calcutta', n.d. The note names those allegedly involved in this lobby, among them: journalists (Inder Malhotra), military officers (Lt General Manekshaw, Lt General Jagjit Singh), officials (P. K. Sen—former Calcutta Commissioner of Police), businessmen (the chief executives of Andrew Yule & Son, Bengal Potteries Ltd, J. Thomas & Co.), politicians (P. C. Ghosh—former chief minister of West Bengal and a number of Congress (O) and socialist luminaries).

105. NMML, Haksar Papers. Instalment III, Subject File Number 248: P. N. Dhar, 'Note' to Haksar.

106. Sen, *Traveller*, 318, 323–4. Once again, the support was laced with criticism. Hiren Mukherji, a CPI member of the Lok Sabha, 'accused the Government of being "intellectually sterile and ideologically destitute" [on Bangladesh]' in July 1971 (*Link*, 4 July 1971, 11).

107. CNS 231, 2 January 1975.

108. Dhar, *Indira Gandhi*, 254.

109. Prime Minister's Report to the 75th Session, 31 December 1975–1 January 1976 in *The Encyclopaedia of the Indian National Congress. Volume Twenty-three, 1974–1975: The Lengthening Shadows*, ed. Moin A. Zaidi (New Delhi: S. Chand and Company Ltd, 1984), 390.

110. Sen, *Traveller*, 344.

111. Harsh Dev Malaviya, *International Conference Against Fascism (Patna: December 4–7, 1975): Western Aid, Multinationals and the CIA* (Delhi: Everest Press, 1975), 17.

112. V. P. Sathe (Congress Lok Sabha member), 'National Crisis & the Role of the Left', *Indian Left Review* 3, no. 2 (April 1974), 12. See also Vidya Charan Shukla, 'The Crisis Ahead', in *Era of Discipline: Documents on Contemporary Reality*, ed. D. V. Gandhi (New Delhi: Samachar Bharati, 1976), 205.

113. See CNS 233, 4 January 1975. The Soviets too regarded a Chile-style military coup in India as a possibility (see Vojtech Mastny, 'The Soviet Union's Partnership with India', *Journal of Cold War Studies*, 12, no. 3 (Summer 2010): 73).

114. CNS 254, 30 January 1975; Sen, *Traveller*, 343.

115. In his account, Sen moves significantly straight on at this point to the anti-Congress movement in Gujarat (Sen, *Traveller*, 336). In 1974, however, Sen had written that Mrs Gandhi was sabotaging the struggle against the Right: 'Here [as opposed to Chile] the right is having its job done for it by the Prime Minister, the chief leader of the centrists, seeking to appease the right by moving against the left' (Mohit Sen, 'Confrontation', *Indian Left Review* 3, no. 8 [November 1974–March 1975]: 5).

116. CPI, *Documents of the 10th*, Report on the International Situation, 54; Sen, 'Confrontation', 3.

117. The account of the JP Movement in Gujarat and Bihar that follows is largely taken from Bipan Chandra's *In the Name of Democracy* and Frankel's *India's Political Economy* unless otherwise indicated.

118. Chandra, *Name*, 37. See also 'Correspondent', 'The Emergency in India', *Bulletin of Concerned Asian Scholars* 7, no. 4 (October–December 1975): '[T]he working class and rural poor remained indifferent to the movement and, largely under the control of the Congress, kept out of opposition politics' (14).

119. 'Correspondent', 'Emergency', 2–16.

120. Chandra, *Name*, 28.

121. Shah points out that in Bihar, rich farmers made a donation of ₹50,000 to the JP Movement (Ghanshyam Shah, *Protest Movements in Two Indian States: A Study of the Gujarat and Bihar Movements* [Delhi: Ajanta Publications, 1977], 104 and 161–62).

122. 'Correspondent', 'Emergency', 16.

123. Unfortunately, Correspondent concludes that this was 'Bonapartism': '[T]he state had moved to crush a section of the ruling class in the interest of the ruling class as a whole.' As should now be clear, I would argue that the state moved in its own interests—with the industrial bourgeoisie in tow.

124. 'In Bihar, the agitation began in March 1974 with the slogan '*Bihar bhi Gujarat Banega*' (Gujarat will be repeated in Bihar) (Shah, *Protest Movements*, vii).

125.   See, for example, Sahgal, *Indira Gandhi*, 113–24.
126.   Chandra, *Name*, 43.
127.   Between March and November 1974 the JPM[ovement] was characterized by almost continuous satyagraha [non-violent non-cooperation] campaigns, student and local bandhs [shut-downs], gheraos of government offices and ministers' and MLAs' houses, and massive meetings, processions and demonstrations in Patna and other towns and cities of Bihar, demanding dissolution of the state assembly. (Chandra, *Name*, 43)

128.   'Correspondent', 'Emergency', 14. Sunil Chakravartty pointed out to the author the number of current political luminaries who received 'their baptism of fire' in the JP Movement—Lalu Prasad Yadav and Nitish Kumar, for example. (Interview with the author, 8 November 2014.)
129.   '… like other Sarvodaya [Gandhian organisations dedicated to 'universal uplift'] members, Jayaprakash claims that he does not believe in any ideologies' (Shah, *Protest Movements*, 103).
130.   'It was essentially an urban middle class agitation. Being unorganized and diffused in its interests, the middle class could not direct the agitation' (Shah, *Protest Movements*, 58).
131.   See Dhar, *Indira Gandhi*, 264; Chandra, *Name*, 139–149.
132.   JP cited in Chandra, *Name*, 145–6; 'JP and RSS,' *New Age*, 23 February 1975, 16. Bipan Chandra points out: 'JP was a democrat and not an authoritarian leader. Nor was the movement he led in 1974–75 yet authoritarian or fascist, but—and this is important—it was capable of creating a space for its fascist component.' (Bipan Chandra, Mridula Mukherjee and Aditya Mukherjee, *India Since Independence* [New Delhi: Penguin, 2008], 317.)
133.   JP said, 'So the contest will be only between two parties—one of those who support the struggle and the other of those who oppose it' (Shah, *Protest Movements*, 119).
134.   Hewitt, *Political Mobilisation*, 108.
135.   P. C. Joshi Archive (JNU), Communism in India, File Number 1974/74. AICC Camp Narora, Background Paper Number 1, 11. The AICC organised the three-day camp in late 1974 '[t]o mobilize the [Congress] party ideologically and organizationally' (Chandra, *Name*, 60). This was followed by a 'wave of Narora-type camps of Congressmen at all levels which covered the entire nation … . History will no doubt record that but for these Narora-type camps the Congress may not have so successfully met the challenge of the false messiahs of "total revolution."' (H. D. Malaviya, 'Implementation and the Party' (Part 2), *Indian Left Review* 3, no. 12 (September 1975): 10.
136.   Sahgal, *Indira Gandhi*, 139; Sen, 'Confrontation', 3.
137.   See, for example, B. C. Bhagwati, *Presidential Address, Indian National Trade Union Congress. 20th Session, Bombay 28 December 1974* (New Delhi: INTUC, 1975).
138.   AICC Camp Narora, Background Number Paper 1, 14–15, P. C. Joshi Archives (JNU), Communism in India.
139.   Sangal, 'People's Mood', 3. See also Mohit Sen on the 'completely justified mass discontent and anger' in early 1974: 'The Perspective of Struggle,' *Indian Left Review* 3, no. 2 (April 1974): 9.
140.   'Blood and Tears in Gujarat', *Link*, 3 February 1974, 9.
141.   Sen, 'Radical Turn, Not Limited Dictatorship,' 4. There remained traces of this approach even at the 10th Congress in early 1975. Gohin Kanar (Howrah) warned that, 'Our negative attitude towards the popular mass struggles may be utilized by the forces of

right reaction and we may be isolated from the masses of the people.' (Amendments to the Political Resolution, 10th Congress. Party Circular Number 41, 30 January 1975, P. C. Joshi Archives [JNU], Communism in India, File Number 1975/46.)

142. C. P. Bhambri, interview with the author 4 November 2014.

143. Srinivas Sardesai, *Student Upsurge and Indian Revolution* (New Delhi: Youth Life Publication, June 1974), 6–7.

144. Sarjoo Pandey (CPI Lok Sabha member), 'The Rightist Threat', *Indian Left Review* 3, no. 2 (April 1974): 15.

145. Indradeep Sinha, *Real Face of JP's 'Total Revolution'* (New Delhi: CPI Publication, 1974), 6; Sen, 'Perspectives of Revolution', CNS 246, 20 January 1975.

146. C. Rajeshwara Rao, Pauly V. Parakal, Sadhan Mukherjee and Shamim Faizee, *Parties of Right Reaction* (New Delhi: Communist Party Publication, August 1975), 5 and 11.

147. Sinha, *Real Face*, 13. *Link* described the non-JS/RSS leaders of the opposition as 'helpless frontmen for the hard-core fascists of the RSS, the cold-blooded compradore capitalists … and the secret American "de-stabilisers" who are in the country in so many guises' (*Link*, 8 June 1975, 7).

148. C. Rajeshwara Rao, 'Awareness of Historical Responsibility', *World Marxist Review* XVIII, no. 5 (May 1975): 23. See also Gupta, *Right Reaction*, 27–31; N.K. Krishnan, 'Main Tasks', *Party Life* XI, no. 2 (22 January 1975): 2–3 in P. C. Joshi Archives (JNU), Communism in India, File Number 1975/43. Sen compared the JP Movement's proposal for a 'party-less democracy' with the system instituted by Field-Marshal Ayub Khan in Pakistan (Sen, *Traveller*, 339).

149. P. C. Joshi, 'Note on Fascist Threat in India' in P. C. Joshi Archives (JNU), Communism in India, File Number 1975/122.

150. CNS 234, 6 January 1975. There had also been incidents of rock throwing against Congress leaders (*Link*, 8 June 1975, 4 and 8) and an attempt on the life of the Chief Justice, A. N. Ray (Dutt, 'Emergency', 1131).

151. Sinha, *Real Face*, 26.

152. Sen, 'New Confrontation', 3. See also Sardesai, *Student Upsurge*, 6.

153. Sen, *Traveller*, 346–47.

154. *World Marxist Review* was a theoretical journal based in Prague and designed for distribution to Soviet-friendly Communist Parties.

155. Sahgal, *Indira Gandhi*, 138.

156. Sen lists Rajeshwara Rao, N. K. Krishnan, Yogendra Sharma, Bhupesh Gupta and Indrajit Gupta as being in this group. In opposition to it were Dange, C. Achuthi Menon, M. N. Govindan Nair, G. Adhikari and N. Rajsekhar Reddy (*Traveller*, 338–39).

157. Sinha, *Real Face*, 45. Bipan Chandra criticised this approach in mid-1974, pointing to the lack of working class and rural poor involvement in the movement: '[A]ny Marxist should be able to see that a political crisis during which the working classes of the cities and villages are politically passive can only lead to fascism, or militarism, or authoritarianism of the more traditional bourgeois parliamentary type (Bipan Chandra, 'Total Rectification', *Seminar* 178 (June 1974): 27). O. P. Sangal agreed, writing that those on the left wanting to join in the anti-Congress agitation were asking the working class to 'accept the urban petty bourgeoisie as its leader and adapt the latter's blind despair as its own guiding ideology' (Sangal, 'People's Mood', 4).

158. Rao, Awareness, 23.

159. Sinha, *Real Face*, 6. See also Rao, *Lenin's Teachings*, 30.

160. Lalan Tiwari, *Democracy and Dissent: A Case Study of the Bihar Movement, 1974–75* (Delhi: Mittal Publications, 1987), 218–220. Mishra said, '[W]e cannot survive alone nor can we be isolated from other progressive forces. Democracy and socialism go together.' Jagjivan Ram replied, '[N]o [other] party should keep in mind that the Congress needed their help for survival.'

161. Sen, *Traveller*, 341.

162. Bhupesh Gupta, 'Behind Rightist Challenge to Parliamentary Democracy', CNS 247, 21 January 1975. See also CNS 241, 14 January 1975.

163. CPI National Council, 'For Intensified United Struggle Against Right-reaction and for Democratic Reforms,' Communist Party of India, *Resolutions and Documents Adopted by the National Council of the Communist Party of India, New Delhi, 1 to 5 April 1975* (New Delhi: Communist Party Publication, May 1975), 4–5.

164. Bhupesh Gupta, 'Behind Rightist Challenge', CNS 247, 21 January 1975.

165. Chandra, *Name*, 44. This was a repeat of what had happened in Gujarat. Once the movement there took up the demand to dissolve the state assembly, *Link* moved from its initial sympathy to a denunciation of 'Fascist Tactics in Gujarat'—and pointed out (either in certainty or hope) that 'the demand for dissolution of the State Assembly does not have the mass backing that the earlier agitation enjoyed.' (*Link*, 24 February 1974, 20–21). Sardesai argued that the CPI was for the right of recall of elected assemblies—but 'exercised in a manner that strengthens our democratic institutions and does not destroy them' (Sardesai, *Student Upsurge*, 8).

166. Reported in *The Indian Nation*, 17 October 1974, 3 cited in Tiwari, *Democracy and Dissent*, 219.

167. Henry C. Hart, 'Introduction', in *Indira Gandhi's India: A Political System Reappraised*, ed. Henry C. Hart (Boulder: Westview Press, 1976), 11.

168. Chandra, *Name*, 55.

169. Tiwari, *Democracy and Dissent*, 218–19.

170. Tiwari, *Democracy and Dissent*, 100. For the CPI view of joint work with the Congress against the JP Movement see CPI National Council, 'For Intensified United Struggle, 4–5.

171. *The Indian Nation*, 17 November 1974 cited in Tiwari, *Democracy and Dissent*, 219.

172. 'Bihar: Party Looks Confidently To Future', *New Age*, 2 February 1975, 6.

173. 'Rajeshwara Rao Explains Objective of the 10th Congress', *New Age*, 2 February 1975, 13. In this context, the General Secretary was reported as saying, '[T]he Communist Party does not want civil war, but if JP's murder politics goes on there would be confrontation which could lead to civil war …. . If reaction uses force, we shall meet that.' To this end, 50,000 volunteers had been trained—and more were to come.

174. Figures cited by Bhogendra Jha (CPI Lok Sabha member), 'Birth and Growth of Communists in Bihar', *Indian Left Review* 4, no. 4 (February 1976): 5.

4

The Emergency

The Course of the Emergency

As if Indira Gandhi did not have troubles enough, on 12 June 1975, Justice Sinha of the Allahabad High Court convicted her of corrupt campaign practices, resulting from a case brought by Raj Narain, her opponent in the 1971 election.[1] Her election was declared invalid and the court determined that she could not seek election or hold office for six years. This judgement received a stay order by Mrs Gandhi's appeal to the Supreme Court. Before this was to be decided on 24 June, she was told that she could remain in office but could not vote in the Lok Sabha. The Supreme Court's decision was not awaited with any degree of optimism in the Congress camp.[2] Mrs Gandhi's response to the Allahabad judgement was, reportedly, to draft an immediate letter of resignation as the prime minister. She was persuaded not to do so by a coterie of close advisers, which included her son, Sanjay.[3] We will encounter Sanjay more substantially in the next chapter, but it is important to note here that, as a firm opponent of any backing down on his mother's part, he assumed at that point a crucial role in the events that were to come. He was constantly by his mother's side during the period between the court's decision and the declaration of Emergency.[4] It was he who told the press, '[T]here was no possibility of the prime minister resigning over such an issue'.[5] It may have been Sanjay who first formulated the idea of an 'emergency'. In mid-June, with Bansi Lal and R. K. Dhawan, he produced a plan to curb the press and arrest the opposition leaders, which he submitted to his mother.[6] The day after the Allahabad court's decision, the Gujarat elections—resulting from the dissolution of the state assembly—were held. The Janata Front (the electoral manifestation of the JP Movement) won 85 seats—10 more than the Congress—and formed the new state government.

These two events gave added impetus to the JP Movement. Since accepting the Congress' electoral challenge, the movement had become fixated on the removal of the Gandhi government and the Congress from power. In March, it had organised a march on the Lok Sabha of some 750,000 people. The Allahabad judgement and the Gujarat result sent the movement once again into top gear. Within hours of the court's decision, according to *Link*, the JS leader, Atal Bihari Vajpayee, was calling on people to 'revolt' against the government.[7] Continuous demonstrations began outside the prime minister's house, calling for her resignation—which were answered by counter-demonstrations in her support.[8] At a massive opposition rally in Delhi on 25 June, JP announced that the movement would not allow Indira Gandhi to function as the prime minister. A national campaign of mobilisation and civil disobedience would commence from 29 June. He appealed to the army, the police and the bureaucracy to refuse illegal or unconstitutional orders.[9] The campaign would culminate after a week, with a *gherao* of the prime minister's house by hundreds and thousands of volunteers.

The Congress government was, therefore, faced with a possible upheaval which may have encompassed mass violence, mutiny and social breakdown—not to mention economic gridlock—presided over by a movement which, at the very least, was influenced by communal and fascist organisations. As Bipan Chandra points out, there was a democratic option for the government here (as there was for the JP Movement—but it is the government's actions that presently concern us):

> … She could have declared that the Lok Sabha would be dissolved and fresh elections to it held in October–November, with her fighting elections subject to the Supreme Court or the Parliament…. If JP and the Opposition accepted this offer the door to a democratic resolution of the political impasse through appeal to the electorate would have been opened.[10]

But the door was not opened. On 26 June, the day after the JP Movement issued its threat, the government proclaimed a State of Emergency under Article 352 of the Constitution. This suspended various sections of the constitution as well as many fundamental rights and civil liberties. Censorship was imposed and preparations were made to put down dissent. Hundreds of opposition leaders were arrested under the Maintenance of Internal Security Act (MISA). The RSS, Anand Marg, Jamaat-i-Islami and the Communist Party of India (Marxist-Leninist) were banned outright.[11] V. P. Dutt claimed that '[a]ny impression that a dictatorship has been foisted on the people is both misconceived and mischievous... . All the constitutional procedures have been abided by'—the problem being, of course, that the constitution allowed for a (limited) dictatorship.[12]

The Congress Working Committee (CWC) approved the Emergency on 14 July and set about rooting out dissent within its ranks.[13] The ex-socialists of the CFSA had already expressed some sympathy with the JP Movement—and were uneasy about Mrs Gandhi's non-resignation after Allahabad. They were warned not to raise any objection to the endorsement of the decision by the meeting of the Congress Parliamentary Party. Subsequently, they stayed away from meetings of the CWC. Many Congress members, who had been radical Leftists or JP Movement supporters, were expelled by the CWC after the Emergency was declared.[14] The Lok Sabha approved the Emergency by 336 votes to 59 on 23 July. Within a few months, Gujarat and Tamil Nadu, the two non-Congress states, had been placed under Presidential rule—thus placing the central government in firm control.

The day following the Emergency declaration, Indira Gandhi attempted an explanation to the people of India through a national radio broadcast. 'The President has proclaimed Emergency. This is nothing to panic about', she instructed them. She said that 'the deep and wide conspiracy' against her government encompassed agitations, violence (including the assassination of L. S. Mishra and the attempt on the Chief Justice) and incitement to mutiny. 'The forces of disintegration are in full play', she declared, 'and communal passions are being aroused.' The government's patience had come to an end.[15]

Not only was the opposition anti-democratic and anti-national, it was also opposed to and enraged by Congress socialism and Indian non-alignment. It included 'businessmen and politicians who have been indicted by tribunals', 'organisations of the rich farmers' and communal elements: the JS and the RSS.[16]

Yashpal Kapoor, a Congress general secretary, painted an idyllic picture of the morning after.

> In the evening of June 25, 1975, when the people went to sleep, it was utter chaos, indiscipline, frustration and a sense of despondency among the people. However, when they got up in the morning of June 26, 1975, they found the life changed to one of national discipline, students going to their schools, teachers taking to their teaching work seriously, the clerical

and other staff going to their offices in time, the workers reaching their factories punctually ...[17]

It is probable that many in India were glad that the calm in the streets had returned—and that the prospect of many more weeks of civil disobedience, strikes, shut-downs and the accompanying violence had been removed. Perhaps, for this reason, the public response to the Emergency was relatively muted.[18] In her initial broadcast, Indira Gandhi was able to claim, 'there is normalcy all over the country except for partial hartal [strike and shut-down] and minor incidents in Gujarat.' A month later she said, 'The people's response to the Emergency has been wholesome.'[19]

Business appeared generally to support the Emergency. Prominent here was Krishna Kumar Birla, a leading industrialist from the Birla family with an interest in politics.[20] It was he who organised a demonstration of businessmen in support of Mrs Gandhi after the Allahabad judgement. He wrote later, 'I have never been an admirer of the Emergency ... . However, considering the way the law and order situation in the country was deteriorating, Indira-ji was perhaps left with no choice.' As a result, said Birla, amongst other things 'punctuality in the running of trains vastly improved'.[21] At the 48th annual session of the Federation of Indian Chambers of Commerce and Industry (FICCI), Birla elaborated on the potential of the Emergency for business. In his presidential address, delivered while Mrs Gandhi was in the audience, he said:

> You had suggested some time back, Madam Prime Minister, that there should be a moratorium on strikes and lockouts for at least five years. I hope that this excellent idea will be given a more concrete shape and a fair trial.[22]

In the meantime, some bright spots did seem to be appearing. Prices improved, inflation declined and strikes and stoppages lessened. In a blaze of publicity, the government cracked down on tax evasion, smuggling and undisclosed investments.[23] But much of this did not result from the reduction of political *stürm und drang*. Toye contended in 1977:

> ... much improvement results from fortuitous influences rather than policies made possible by the declaration of the Emergency ... . The most important single fact about the Indian economy is that the 1975–76 harvests have been an all-time record ... . This expectation helped to end the vicious circle of food scarcity, hoarding, price rises and commodity speculation which had built up in the two preceding drought years.[24]

Furthermore, we should not forget that this slight alleviation in the condition of the Indian people took place against a backdrop of repression—arrests, censorship and mistreatment of detainees. During the Emergency, over 100,000 people were arrested under MISA and the Defence of India Rules. India's gaols did not offer comfort at the best of times—and neither did her police curb their zeal in carrying out the authorities' bidding.

A secondary aspect of the Emergency was the economic programme that was introduced simultaneously with it. The prime minister noted in August 1975, 'The economic programme now announced was not the reason for Emergency but Emergency has created the right climate for its implementation.'[25] On the day the Emergency was announced, the cabinet decided that it should be followed by radical economic measures. In her broadcast, Mrs Gandhi promised 'further measures to strengthen the economy and to relieve that hardship of various sections, particularly the poor and vulnerable, and those with fixed incomes'.[26] When the measures came, on 21 July, they took the form of the 20-Point Programme. Its most important features included: measures to keep prices down; the implementation of land ceiling laws and the distribution of surplus land; liquidation of rural indebtedness; a rise in the minimum agricultural wage; outlawing of bonded labour; measures to increase production; measures against land speculation and tax evasion (with summary trials and stern punishment for the latter) and workers' participation in industry.[27]

This represented, on paper at any rate, a serious attempt at the economic uplift of the poor—especially in rural areas—and at the further development of the Indian economy.[28] Certainly, the Congress Left saw it as a new stage in the progressive direction of the government. Congress Lok Sabha member, Amrit Nahata wrote, 'The twenty-point programme should be viewed ... as a part of the larger task of building a socialist society.' He went on to advocate the nationalisation of the textile, jute and automobile industries and the establishment of an effective public distribution system.[29]

There were, however, difficulties in its implementation. Mrs Gandhi blamed these on '[p]owerful classes and interests ... sabotaging the 20-point program'—and no doubt these forces were at work.[30] But the only way that they could be fought was by popular mobilisation in favour of the programme. Elements in the Congress seemed to realise this. Malaviya wrote, 'Popular committees, at all levels, having statutory powers would have to be set up so that reliance is placed not solely on the bureaucracy, but the people may exercise control and be actively involved in implementation.'[31] The CWC met on 14 July and its president, Barooah 'requested the Prime Minister to give some guidelines as to how to involve the people and the Party workers in the implementation of the economic programme announced by her'. Mrs Gandhi agreed that the involvement of Congress workers and 'like-minded parties and persons' was a good idea—but warned, 'We cannot allow the programme to go into the hands of those who do not agree with our policies or those who are opposed to us.' The committees would have to be supervised by agents of the Congress president—and would be established from the top down, by the chief ministers of the states.[32] A sub-committee under Barooah was set up to work out the details.[33] A week or so later, Congress General Secretary P. V. Narasimha Rao confirmed that the sub-committee was working on its report. In early August, the report was submitted to the prime minister for final approval. After that, the report and the sub-committee disappeared without a trace.[34] In the All-India Congress Committee (AICC), Barooah had stopped talking about 'people's committees' by early 1976.[35]

Following Mrs Gandhi's model, the Assam government established four 'task forces' to implement the economic programme, consisting entirely of state bureaucrats.[36] By August, the prime minister was becoming hesitant about 'popular committees': '[T]here will have to be perhaps some such committees, but this cannot be done suddenly.'[37] Eventually, a sub-committee of the CWC issued guidelines on the formation of committees at state, district and sub-district level. Amongst the chief ministers, state ministers, Congress officials and local members of Legislative Assemblies and Legislative Councils, who were to make up these committees, one searches in vain for any real grass-roots involvement in the committee structure.[38] For the rest of the month, Mrs Gandhi maintained that 'we are making an effort to have people's committees so that more people are involved' (to a no doubt enthusiastic audience of chief secretaries and chief commissioners) and that '[c]itizens' groups are being formed to co-operate constructively with officials'.[39] Barooah declared in February 1976, 'I hope by this time the implementation committees at various levels must have been set up in your State and they are functioning properly' (to a probably startled audience of Congress chief ministers and state Congress committee presidents).[40]

A problem here was that the Emergency had promised stability and an end to street politics. The government therefore did not take measures to encourage popular mobilisation or participation in the implementation of the economic programme. It was left issuing 'quixotic commands for putting in place a grass-roots organization for popular mobilization by fiat from above'.[41] Haksar noted towards the end of the Emergency:

[T]he [economic] programme is being implemented in the most routine manner by the Administration, with hardly any political support being mobilised for it, and [the] benefits already provided under it are so micro-scopic that they are almost unmeaningful ...[42]

We will return to the question of participation in the implementation of the programme in the countryside shortly. Before that, we should consider briefly the immediate effects of the Emergency on urban workers. Mrs Gandhi told the Rajya Sabha, on 22 July 1975, that before the Emergency:

Amongst industrial workers there was a tendency to go on strike, to make demands. The employers on their side also felt that they could take advan-tage of the situation and they did take advantage.[43]

The state, it appeared, would arbitrate between the two. There was no immediate attack on workers—trade unions, for example, were not banned. The prime minister told representatives of FICCI, the Associated Chambers of Commerce and the All-India Manufacturers' Organisation that they should 'promptly concede legitimate demands of the workers'.[44] Some wage rises were granted. *Link* reported on 'the creation of a mecha-nism for the active participation of workers in industrial production'.[45] When there were extensive layoffs in the private industry during the first six months of the Emergency, the government brought in the Industrial Disputes Act, which required enterprises with more than 300 workers to obtain government approval before layoffs, retrenchments or closures were instituted.[46] Mrs Gandhi called for better conditions for factory workers at a meeting of the AICC in November 1976.[47]

But as Toye points out, the Congress government had been locked in combat with the Indian workers' movement for several years before the Emergency. The Indian Airlines lockout, the Life Insurance Corporation dispute and the railway strike were defeats for the workers and, as we have seen, the sound and fury of the JP Movement did little to raise their class spirit. By 1975, the labour movement was 'out-manoeuvred and demoral-ized', according to Toye. Little wonder then that the Emergency was met with 'total passivity amongst organized labour' despite Mrs Gandhi's assur-ance that 'workers from all over the country have welcomed our move and have given us their full support'.[48] The Emergency's economic programme was aimed, in part, at increasing production—and this inevitably meant inroads into workers' conditions.[49] Government workers 'were put under speed-up pressure and forced to meet time-clocks in a way they had not for some time'.[50] Sanjay told a joint convention of the Youth Congress, the National Students' Union of India and the All-India Trade Union Congress (AITUC) Youth Front, at the beginning of 1976, that an important aim was 'the stopping of wage increases'.[51]

In September 1975, by presidential ordinance, the government cut the traditional annual bonus for industrial workers from 8.33 per cent to 4.5 per cent (for 1974–75) and then abolished it. The AITUC came out against the decision (as did Indian National Trade Union Congress [INTUC], the Congress-aligned union federation) and called a protest strike against it. In Delhi, 16,000 strikers courted arrest.[52] But that was as far as the resistance went. Haksar noted that the workers did not have leaders 'who would have taken advantage of the situation and led them to a violent struggle. Such leaders have been detained'. Prakash Ray, in a note for the 11th (post-Emergency) CPI Congress, alleged that 'at the Delhi Boat Club all our leaders including the party chairman and 20 parliament members withdrew just at the appearance of [a] few police inspectors'.[53]

In fact, it was only really in the areas of increased production, harder work and speed-up that popular mobilisation was attempted. The Congress leadership, for example, organised various 'National Days' in order to emphasise this or that aspect of the Emergency programme—'National Discipline Day', 'Increased Production Day', 'Rural Labour Day' and so on. The number of these soon reached epic proportions. Between June and December 1976, there were no less than 27 National Days—including 'National Dedication Day', '20-Point Economic Programme Day', 'National Self-Reliance Day' and 'Family Planning Day' (twice).[54]

It was in the rural areas that the Emergency economic programme produced the greatest hopes and the greatest disappointment. Five points of the 20-Point programme were concerned with alleviating the plight of the rural poor. Haksar, suggesting a detailed land reform programme, told the prime minister a few days after the Emergency was declared:

> ... no programme which does not go deeply into the rural areas of India can have any meaning or purpose ... . Difficult, hard decisions have to be made. Otherwise, the argument advanced by [the] Prime Minister that [the opposition] has been thwarting all her efforts to carry out radical programmes would sound hollow.[55]

However, Congress faced the same dilemma here as with the 'people's committees' considered earlier. A decade before the Emergency, Nigel Harris wrote, '[I]n India, the small ruling group has consistently been afraid of the possible results of permitting more conflict than it already has ... Accordingly, no appeal to the poor peasants or landless labourers is possible.'[56] Yet, this was what was needed. Successful reforms had to be driven by a government 'that derives its strength from the dispossessed'.[57] The Congress government, in all likelihood, did derive some of its strength from that source—but the source had to be mobilised to implement the programme. The business magazine *Commerce* was moved to declare in 1973, that agrarian reform needed

> a cadre organisation 'something like' a communist party to mobilize people to force the bureaucracy to serve their interests, force implementation of the programs, to carry through land reforms necessary to destroy the dominance of an unproductive elite and to fight 'traditionalistic fatalism' ... holding back development.[58]

Words to this effect there were aplenty. Barooah (never short of them) declared that the rural programme 'is bound to change the face of rural India in a manner truly revolutionary ... it will give a much needed rural face to our socialism'.[59] The chief ministers met in March 1976 to review the implementation of land reform. Indira Gandhi detected a 'certain amount of lethargy and hesitation' in their approach. She conceded that, while local people should be involved, this could not be done 'at once'. 'But this is the direction in which we should work.'[60] Barooah felt able to claim that land reform, abolition of bonded labour and provision of house sites were 'outstanding examples of progress' by August 1976.[61]

Actual mobilisation, however, was a good deal more difficult than loud declarations. One of the difficulties was the Congress organisation itself. Malaviya pointed out that 'the [Congress] party units in the rural areas are more often than not dominated by land owners and other rural vested interests, and none could care less about rousing the agricultural labourers and the poor peasants'.[62] In fact, the Emergency worsened this situation somewhat. According to Frankel, in the absence of democracy, 'the ruling party had become more than ever dependent upon the very local elites it was presumably committed to displace in order to carry out its "growth"-oriented policies'.[63]

The agricultural sections of the Emergency programme were, therefore, destined to disappoint—whatever may have been the intentions of their advocates. By mid-March 1976, 136,000 acres of land had been given to the landless. But this was 'a mere 3 per cent of the 3.8–4.0 million acres which were estimated to be rendered surplus under the July 1972 guidelines'.[64] The 20-Point programme had promised to abolish bonded labour, but by September 1976, only 62,500 bonded labourers had been identified, out of an estimated 2.62 million.[65] When landless peasants demanded more, there were cases of them being set upon by landlords and their agents, as well as being lathi-charged (an occasion when a large group of police run forward in an attacking movement carrying their sticks), shot at and gaoled by police.[66] Blair concludes:

> Overall then, in the agricultural sector, the Emergency meant essentially a continuation of the status quo that benefitted the bigger farmers and held down other strata.[67]

Within 12 months, the visible benefits of the Emergency, such as they were, began to fade. Radical economic reforms were not implemented; government office timeliness eroded; land reform ground to a halt.[68] The Congress itself, as essentially a parliamentary and patronage organisation, was now no longer needed for the former function—while the latter one was generally an obstruction to the Emergency programme.[69] Mrs Gandhi herself told the AICC in November 1976:

> … We have not been able to change our Congress party to meet the changing needs of the country. We do not find the Party that sharp instrument of action, that instrument of change and of our silent peaceful revolution which we have to bring about.[70]

Worse still, the Congress was being infiltrated by its erstwhile political opponents.[71] Malaviya offered the time-honoured remedy of the Congress Left to combat the menace: '[A] thorough purge of the factional bosses and corrupt elements from the Congress organisation at all levels is essential for winning the traditional mass support of the Congress among the people.'[72] But the purge did not come. In the meantime, there was a steady increase in the importance placed on the personality and personal qualities of the leader—and, in time, on those of her son, Sanjay. Barooah's remarks at the 75th Congress session at the end of 1975 were typical:

I am also sustained by the shining example of our leader, Shrimati Indira Gandhi, who has steered the ship of the nation clear of rocks in the stormiest of times in free India's history. She has set for us standards of unflinching patriotism, undaunted courage and undimmed political vision.[73]

The CPI and the Emergency

It will come as no surprise to the reader that India's communists supported the declaration, intention and thrust of the Emergency when it was declared in June 1975.

From the beginning of the year, they had remained in a state of heightened mobilisation against the JP Movement and in favour of more radical economic policies. In mid-May, the Party launched three national campaigns—for the implementation of land reform, for the creation of a viable public distribution system and against the 'pincer attack' of US imperialism and Right-reaction. In an early indication of how the Party hoped events would unfold, *Link* reported that 'in several States even Congressmen are cooperating with the CPI in these campaigns'.[74] Gargi Chakravartty, an activist in the CPI teachers' organisation tells of how CPI and Congress women co-operated in the preparation of a government publication, to mark International Women's Year in 1975.[75]

When the Allahabad judgement was handed down, the CPI rejected the notion that Indira Gandhi should resign.[76] The Bihar unit of the Party saw in the demand for her resignation, 'a conspiracy to destabilize the Government and usher in a rightist and pro-American regime'.[77] But the Party pointed out that it was not enough for the Congress to resort 'to political manoeuvres or court procedures'. Its popularity had been eroded by the failure to implement its election promises—and this had 'created fertile soil among the masses for the operations of right reactionary forces'. What was required was 'the sincere implementation of the pledges made … to the people'.[78] The Party intended to continue with its three campaigns, as well as its appeal for Congress participation in them. On the eve of the Emergency, it announced land occupations in Andhra Pradesh, Rajasthan, Hyderabad and West Bengal.[79]

The Party's Central Executive Committee (CEC) endorsed the Emergency in early July. Its trade union organisation, AITUC, did so at the same time.[80] The role of Mrs Gandhi and the Congress—without whom 'it would have been impossible to defeat the conspiracies of reaction'—was duly acknowledged.[81] *Link* looked forward to 'a healthy change in values in crucial areas of national endeavour … [The Emergency] has put an end to the psychology of drift and helplessness which seemed to be overtaking the country in recent months'.[82] The Party also endorsed the 20-Point Programme, pointing out that it represented 'measures for which the CPI and the mass organisations under its influence have been campaigning and fighting in the recent period through all-India mass struggles'.[83] The CPI stressed again the importance of seeing the Indian crisis and the Emergency in an international context. In August the NC declared:

> The present events in Portugal, the developments in India that led to the promulgation of the Emergency, the assassination of Sheikh Mujibur Rahman and the Rightist coup in Bangladesh, all form links in one single chain of US imperialist global strategy today.[84]

It concluded, 'The contradiction between world imperialism, especially US imperialism, and the nation, *including the ruling class*, is sharpening.'[85] Such an analysis put the ruling class—the national bourgeoisie—back in the driver's seat of the national democratic revolution.

The Party quickly returned to the question of popular mobilisation. The announcement of the Emergency and the 20-Point Programme had to be followed by:

- Measures to curb and weaken the social base of Right-reaction.
- Measures against neo-colonialists, monopolists, landlords, hoarders and speculators.
- Measures to bring down prices.
- Vigilance that the bureaucracy and Right-reaction 'do not use the Emergency to restrict the rights and liberties of the working people and other democratic forces or democratic activity'.
- Purging the state apparatus of those 'in league with right-reactionary forces and imperialist agencies'.[86]

The key was to move from announcement to implementation with all possible speed—and for this, popular mobilisation committees were essential.[87] For its part, the CPI continued to be involved in numerous campaigns for land reform, land distribution and the enforcement of land ceilings—at least for much of June 1975. In August, it organised a mass rally at Shahir Minar—'the first organised by any political party after the declaration of Emergency'—calling for the implementation of the 20-Point Programme.[88]

The Party leadership, however, was starting to think that this kind of mobilisation—land seizures, protest demonstrations, oppositional slogans—was no longer what was required. After all, in many ways, the Emergency represented a dream scenario for the CPI. It brought to fruition just what they had been predicting for 20 years. The bourgeoisie had divided into its monopolist and national elements. The Congress had followed suit. The progressive elements of the Congress, led by Indira Gandhi and representing the national bourgeoisie, provoked by Right-reaction and imperialism, had now taken decisive action against them and, to all outward appearances, seemed ready to use the state to implement radical economic policies. If this was the case, then the communists had surely to place themselves on the side of the state in that implementation. This would necessitate a fundamental reorientation of the CPI's work and its methods. On the other hand, if the Emergency represented an attempt by the Congress state to defend itself against all comers (as this author believes)—rich farmers, the Right and the forces of globalisation—by doing that state's bidding, the CPI was heading for trouble.[89] As we shall see, the Party's initial reaction was to reorient itself as outlined earlier.

The communists argued that the Emergency signified a new stage in the conflict within the bourgeoisie:

> [T]hose representing the anti-imperialist democratic sections of the bourgeoisie have been forced into using the repressive organs of state power against those representing the proimperialist, prolandlord, anti-communist sections.[90]

Link advised its readers that 'this new thrust in the use of state power must be appreciated'.[91] It is worth noting that such an appreciation led the Party and some of its supporters into politically murky waters. In the 'Emergency' issue of *Indian Left Review* (August 1975), Srinivas Sardesai (a CPI MP) warned that 'a mechanical conception of civil liberties based on an abstract theory of individual freedom will have to be changed... . In a period like the present one it is inevitable that immense executive powers have to be given to the government'.[92] Published in the same issue was an article by the American communist William Pomeroy, praising the Filipino martial law regime under Ferdinand Marcos. This apparently served the national bourgeoisie and opposed the feudal elements—the lessons for India (though not spelt out) were obvious.[93] In the same month Central News Service (CNS) reported, 'State CPI secretary Gopal Banerjee said that the Anglo-Saxon concept of democracy was an anachronism in these days of people's awareness.'[94]

More benignly perhaps, the Party's style of work had to change. 'The style of mass work we are used to, that is of all-India and state political and mass campaigns and struggles, will no longer suffice,' declared the CEC. It had to be replaced with 'persevering day-to-day grassroots level constructive work, utilising the concrete schemes of the government in the interests of the masses'.[95] The Party had to shift from the oppositional agitation to the practical implementation of government policy. 'The traditional agitational approach, mass rallies and demonstration, do not suit the spirit of the times', said *Link*. Instead, 'the duty of the left and democratic forces today appears to be to see that these promises [of the 20-Point Programme] are transformed into quick and fair action'.[96] The general secretary pointed out that this approach ('persevering constructive work') had antecedents in a previous successful period of the Party's history ('the 1943–47 period'): 'We gave this up during the 1948–52 period and we have failed to reintroduce it again after that.'[97]

To this end, the campaigns that the Party had launched in the period up to the Emergency were called off. The proposed power workers' strike was 'withdrawn' by their (CPI-controlled) union. Meanwhile, the All-India Bank Employees' Association directed its members into a charm offensive during a 'service week' from 19 July.[98] In the countryside, the mass agitations for land reform in Assam and Bihar, scheduled to start on 1 July, were called off.[99] The Party leadership decided on 3 July that 'the national land movement in its present form of occupation of surplus land [should] be replaced by a nationwide united mass movement for the speedy implementation of the 20-point programme given by the Prime Minister'.[100]

Given its increasingly positive attitude towards the government and the state, it seemed only natural that the CPI should seek some kind of political unity with the Congress. The Party seems to have initially rather overestimated the influence it would have in this regard. Arjun Dev told the author:

> After the declaration of the Emergency, there was a meeting for Party cadres in Delhi ... some people (including me) were quite unhappy that [the secretary of the Party] tried to suggest that the 20-Point Programme had been given to Indira Gandhi by us. This was, I thought, a highly exaggerated view of one's own relevance in that field. The Party was in no position to dictate the policy framework that Indira Gandhi wanted. For some time, the CPI continued to have this illusion.[101]

Soon after the Emergency was declared, the Party revealed that leaders of the CPI, the Congress and the All-India Dravida Munnetra Kazhagam (AIADMK), a southern regional party, had 'chalked out a joint campaign in furtherance of their common stand, together with other left and democratic parties.... . In some districts, joint committees have already been formed for this purpose'.[102] *Link* reported that 'indications that efforts would also be made to forge a united front at the lower levels between the Congress and other democratic and left forces'.[103] For the next year at least the communists would continue to pursue joint work with Congress members and leaders. Much of this, however, would prove to be illusory—because the Congress remained unwilling to cede its state machine to CPI cadres in order to implement the economic measures of the Emergency.

The CPI-controlled Central News Service (CNS) was fulsome in its coverage of anything resembling Communist/Congress joint work. It reported a 'joint convention' of the parties in Chandigarh that agreed 'to set up effective machinery from top to bottom' to fight Right-reaction and implement the 20-points. A central committee was set up and 'sectorwise committees in the towns' were promised. In Punjab, the two parties agreed to 'better coordination' and to meet again to discuss implementation of the programme. Joint conventions were held in Chandigarh, Amritsar and Midnapore, with hopes for future joint action expressed all round. In Assam, joint co-ordination committees were to be established at central, district and sub-divisional levels, while in Orissa, 'a high power coordination committee of 14 leaders belonging to the Congress and the CPI' was formed (two of its members were from the CPI).[104]

In similar style, *Link* filled its pages with positive reports about ongoing exercises in joint work. 'In State after State', it proclaimed in June 1976, 'local Congress and CPI workers have joined hands for the implementation of the 20-point programme.' There were increasing references to 'the main national stream'—meaning the Congress–Communist combine.[105]

Joint campaigns and committees were extolled in Uttar Pradesh, Bihar, Rajasthan, West Bengal, Punjab and Madhya Pradesh.[106] An All-India Conference on the 20-Point Programme and National Development, 'held in close cooperation between the Congress and the CPI', was staged in Indore in September 1976, which 'bore testimony to the close understanding between the Congress and the CPI'.[107] In trade union and youth work too, moves were made to bring the respective leaderships into alignment.[108]

But some of it remained as mere words, some of it remained on paper—and a good deal of it was frankly illusory.[109] Digging deeper into these reports, it will be found that many of them are simply about a convergence of *views* between the CPI and the Congress and not about the concrete construction of political unity at all. The Congress was prepared to have joint leadership meetings (between parties, trade unions and youth organisations), to issue statements, to attend implementation conventions and to speak at rallies—but not to join with the communists in creating new administrative machinery to make the 20-Point Programme a reality. Beyond the declaration, the statement and the call, political action at the grassroots did not amount to very much.[110] The Congress was not about to share its domination of the state. Barooah said in August 1975, 'the main responsibility has fallen on the shoulders of the Congress. The Congress, as the premier national organisation has again to stand in the forefront'. The president of the West Bengal Youth Congress was rather blunter in December: 'The Congress and the CPI are two different organizations. Our ideologies and programs are different.... . The question of a joint movement does not arise.'[111] At a national conference on the 20-point Programme in September 1976, the CPI appealed for unity with the Congress. CNS reported:

> AICC general secretary Purabi Mukherjee said that the Congress would certainly like to work with those parties *which believe in the objectives and programmes and policies of the Congress Party*.[112]

The CPI was disappointed to discover that, on the agenda for the AICC in November 1976, 'there is a significant omission about the attitude of Congress towards like-minded secular and progressive forces outside the Congress'.[113] Meanwhile in Punjab, although 'a 150-member broad-based committee' to implement the reforms was set up in August 1975, 'consisting of the Congress, CPI and other like-minded parties', it was side-lined two weeks later by an exclusively Congress committee formed from the top downwards. The aforementioned joint committee (which had yet to be established—and, I suspect, never was) was relegated to a 'watch and steer' role.[114] The CPI and its supporters blamed this kind of obstruction on 'Rightist forces inside and outside the Congress' and on some state governments.[115] Yet, it was clear that opposition to communist participation in the Emergency programme (as opposed to providing warm bodies for demonstrations and helping to maintain stability) was located in the highest reaches of the Congress government.

Two further responses were forthcoming from the CPI. Both represented an attempt to create the illusion of joint work. The first was the organisation of Anti-Fascist Conferences. These had begun before the Emergency. They were sometimes organised jointly with local Congress forces. A number of state-wide conferences culminated in the World Anti-Fascist Conference in Patna in October 1975.[116] These conferences—with the attendant publicity and mass participation—were relatively easy for the Party to organise and the Congress had no objection to (albeit a rather passive) involvement. For that reason, for the CPI, they assumed an importance out of all proportion to their actual significance. They were continually extolled as shining examples of the joint work which was not happening elsewhere. The NC reported in February 1976 that the conferences, 'which reached a great climax in the Patna international antifascist conference', were 'The single biggest achievement of the party' during this period. They forged 'bonds of mutual understanding, common objectives and desire for joint work and action' between Congress and the CPI.[117] However, *Link* rather ruefully (but correctly) remarked that 'joint activity by progressive forces is now mainly confined to anti-imperialist issues. Domestic, economic and other issues do not seem to attract much attention'.[118]

The second response was a kind of sleight-of-hand in reporting events during the Emergency. In the absence of real joint work, as opposed to its declaratory form (and that absence became greater as the Emergency went on), an illusion of it was created by simply juxtaposing CPI and Congress activities to each other as if they were connected. *Link* was particularly adept at this technique. For example, an article on Congress plans to transform itself into a 'cadre' party was slapped together with some CPI views on its own changes, jointly headlined 'Cadres for New Tasks' and made to look as though it were a joint perspective.[119] Interviews with prominent Congress leaders (especially Barooah) were placed side-by-side with an article by or interview with a CPI leader to give the impression of a joint approach.[120] Totally separate events were also conflated in this way. *Link* told its readers in June 1976 that 'two major steps planned to be taken by the Congress and the CPI are important'—and went on to describe a Congress decision on party training and a CPI discussion on the mobilisation of Party members to implement the 20-Point Programme.[121]

If the CPI were to successfully implement its new strategy of helping to put government policy into practice, it needed structures through which to do it. The NC said, 'We should fight for establishment of committees consisting of representatives of parties and mass organisations prepared to fight reaction and implement the 20-point programme.'[122] The committees were essential to the Party's approach because, although now implementing state (Congress) policy, it still mightily distrusted the state bureaucracy—especially in places far from New Delhi; 'some mechanism has to be evolved which ensures that they [the 20 Points] are not watered down in bureaucratic processes.'[123] If such committees were set up, great things could be expected of them, even beyond implementation. They could be 'used as political levers for taking the country forward along socialist lines', as well as playing a major role in laying 'the basis for a new power structure'.[124] As with the prospects of joint work with Congress, the communists seized optimistically on any indication that the popular committees were coming into being. They believed that their inspiration came from the top: 'With unshakeable faith in the people and their participation in the decision making process at every level, she [Mrs Gandhi] has evolved a concept of popular committees at every level.'[125] The Party reported that committees had actually been established in various states.[126] But it is open to question whether these reports were accurate—or whether the committees thus formed consisted of anything more than the local bureaucracy rebadged. The Party and its supporters had to admit in early 1976 that 'the burden of the job [implementation of the economic programme] has rested with the district administrators'. They concluded:

> It is unfortunate that the Government has not come forward to set up statutory popular committees at various levels with representatives belonging to the Congress, CPI and other democratic sections, including mass organisations of the people. As a result, mass enthusiasm and mass participation in the programme is getting dampened.[127]

As we have noted earlier, the lack of popular mobilisation was also felt in the area of land reform. The CEC, in its first major statement on the Emergency, called for 'special machinery' to implement the land reform measures.[128] But, whatever promises the CPI thought it had from the Congress on this score were steadily watered down as the Emergency progressed. In Bihar and Assam, land reform committees were 'instigated' in the former and 'accepted' in the latter and it was on this basis that the Party agreed to call off its pre-Emergency land campaigns in those states. But little was heard of those committees after that.[129]

The sense of disappointment over land reform is palpable in *Link*: '[E]ven in those places where popular committees have been set up, by and large they are lagging behind the mass enthusiasm.' This was, undoubtedly, due to the fact that 'most villages are still dominated by a few powerful vested interests, who easily manipulate things'.[130] And not a few of those vested interests were linked to the Congress itself. The reality was, as Chandra put it:

> The regional Congress leaders as also Mrs Gandhi had no intention of either organizing joint political actions with the CPI or letting it go down among the people and gain from the political harvest to be reaped from the implementation of the 20-Point Programme.[131]

In the face of these difficulties, the communist position did not remain fixed in its approval of the Emergency and its methods. Its attitude became rapidly more critical: '[I]n less than two months, it began attacking the negative features of the emergency and the growth of a caucus within the Congress.'[132] Most importantly, the CPI attacked the non-mobilisation of the people in implementing the 20-Point Programme, its land reform aspects in particular. Everywhere, it discovered the government relying on the state bureaucracy to carry out 'reform'. With no people's committees and reliance on state and local officials, it accused the government of implementing reform 'at a snail's pace'.[133]

Furthermore, there were areas in which the government was misusing and abusing the powers granted to it by the Emergency. The two main areas of abuse, as the CPI discovered, were family planning and slum clearance.[134] These will be dealt with in the next chapter. As early as August 1975, the NC brought forth an extensive indictment of Emergency misuse by the authorities which included: the insistence on punctuality by workers, but no provision of extra transport; Delhi teachers being forced to work on Sundays; police demanding bribes in order to refrain from detaining people under MISA; forcible cutting of long hair and wide trousers; and the harassment of small traders.[135] The Party also complained about political repression, censorship and denial of civil liberties (including the arrest of CPI workers).[136] However, according to Chandra, '[T]he CPI was virtually sidelined and was hamstrung and thwarted in its efforts to take up popular grievances.'[137] In 1976 therefore, the communists opposed the moves of some in the Congress towards a presidential form of government and those aimed at the institutionalisation of censorship—as well as the decision of the government to postpone the election which was due early in that year.[138]

The CPI was also unhappy about the lot of workers under the Emergency. As we have seen, the AITUC, meeting on the Emergency's first day, pledged support. It warned that 'the Emergency powers must not be used to suppress or curb [the] trade-union rights of the working class'.[139] The following year, the Bihar state government attempted to impose conditions on the AITUC session, due in October. AITUC were instructed that the session must not be converted into any kind of public meeting, demonstration or march. Furthermore, '[t]he participants in the conference shall not criticise any policy of the government'. After strenuous protests, the restrictions were withdrawn. Dange was thus able to tell the session that 'the working class in general [is] angry and sullen due to a decline in their purchasing power and [he] warned the Government that their discontent and frustration were being utilised by reactionary forces to undermine their faith in the Emergency and the 20-point programme'.[140] AITUC pointed to a steady deterioration in workers' rights.[141] Even '[t]he much-advertized scheme for workers' participation in management turned out to be nothing more than participation in production'.[142]

Despite this gloomy outlook (or perhaps because of it), the Party carried out some independent action on land reform in spite of the lack of committees and of local state obstruction.[143] In fact, as the Party's hopes for official mobilisation faded, it undertook some mobilisation of its own. A series of *padayatras*—literally, 'travelling by foot', in which Party activists walked from village to village, promoting land reform and examining the local situations—was organised in the rural areas in the first half of 1976, most successfully in Kerala, Assam and Punjab. On arriving at a village, activists would locate surplus land for distribution; investigate the distribution of house sites to the landless and galvanise support for better services.[144] There were instances of local Congress activists joining in—together with Congress MPs and even Ministers in Andhra Pradesh.[145] What they discovered in the *padayatra* (journey by foot) process made the communists more critical of the Emergency and of the progress of implementation. The general secretary discovered 'grave shortcomings' due to the fact that moneylenders, rich farmers and bureaucrats were interfering in the programme. In Assam, 'the rural poor are quite defenceless against the exploitation and terrorization [by] the landowners and moneylenders … and the unfeeling and insincere bureaucracy'.[146]

From this point, the Party was more inclined to pursue political campaigns outside the (hardly breathing) popular committees, beyond the 20 Points and without the Congress. Rajeshwara Rao had said in August 1975:

> One need not wait for overall unity with the Congress as such. We should go in for such united mass actions with congressmen wherever it is possible. That will gradually extend to the whole of the country.[147]

As well as continuing land action and the *padayatras*, the Party—together with its trade union, peasant, youth and student organisations—launched a campaign against price rises in late 1976.[148]

The Party claimed considerable success for its mobilisation efforts: the participation of over 200,000 CPI members, fanning out over 44,000 villages across 270 districts, holding thousands of meetings and demonstrations.[149] By mid-1976, the Party estimated that its membership had grown by 130,000 over one year to 550,000.[150]

Conclusion

Quite suddenly, on 18 January 1977, Mrs Gandhi announced that there would be a general election in March. Repression of opposition parties and censorship of the press was ended. Political prisoners were released. The decision may have been the result of lengthy political deliberation within the prime minister's circles, but it came as a surprise to the vast majority of Congress members and to India as a whole. Until Indira Gandhi's papers are open to public scrutiny, we will not know with any certainty what her motives were for ending the Emergency at this time. Bipan Chandra is probably right to suggest that among those motives was a residual commitment to parliamentary democracy, a conviction that she could win the election and a realisation that the aims of the Emergency needed re-legitimising.[151] There is, however, one piece of archival evidence that is to hand and may well have had a major influence on the prime minister's decision. P. N. Haksar wrote a ('Top Secret') 'Note to the PM as Principal Secretary', sketching out the pros and cons of holding elections.[152] As we have noted, Haksar himself was opposed to the Emergency—and was presumably in favour of bringing it to an end. His note, therefore, sets out on the one hand to paint a generally positive picture of the political and economic situation in order to encourage Mrs Gandhi to call elections.

> The general situation in the country is favourable to the Prime Minister and is not unfavourable to either the Government or the Congress Party.[153]

The opposition parties were 'thoroughly disorganised' and 'unable to decide what they should do in the absence of elections'. Furthermore, '[t]here is little chance of unity among the opposition parties'. Calling elections might give the impression that the grip of the government was weakening—'But this will only be a superficial and temporary phenomenon.' In fact:

> On the basis of the hope among the rural poor alone the Congress has a very good chance of success. An effective election slogan could be: 'Prime Minister brought down prices and helped the poor. To keep prices down and benefit poor, strengthen PM's hands'.

On the other hand, Haksar was at pains to point out the seriousness of the situation in order to convince his bosses that elections *had* to be called. To this end, he made the points about non-implementation of the 20-Point programme and general disenchantment with the Emergency, particularly in the rural areas, that have been cited earlier in this chapter. He added, 'If the elections are held, they will successfully divert the attention of the people from the economic situation.'

So, in a mood of misplaced confidence, justified apprehension and foolhardy bravado, the Congress went to the elections in March 1977—and lost. We will examine the effects of that loss—particularly on the CPI—in Chapter 6.

Proclamation of the Emergency was the Congress' reaction to economic crisis (produced by globalisation) and political dissent (produced by economic crisis). It was an attempt by the government to combat these crises with a reassertion of state power.

At the outset, the CPI was equipped with a belief that the stronger the economic power of the state, the more progressive it was likely to be. It went into the Emergency believing that if the state were controlled by 'progressive' forces—albeit it in a stern, authoritarian and centrally-directed way—then it could be used to carry out radical policies which would improve the lot of the Indian people.

In India, the Congress was the state. But parts of it were tied to the central and local bureaucracies, parts to big business enterprises and parts to rich farmers. Its central aim was its own preservation in the face of the dangers that surrounded it. It could not be used in ways that would threaten its own pillars of support.

The communists believed that stern measures had to be taken to turn back the JP Movement—and that those measures could also be used to implement radical reform. Radical reform proved to be impossible—and so, only the stern measures remained.

Notes

1. The editor of *Mainstream*, Nikhil Chakravarty commented: 'the irony of the situation is that Smt Gandhi has been indicted of corrupt electoral practices by a court of law on the petition of a person whose record in polluting public life is undisputed' (Nikhil Chakravarty, 'Indira Gandhi: Moment of Truth', *Mainstream*, 21 June 1975, www.mainstreamweekly.net/article2869.html [last accessed on 3 September 2015]).
2. Carras tells us:

    By the 1960s, it was clear to most impartial observers that the Supreme Court was the most effective shelter of businessmen and big landlords … the nineteenth-century economic philosophies of most of the judges … closely resemble[d] the political and economic outlooks of the conservative Jan Sangh and Swatantra parties. (Mary C. Carras, *Indira Gandhi: In the Crucible of Leadership* [Bombay. Jaico Press Private Ltd, 1980], 130)

3. Hewitt names the others as S. S. Ray (chief minister of West Bengal), H. R. Gokhale, Om Mehta and D. K. Barooah (Congress president) (Vernon Hewitt, *Political Mobilisation and Democracy in India: States of Emergency* [New York: Routledge, 2008], 116).
4. According to Mehta, Sanjay 'took over the show' (Vinod Mehta, *The Sanjay Story* (New Delhi: Harper Collins Publishers, 2012 [1978], 97). At the Shah Commission, 'S.S. Ray recalled how this meeting [between himself, Barooah and Mrs Gandhi] had been interrupted continually by Sanjay Gandhi, who would insist on talking to his mother in private' (Hewitt, *Political Mobilisation*, 121).
5. *Times of India* 13 June 1975 in Hewitt, *Political Mobilisation*, 116.

6. Mehta, *Sanjay*, 98–99; see also Francine R. Frankel, *India's Political Economy, 1947–1977: The Gradual Revolution* (Princeton: Princeton University Press, 1978), 543. Other culprits have been put forward. Janak Raj Jai (a civil servant closely associated with Mrs Gandhi until 1969, detained under MISA during the Emergency), suggests that Yashpal Kapur (Mrs Gandhi's 1971 election agent) was 'the main person' behind it; and then, S. S. Ray 'perhaps was the author of the Emergency' (Nehru Memorial Museum and Library (henceforward NMML) Oral History transcript: Dr Janak Raj Jai, 10 November 1994).

7. 'A Serious New Confrontation', *Link*, 15 June 1975, 8.

8. These were organised by Sanjay through pliant chief ministers (Mehta, *Sanjay*, 97). Chakravarty commented:

    The element of spontaneity of support to her, genuinely felt by the multitude in this country is submerged in the tamasha [singing and dancing show] that the Chief Ministers from nearby States have been helping the organisers put up. In fact, a virtual competition in collecting trucks and buses has been going on. (Chakravarty, 'Moment of Truth')

9. On this call—of which both the Congress and the CPI made much—Sumit Chakravartty said, 'It was a call generally because JP was trying to say that these people [the Congress government] were corrupt so you need not obey their orders in that sense. But this was not a call for insurrection. That would be too far-fetched' (interview with the author, 8 November 2014).

10. Bipan Chandra, *In the Name of Democracy: JP Movement and the Emergency* (New Delhi: Penguin Books, 2003), 88–93. For the democratic option open to the JP Movement, see 85–88.

11. Although, according to Khushiram Nebhraj Vaswani (an editor of Gandhi's *Collected Works* and an opponent of the Emergency), Mrs Gandhi kept channels open to Balasaheb Deoras, the RSS leader, while he was under arrest: '... Indira wanted some peace-talks with Balasaheb ... she wanted to come to some terms with the RSS' (NMML Oral History transcript: Professor Khushiram Nebhraj Vaswani, 31 March 1999). In all, 26 organisations were banned. *Link* carried lurid tales of raids on RSS and Anand Marg premises, describing the discovery of 'swords, spears, human skulls ... live cartridges with US markings, secret army maps and enough swords, spears and similar weapons and heavy clothing to outfit a whole battalion' (*Link*, 13 July 1975, 6).

12. V. P. Dutt, 'The Emergency in India: Background and Rationale,' *Asian Survey* 16, no. 12 (December 1976): 1136.

13. See Moin A. Zaidi, ed., *The Encyclopaedia of the Indian National Congress. Volume 23, 1974–1975: The Lengthening Shadows* (New Delhi: S. Chand and Company Ltd, 1984), 475–78.

14. Hewitt, *Political Mobilisation*, 118 and 137. Chandra Shekhar's expulsion for 10 years for 'anti-Congress activities' is recorded in the CWC minutes for 28 May 1976 (Moin A. Zaidi, ed., *The Encyclopaedia of the Indian National Congress. Volume 24, 1976–1977: Amid Encircling Gloom* (New Delhi: S. Chand and Company Ltd, 1984), 146).

15. Indira Gandhi, 'Emergency' 26 June 1975, in *Democracy and Discipline: Speeches of Shrimati Indira Gandhi* [1975] (New Delhi: Ministry of Information and Broadcasting, Government of India, n.d.), 1.

16. Businessmen: 8 July 1975, *Democracy and Discipline*, 16; rich farmers: 2 August 1975, 58; communal elements: 22 July 1975, 28–32. Naturally enough, her opponents put forward other explanations for the Emergency. According to JP, it was a plot by 'Indiraji, the disguised communists in her party, the CPI and, behind the scene, Soviet agents' to impose 'a totalitarian system' ('Prison Diary' in Chandra, *Name*, 75–76). According to Janak Raj Jai, it was designed 'to perpetuate herself in the saddle for all times to come … it was a Hitler-like action' (NMML Oral History transcript: Dr Janak Raj Jai, 10 November 1994).

17. AICC Circular, 3 June 1976 in Zaidi, *Encyclopaedia of the INC Volume 24*, 178.

18. '… the large majority of Indians … responded to it with apathy and passivity, acquiescence and obedience; in some cases they even welcomed and supported it but were not overenthusiastic' (Chandra, *Name*, 171).

19. Indira Gandhi, *Democracy and Discipline*, 27 June 1975, 3; 22 July 1975, 35.

20. For K. K. Birla's background see Medha M. Kudaisya, *The Life and Times of G.D. Birla* (New Delhi: Oxford University Press, 2003), chapters 16 and 17.

21. Krishna Kumar Birla, *Brushes with History: An Autobiography* (New Delhi: Penguin Viking, 2007), 174 and 176. Birla was not alone in seeing railway timeliness as an important index of discipline and well-being. The AICC circular, quoted above, pointed out that on the first day of the Emergency, the people 'found … the trains and buses running in time' (AICC circular, 3 June 1976 in Zaidi, *Encyclopaedia of the INC Volume 24*, 179). The CPI's NC reported in August 1975 that 'Trains have started running on time' (CPI, National Council, *Resolutions and Report Adopted by the National Council of the Communist Party of India (New Delhi, August 1975)* (New Delhi: Communist Party Publication, September 1975, 25). Mohit Sen wrote later that 'Discipline was restored, law and order prevailed, trains ran on time and work was done in government offices and elsewhere' (Mohit Sen, *A Traveller and the Road: The Journey of an Indian Communist* [New Delhi: Rupa & Co., 2003], 350).

22. Birla, *Brushes*, 645. *Link*, however, doubted that business was unanimous in its support for the government. After a meeting between Mrs Gandhi and industrialists, it reported that 'there appears to be a rift among the top industrialists. One group is reported to be of the view that political stability is necessary for the country's progress while another appears to support the extreme right' ('Proper Frame for Economic Plan', *Link*, 13 July 1975, 9). Given our earlier discussion on the relationship between industrialists and the JP Movement, this would appear unlikely. We shall return to the nature of big business support for the Emergency in Chapter 7.

23. Frankel, *India's Political Economy*, 554–56.

24. J. F. J. Toye, 'Economic Trends and Policies in India during the Emergency', *World Development* 5, no. 4 (1977): 303–06.

25. Chandra, *Name*, 80.

26. Hewitt, *Political Mobilisation*, 124; Indira Gandhi, *Democracy and Discipline*, 26 June 1975, 1.

27. Indira Gandhi, *Democracy and Discipline*, 1 July 1975, 7–8. A full list of all 20 points can be found in Trevor Drieberg and Sarala Jag Mohan, *Emergency in India* (New Delhi: Manas Publications, 1975), 77–78. According to Mohit Sen, the original 20-Point programme also included the nationalisation of the textile industry—a suggestion from the CPI. However, 'Haksar … vehemently opposed the nationalization proposal. He said that it would add economic adventurism to the political adventurism which the Emergency was … It was Haksar's opinion that eventually prevailed' (*Traveller*, 348–9).

Haksar, in fact, opposed the whole Emergency strategy. He discussed it very little, at least on paper, from 1975 to 1977 (see NMML, P. N. Haksar Papers. Instalment III. Subject Files, 342, 360, 363, 372)—and was subject to some official harassment for his opposition (Sen, *Traveller*, 355).

28.   See 'Correspondent', 'The Emergency in India', *Bulletin of Concerned Asian Scholars* 7, no. 4 (October–December) 1975: 4–6; Hewitt, *Political Mobilisation*, 99; Chandra, *Name*, 176.

29.   Amrit Nahata, 'Now, Or Never' *Indian Left Review* 3, no. 11 (August 1975): 14–16.

30.   *Economic Times*, 10 January 1976 cited in Henry C. Hart, 'Introduction', in *Indira Gandhi's India: A Political System Reappraised*, ed. Henry C. Hart (Boulder: Westview Press, 1976), 29.

31.   H. D. Malaviya, 'Implementation and the Party' Part 1, *Indian Left Review* 3, no. 11 (August 1975), 28.

32.   CWC proceedings, 14 July 1975, Zaidi, *Encyclopaedia of the INC Volume 23*, 472–73 & 480–81. Much to the CPI's surprise, the 'like-minded parties' turned out to be solely and peculiarly the Republican Party of India (AICC circular, 20 April 1976, Zaidi, *Encyclopaedia of the INC Volume 24*, 175).

33.   According to *Link*, 20 July 1975, 6—although there is no record of this sub-committee in the CWC's published proceedings (CWC, 14 July 1975, Zaidi, *Encyclopaedia of the INC Volume 23*, 470–82).

34.   *Link*, 20 July 1975, 3, 5 and 6; 'Promise of New Social Order', 3 August 1975, 2 and 10; 10 August 1975, 7; 31 August 1975, 7.

35.   'Stress on Land Reforms', *Link*, 15 February 1976, 6.

36.   The Commissioner, the Director-General of Police, the joint director of supply, the joint regulator of co-operative societies and the revenue officer ('Task Forces in Assam', *Link*, 27 July 1975, 24).

37.   Interview with *Blitz*, 16 August 1975 in Indira Gandhi, *Democracy and Discipline*, 106.

38.   Guidelines, 26 August 1975, Zaidi, *Encyclopaedia of the INC Volume 24*, 471–79.

39.   Speech at a conference of chief secretaries and chief commissioners, 29 August 1975, in *Democracy and Discipline*, 133; interview with *Socialist India* (a Congress weekly), August 1975, in *Democracy and Discipline*, 98.

40.   AICC circular, 9 February 1976, Zaidi, *Encyclopaedia of the INC Volume 24*, 173.

41.   Frankel, *India's Political Economy*, 551.

42.   NMML: P. N. Haksar papers. Subject File Number 57, 'Note to the PM as Principal Secretary,' 1977. He added that the 20-Point programme 'has succeeded in generating, among the rural poor in particular, waves of hope beyond all rational thinking and expectations'.

43.   Indira Gandhi, Speech in the Rajya Sabha, 22 July 1975 in *Democracy and Discipline*, 38.

44.   Reported in *Link*, 13 July 1975, 9.

45.   *Link*, 3 August 1975, 10.

46.   Toye, 'Economic Trends', 310.

47.   AICC meeting, 21 November 1976, Zaidi, *Encyclopaedia of the INC, Volume 24*, 107.

48.   Toye, 'Economic Trends', 310; Indira Gandhi in the Lok Sabha, 22 July 1975, in *Democracy and Discipline*, 27.

49.   See V. P. Dutt, 'The Emergency in India: Background and Rationale', *Asian Survey* 16, no. 12 (December 1976): 1137–38.

50.   Correspondent, 'Emergency in India', 3.

51. David Selbourne, *An Eye to India: the Unmasking of a Tyranny* (Harmondsworth: Penguin, 1977), 304.

52. CPI, National Council, *Report and Resolutions Adopted by the National Council of the Communist Party of India (Trivandrum, 7–11 February 1976)* (New Delhi: Communist Party Publication, 1976), 30–32; Communist Party of India, *Documents of the 11th Congress of the Communist Party of India, Bhakna Nagar, Bhatinda, 31 March to 7 April, 1978* (New Delhi: Communist Party Publication, July 1978), 60–62; Bhabani Sen Gupta, 'Communism Further Divided', in *Indira Gandhi's India: A Political System Reappraised*, ed. Henry C. Hart (Boulder: Westview Press, 1976), 171.

53. NMML: P. N. Haksar papers. Subject File Number 57, 'Note to the PM as Principal Secretary,' 1977, 12; Prakash Ray, 'A Critical Note for Eleventh Party Congress', in P. C. Joshi Archive (JNU), Communism in India, File 1978/9013, 19.

54. A full list of these can be found in AICC circulars for 3 June, 30 June and 19 October 1976, Zaidi, *Encyclopaedia of the INC, Volume 24*, 177–84, 194–95 and 203–05.

55. NMML: P. N. Haksar papers. Instalment III, Subject File Number 342: Letter to Indira Gandhi, 30 June 1975.

56. Nigel Harris, 'India: Part One', *International Socialism* (1st series), no. 17 (Summer 1964) at www.marxists.org/history/etol/writers/harris/1964/xx/india3.htm.

57. Arun Shourie, 'Growth, Poverty and Inequalities', *Foreign Affairs* (January 1973): 344–45.

58. *Commerce*, Annual Review of Agriculture 1973 summarised by Correspondent, 'Emergency in India', 6.

59. Presidential address to 75th Congress session, 31 December 1975, Zaidi, *Encyclopaedia of the INC Volume 23*, 428. History (and historians) have not treated D. K. Barooah kindly. Seen as a Leftist appointment to the Congress presidency (Uma Vasudev, *Two Faces of Indira Gandhi* (New Delhi, Vikas Publishing House, 1977), 56). Chandra says that he 'hardly carried any weight in the party or the government' (*Name*, 161). Dhar is damning: 'The Congress president, Dev Kant Barooah, was more a sycophant than a leader. He could not go beyond laboured witticisms which made him seem some sort of amiable court jester' (P. N. Dhar, *Indira Gandhi, the 'Emergency', and Indian Democracy* [New Delhi: Oxford India Paperbacks, 2001], 266).

60. Reports in *Link*, 14 March 1976, 2 and 6–7; 27 June 1976, 15.

61. *Link*, 15 August 1976, 17. Haksar, on the other hand, noticed billboards in rural areas calling for the implementation of the 20-Point programme—but with no explanation of what it was. When he asked rural officials, what it was they were implementing, 'They had difficulty in providing me with more than four or five points' (NMML: Haksar Note 1977, 14).

62. Harsh Dev Malaviya, 'Implementation and the Party (Part 2)', *Indian Left Review* 3, no. 12 (September 1975): 12. Dhar agrees: 'The lower rungs of the party continued to be dominated by agrarian interests which would have been hurt by such reforms' (Dhar, *Indira Gandhi*, 266). Back in 1973, senior World Bank official William M. Gilmartin had told WB president McNamara that land reforms 'run head-on into the interests of those who constitute the real power foundations of the Congress Party: the larger and better-off farmers and landowners of rural India.' He went on to describe the Congress as a 'government of kulaks' (Devesh Kapur, John P. Lewis and Richard Webb, *The World Bank: Its First Half Century* (Washington: The Brookings Institution, 1997), 294. See also Bipan Chandra, Mridula Mukherjee and Aditya Mukherjee, *India Since Independence* (New Delhi: Penguin, 2008), 325.

63.   Frankel, *India's Political Economy*, 561. Chandra claims that 'Popular committees were set up', but that these 'worked only in a few places and that too only in the initial months of the Emergency' (*Name*, 187). An analysis of the communist experience of these committees follows in the second section of this chapter.

64.   Toye, 'Economic Trends', 306.

65.   Harry W. Blair, 'Mrs Gandhi's Emergency, The Indian Elections of 1977, Pluralism and Marxism: Problems with Paradigms', *Modern Asian Studies*, 14, no. 2 (1980): 256. Estimate of total bonded labour (1978 figure): Ravi S. Srivastava, 'Bonded Labor in India: Its Incidence and Pattern' (4 January 2005), www.digitalcommons.ilr.cornell. edu (last accessed on 03 September 2015). Sunil Chakravartty argued that 'mere abolition of bonded labour does not help—because these people will have to finally again go back to bonded labour unless you give them resources… . It is not the bureaucracy that can carry out these tasks. There has to be another way' (interview with the author 8 November 2014).

66.   Primila Lewis, *Reason Wounded: An Experience of India's Emergency* (London: George Allen & Unwin Ltd, 1978), 26.

67.   Blair, 'Mrs Gandhi's Emergency', 257.

68.   Haksar noted to the prime minister 'since March/April [1976] these benefits are getting eroded and the people have begun to feel dissatisfied again.' He also pointed out: 'In Uttar Pradesh where the [government] office goers do come in on time, they now tend to go out and spend quite a bit of their time in canteens' (NMML: Haksar Note 1977, 8–9).

69.   'The party structure was thus so completely weakened that it was incapable of even being used as the agency for popularizing and implementing the 20-Point Programme of the government' (Chandra, *Name*, 161). Haksar said 'in the absence of elections, they [Congress members] do not know what to do, as no other programme has been given to them' (NMML: Haksar Note 1977, 2).

70.   Indira Gandhi to the AICC, 21 November 1976 in Zaidi, *Encyclopaedia of the INC Volume 24*, 105. Hewitt says that Barooah set up a 7-person committee to look at turning the Congress into a 'cadre party'. Others favoured handing over the activism to the Youth Congress (Hewitt, *Political Mobilisation*, 132).

71.   See *Link*, 21 March 1976, 5; Indira Gandhi cited in Frankel, *India's Political Economy*, 553.

72.   Malaviya, 'Implementation Part 2', 12.

73.   Zaidi, *Encyclopaedia of the INC*, 23, 412. See also 'The Indian Road' (interview with Barooah) in *Link*, 15 August 1976, 18.

74.   *Link*, 25 May 1975, 8–9.

75.   Gargi Chakravartty, interview with the author 6 November 2014.

76.   'CPI Statement on Allahabad High Court Verdict and Intensified Rightist Offensive', CNS Number 364, 13 June 1975; see also CNS Number 374, 25 June 1975.

77.   *Link*, 22 June 1975, 21.

78.   CPI Statement on Allahabad; N. K. Krishnan, 'Time for Action', CNS Number 368, 18 June 1975.

79.   CNS Number 373, 24 June 1975.

80.   CEC, CPI, 'National Emergency and Our Party's Tasks', *New Age*, 6 July 1975; N. K. Krishnan, Raj Bahadur Gour and T. N. Siddhanta, *Working Class and the Emergency* (New Delhi: Communist Party Publication, August 1975), 3. Amarjit Kaur adds: 'When the Emergency was declared, the Party made a statement [but] the National Council

or Executive had not met ... the Secretariat made the decision ... . We needed to have a serious debate' (interview with the author, 15 January 2014).

81. Rajeshwara Rao, 'Challenge and Possibilities Before People', *New Age*, 17 August 1975, 1.

82. 'Towards a Healthy Change', *Link*, 6 July 1975, 8.

83. N. K. Krishnan, 'A Sharp Turn', *World Marxist Review* XVIII, no. 10 (October 1975): 11.

84. CPI National Council resolution, 'On Portugal' 25–28 August 1975, located in P. C. Joshi Archive (JNU). Communism in India, CNS file, 1975/879F.

85. CPI, National Council, *Report and Resolutions*, February 1976, 45 (emphasis added); see also CPI, National Council, *Reports and Resolution Adopted by the National Council of the Communist Party of India. Hyderabad, 4–8 August 1976* (New Delhi: Communist Party Publication, 1976), 30.

86. CPI, *National Emergency and Our Tasks. Resolution adopted by the Central Executive Committee, Communist Party of India, New Delhi, 30 June to 2 July 1975* (New Delhi: Communist Party Publication, July 1975), 4.

87. Krishnan, 'Sharp Turn', 11. The CEC called for joint mobilisation of the CPI, Congress and other left and democratic forces. *Link* noted, however, that 'in terms of political mobilization to face this challenge, the performance of the left and democratic forces both within Congress and outside has been disappointing' (*Link*, 6 July 1975, 9).

88. See CNS reports for June 1975 in JNU: P. C. Joshi Archive (JNU). Communism in India, *New Age*, 17 August 1975, 15.

89. Toye describes the Emergency as 'a rally of the forces of populist nationalism in an effort to reassert the sovereignty of the overdeveloped state' (Toye, 'Economic Trends', 315). The Rudolphs argue that it was an 'attempt to re-establish an autonomous state based on command politics' (Lloyd I. Rudolph and Susanne Hoeber Rudolph, *In Pursuit of Lakshmi: The Political Economy of the Indian State* (Hyderabad: Orient Longman, 1987), 63).

90. CPI, *Emergency and Our Tasks*, 6; see also Krishnan, 'Sharp Turn', 12.

91. 'An Eventful One Year', *Link*, 27 June 1976, 10.

92. Srinivas Sardesai, 'The Path Ahead', *Indian Left Review* 3, no. 11 (August 1975): 26.

93. William Pomeroy, 'Martial Law and the National Democratic Struggle in the Philippines', *Indian Left Review* 3, no. 11 (August 1975): 30–42.

94. CNS Number 414, 11 August 1975.

95. CPI, *Emergency and Our Tasks*, 9.

96. 'Andhra Pradesh Peasants' Problems', *Link*, 18 April 1976, 19.

97. C. Rajeshwara Rao, Bhupesh Gupta and Mohit Sen, *Emergency and the Communist Party* (New Delhi: Communist Party Publication, August 1975), 10.

98. 'Punctual attendance at the stipulated opening hours; prompt attendance of customers at all counters, with the least possible delay over procedures; respect, courtesy and friendliness to be shown to all customers' (CNS Number 389, 12 July 1975; see also Haksar on the CPI and workers' struggles in the late Emergency (NMML: P. N. Haksar papers, Instalment III, Subject File Number 57, 1977, 'Note to the Prime Minister as Principal Secretary', 33).

99. CNS Number 379, 1 July 1975.

100. CNS Number 381, 3 July 1975.

101. Arjun Dev, interview with the author 15 January 2014.

102.   CNS Number 392, 16 July 1975.
103.   *Link*, 6 July 1975, 9.
104.   CNS Numbers 394, 18 July 1975; 398, 23 July 1975; 402, 28 July 1975; 411, 7 August 1975; 414, 11 August 1975; 417, 14 August 1975.
105.   'Many Positive Trends', *Link*, 27 June 1976, 14.
106.   'Left, Democratic Unity', *Link*, 27 July 1975, 6; 'In the States', *Link*, 4 January 1976, 15; 'Tehsil Level Committees in M.P.', *Link*, 25 April 1976, 16.
107.   *Link*, 3 October 1976, 20–21.
108.   Between AITUC and INTUC; and between the All-India Youth Federation and All-India Student Federation (CPI) on the one hand and the Youth Congress and the National Students' Union of India (Congress) on the other (CPI, National Council, *Resolutions and Report*, 12–13. See also CNS Number 401, 26 July 1975; *Link*, 13 July 1975, 9).
109.   As early as August 1975, the CPI's National Council reported that 'there seems to be resistance not only from the side of the bureaucracy, but also from sections of the Congress leadership and the bourgeois state to joint work with the CPI and other healthy democratic parties' (CPI, National Council, *Report and Resolutions*, August 1975, 25).
110.   'The [Congress] state governments have sought to give the CPI only a minor role in the implementation committees' (Gupta, 'Communism Further Divided', 173). In the West Bengal implementation committee, out of 51 members, the communists had 4; in the Andhra Pradesh Land Reform committee, they had no representatives at all.
111.   'A New Political, Social Structure' (interview with Barooah), *Link*, 15 August 1975; Youth Congress speaker in Gupta, 'Communism Further Divided', 173.
112.   CNS 18 September 1976—emphasis added.
113.   'For the AICC', *Link*, 21 November 1976, 19.
114.   'Structured Change in the Economy', *Link*, 15 August 1975, 55; 'Punjab: Action on the Economic Front', *Link*, 24 August 1975, 16.
115.   'Reaction Not Yet Defeated', *Link*, 15 August 1976, 21; *Link*, 4 January 1976, 15.
116.   CPI, *Emergency and Our Tasks*, 7; CPI, National Council, *Report and Resolutions*, August 1975, 22; 'Congress-CPI Joint Action in Assam', *New Age*, 17 August 1975.
117.   CPI, National Council, *Report and Resolutions*, February 1976, 14–15.
118.   'An Eventful One Year', *Link*, 27 June 1976, 10.
119.   *Link*, 10 August 1975, 12–13.
120.   Barooah and Rajeshwara Rao, *Link*,15 August 1975, 32–39; Dange (CPI & AITUC) and B. C. Bhagawati (Congress & INTUC), *Link*, 15 August 1975, 65–69; Barooah and Rajeshwara Rao (again), *Link*, 26 January 1976, 21–26; (and again) *Link*, 27 June 1976, 12–14.
121.   'The Next Decade', *Link*, 26 January 1976, 18.
122.   CPI, National Council, *Report and Resolutions*, August 1975, 16.
123.   *Link*, 6 July 1975, 9.
124.   *Link*, 3 August 1975, 10; 'Significant Freedom Anniversary', *Link*, 15 August 1975, 27.
125.   *Link*, 3 August 1975, 10.
126.   The National Council reported committees in Assam, Punjab, West Bengal and Orissa (CPI, National Council, *Report and Resolutions*, August 1975, 23); CNS in Haryana

(Number 385, 8 July 1975) and Assam (Number 415, 12 August 1975); and *Link* in Gujarat (11 July 1976, 14).

127. *Link*, 7 March 1976, 7; *Link*, 18 April 1976, 19.
128. CPI, *Emergency and Our Tasks*, 11. See also CNS Number 394, 18 July 1975.
129. CNS Number, 379 1 July 1975.
130. 'Change in Rural Areas', *Link*, 22 January 1975, 6; 'Gujarat Launches Two Schemes', *Link*, 11 July 1976, 14–15.
131. Chandra, *Name*, 220.
132. *Link*, 26 June 1977, 14. The 'caucus' refers to the activities of Sanjay Gandhi and his supporters—for which, see the next chapter.
133. See Rajeshwara Rao, 'Path of Democratic Advance', *Link*, 15 August 1975, 38; Mohit Sen, 'Emergency Balance Sheet', *Indian Left Review* 4, no. 1 (October 1975): 3–5; *Link*, 4 January 1976, 12–14; 26 January 1976, 83; 6 June 1976, 13; 20 June 1976, 41; 15 August 1976, 21 and 59.
134. Initially, Party comment on this was somewhat cryptic—referring to 'measures which should either have not been taken up at all or certainly been postponed' and then to 'certain anti-people actions of the Government' (Mohit Sen, 'Spring-board for Democratic Advance', *Indian Left Review* 3, no. 12 (September 1975): 5; CPI quoted in *Link*, 18 July 1976, 7).
135. CPI, National Council, *Report and Resolutions*, August 1975, 26.
136. CPI, National Council, *Report and Resolutions*, August 1975, 15; Hewitt, *Political Mobilisation*, 124; interview with N. K. Krishnan in *Link*, 15 August 1976, 21.
137. Chandra, *Name*, 188.
138. Bhabani Sen Gupta, 'Communism Further Divided', in *Indira Gandhi's India: A Political System Reappraised*, ed. Henry C. Hart (Boulder: Westview Press, 1976), 172; Mohit Sen, *Traveller*, 355.
139. AITUC resolution cited in Krishnan, Gour and Siddhanta, *Working Class and Emergency*, 4.
140. CNS 29 September 1976 and 14 October 1976.
141. See 'Two Conferences', *Link*, 10 October 1976, 6; 'Need for New Paths', *Link*, 17 October 1976, 14–15.
142. Report on AITUC conference (13–17 October), *Link*, 17 October 1976, 15.
143. See 'Action on Land Continues in Andhra Pradesh', CNS Number 379, 1 July 1975.
144. 'Significance of Padayatras', *Link*, 2 May 1976, 20; 'CPI Padayatras in Punjab', *Link*, 27 June 1976, 35. See also CNS 17 March 1976.
145. 'A.P. Congress Chief's Fear', *Link* 27 June 1976, 35.
146. 'M.P.—Obstacles to 20-point Programme', *Link*, 16 May 1976, 14–15; 'Assam: Some Stark Facts', *Link*, 30 May 1976, 43; *Link*, 2 May 1976, 20.
147. Rajeshwara Rao, Gupta and Sen, *Emergency and the Communist Party*, 6.
148. *Link*, 12 December 1976, 4; 9 January 1977, 2.
149. Figures from Yogindra Sharma, M.Farooqi and N. Rajasekhara Reddy, *The Struggle for Building a Mass Communist Party*, (New Delhi, CPI publication, 1976), cited in Joseph Varkey, 'The CPI–Congress Alliance in India', *Asian Survey* 19, no. 9 (September 1979): 884. See also CEC meeting 19–22 June 1976 reported in 'CPI's Assessment', *Link*, 27 June 1976, 31.
150. 'CPI's Strength', *Link*, 18 July 1976, 7.

151. See Chandra, Mukherjee and Mukherjee, *Since Independence*, 328. C. P. Bhambri tells us that after the Emergency a journalist asked Sanjay, in his mother's presence, 'Why did you declare the end of the Emergency?' 'Ask this woman', Sanjay replied (Interview with the author 4 November 2014).
152. The Note is undated but appears in a file marked '1977'. However, given its general tone and the fact that it assumes that no election has been called, it must have been written before 18 January 1977. It refers to the JP Movement as occurring 'last year'. I would, therefore, estimate that it was written in late 1976.
153. All subsequent citations from Haksar's Note from NMML: P. N. Haksar papers, Instalment III, Subject File Number 57, 1977, 'Note to the Prime Minister as Principal Secretary'.

5

Excesses

Once democracy was held in abeyance, whatever the provocation, its inevitable misuse was to follow, what we now remember as the 'excesses'.[1]

In this chapter, we will look at those excesses, particularly in the areas of family planning and slum clearance, together with the communist reaction to them—and the falling-out between Congress and the CPI that ensued.

The excesses of the Emergency cannot be divorced from the rise to fame and influence of the prime minister's second son, Sanjay Gandhi. Sanjay's views on economic matters—which were a crucial piece of the Emergency jigsaw—will be dealt with in the next chapter. It is his political career that interests us for the present. But that started out around the politics of business—specifically, around the Maruti car project. From the late 1950s onwards, the idea of producing a small and cheap car designed for Indian conditions had been under discussion. One committee on the subject followed another, until it was eventually decided that production of the car would be assigned to the private sector. Proposals were called for and, out of 18 entries, the licence to manufacture the small car was given in November 1970 to Sanjay Gandhi.

Sanjay was 23 years old at that time and his only real qualification for the job seemed to be a 'two-thirds Rolls Royce apprenticeship'. The decision was widely regarded as nepotism of the worst sort.[2] Further help from those in power was forthcoming. The chief minister of Haryana, Bansi Lal (in the process of becoming Sanjay's firm political friend), provided land for the Maruti factory at a bargain price. The capital was provided by sympathetic businessmen, with K. K. Birla in the lead.[3] The nationalised banks proffered preferential loans. But the car itself never appeared.[4] This was an inauspicious beginning. But it was not Mrs Gandhi's intention to leave Sanjay languishing in the ranks of failed entrepreneurs. Politics was where she wanted him—in her footsteps and at her side.[5]

It was never really clear what motivated Sanjay politically—apart from the exercise of power, which, as we shall see, he took to with a will.[6] He positively rejected ideology. He was an anti-intellectual. It was reported that '[i]n none of his speeches did he refer to any "isms". His accent was on constructive work.' Furthermore, 'any discussion of ideology was made taboo.'[7] Even socialism was, for him, non-ideological. It was, he declared, 'any ideology that would help uplift the poor and downtrodden—whether it is Left, Right or Centre is not important, but we should consider it socialism.'[8] He clearly had authoritarian tendencies. It is said that he was an admirer of Ferdinand Marcos, the Filipino dictator.[9] Marcos had described his own regime as 'a reform government under martial law. The purpose is … to bring about urgently needed radical or revolutionary reforms and changes in society.'[10] It would appear that Sanjay took the same sort of approach to the Indian polity in the early 1970s. Once the Emergency was underway, he stated, '[f]uture generations will not remember us by how many elections we had, but by the progress we have made.'[11]

With his mother's help and encouragement, Sanjay managed to establish a position of considerable political influence—both through her administration and through the Youth Congress. By 1974 his group of followers, which included Bansi Lal (defence minister from December 1975), Om Mehta (home minister), Kishen Chand (lieutenant-governor of Delhi) and R. K. Dhawan (additional private secretary to the Prime Minister), was operating through the Prime Minister's House. This had, according to Dhar, 'started functioning like a well-oiled extra-constitutional authority'.[12] Its interference in government and administration was reinforced by Sanjay's role in the Emergency, which also provided opportunities for the expansion of his power. Janak Raj Jai told the Oral History Project:

> During the Emergency, Sanjay Gandhi was all in all. He was the defacto Prime Minister… . All the senior officers from almost all the Departments used to be present at the Prime Minister's House to seek direction from Sanjay Gandhi.[13]

Elsewhere in the Prime Minister's administration, some senior officials were not so easily impressed. P. N. Haksar (the then deputy chairman of the Planning Commission) kept a file of '[P]ress Clippings related to the various activities of Sanjay Gandhi' from 1975 to 1976, clearly with a view to keeping a watching brief on Sanjay's rise and misdeeds.[14]

Powerful though the Prime Minister's House was, it was in the Youth Congress that Sanjay, most spectacularly, came into his own. He was appointed to the Executive Council of the Youth Congress in December

1975 and initiated a 'crash programme', which claimed to have raised the organisation to six million members by February 1977. It was unfortunate for the political composition of the Youth Congress, but of considerable advantage to Sanjay, that the membership drive opened it up to 'a variety of goondas, thugs, pick-pockets and criminals'. The Youth Congress president, Ambika Soni (a strong supporter of Sanjay) said, 'The Youth Congress had been infiltrated by hoodlums and gangsters'. In addition, according to Arjun Dev, 'from 1976–77 onwards, RSS cadres had massively joined him.' Amarjit Kaur adds: 'There was a clear-cut call by the RSS chief to his youth to go and join the Sanjay brigade.'[15]

Since the Congress itself was in such a weakened political state, some of its leaders—clearly including Mrs Gandhi —believed that the Youth Congress could step up to fulfil the role of a political mobiliser. Sanjay himself was certainly of that opinion. He believed that 'Youth Congress offices should be set up in every block and ultimately each village should have a Youth Congress office.'[16] Furthermore, the Youth Congress should act as a 'watchdog' over the state governments to ensure that they carried out the behests of the Congress High Command.[17] Youth Congress committees did indeed start to supplant the Congress organisation at the block level (between villages and districts) during the Emergency. The Youth Congress was able to intimidate and, at times, override many of the state governments.[18]

In July 1976, Sanjay had the Youth Congress adopt a '5-Point Programme', which called for:

- Family planning
- Planting trees and cleaning the environment (this seems to have been the basis for slum clearance)
- Refusal of dowry
- Promotion of adult literacy
- Abolition of caste[19]

The AICC told the Congress that the five points were 'of vital importance in the context of the social and economic changes in the fabric of society', and instructed all units and all legislative parties to adopt them.[20] Congress leaders, with Indira Gandhi at their head, were soon referring to the '25-Point Programme'.[21] Mrs Gandhi drew attention to the less confrontational nature of the five points—things that *individuals* could put into practice, without the trouble and strife of political mobilisation.

> Land reform is a good programme but a citizen cannot do anything about
> it; it is for the Government to do it. Similarly for debt relief ... . But the
> 5-Point Programme is a more personal problem where each person has
> to say for example: I am not going to take dowry; I am going to fight the
> caste system; I am going to plant the tree; I am going to see that the trees
> are not cut down.[22]

This may have been the view of many in the adult organisation. As it turned
out, Sanjay was not going to leave his points to individual implementation.

As already noted, Sanjay reached the height of his power during the
Emergency. One reason for this was that the Prime Minister had handed
over the running of, and planning for, the city of Delhi to her son.[23] Viewed
through the prism of Sanjay's five points, the city was a den of iniquity:
too many people (and too many of them poor, illiterate and caste-bound),
too few trees, too many slums, too much backwardness—'in short,' says
Mehta, 'all the urban ills.'[24] Even before slum clearance and sterilisation
were visited upon the city's hapless citizens, they were subject to routine
harassment and intimidation by the thugs of the Youth Congress.[25]

The Youth Congress tactics reached the Congress itself. The renewed
Youth Congress held its first convention in Guwahati (Assam) in late
November 1976, just before a meeting of the AICC in the same city.[26] The
former was planned by the Youth Congress leadership to overshadow the
latter. As the convention drew near, posters appeared in the city: 'Sanjay
Gandhi, you are the helmsman of our new India, the country's last resort'
and 'Welcome, future light of India'. According to Mehta, the objective of
'Sanjay and his brigade' was 'to ridicule, mock, terrorize and finally take
over the Party'. Sanjay illustrated his opinion of the relative importance
of the two organisations.

> A year ago [he told the Youth Congress convention], the Congress held
> its session in Chandigarh while the Youth Congress held a cell meeting.
> This year the Youth Congress is holding its session while the Congress [in
> reality, the AICC] will hold a small meeting.

But more important was his political message to the Youth Congress.
Referring to the state government and the Congress committees, he said:

> They only want to hold you back... . What do we want? If we want to
> remain *chelas* and *chamchas* [slaves and lackeys] of others let us continue
> to take their help and follow them as their tail. But if you want the Youth

Congress to be a work-oriented organization determined to shape the future
of India, then we can't follow someone holding his tail.

The Youth Congress president, Ambika Soni, chimed in, accusing Congress
leaders and officials of obstructing the 5-Point Programme and 'the constructive programme of the Youth Congress', in general.

This all appeared to be an attempt to replace a moribund Congress
organisation with its youthful (and more dynamic) counterpart. And on the
last day of the convention, the attempt was endorsed by Mrs Gandhi. 'You
have stolen our thunder,' she said, 'and it should be that way. I have firm
faith in the youth of India.' Marking a change in his status, the government
censors directed that from this point Sanjay should stop being referred
to merely as a 'youth leader'. Mehta argues that after Guwahati, Congress
leaders were running scared at '[t]he prospect of hordes of gruff young
men and women seizing the party structure from the grassroots upwards.'

Sanjay, with his Youth Congress associates and his placement in Mrs
Gandhi's administration, remained a powerful force in the Emergency to
the end. Particularly in north India, it was he who operated the Emergency
regime.[27] His influence was accompanied by a personality cult of considerable proportions and reinforced by the sycophancy of Congress officials.
On a visit to Jaipur in January 1976, he was welcomed at the airport by
the chief minister, the entire cabinet of Rajasthan, leaders of the Youth
Congress, senior bureaucrats, social workers and 'eminent personalities'.
Meanwhile, the city itself had been decorated with no less than 501 gates
and arches in his honour.[28] His position was defended by a pliant press.
The *Amrita Bazar Patrika* reported in December 1975:

> Systematic propaganda against Mr Sanjay Gandhi is being carried on by
> opponents of the Prime Minister.... The sole aim of this campaign is to
> create confusion not only among the people but also among Congressmen...
> . All these propagandas are no doubt absolutely baseless and untrue.[29]

Madhu Dandavate was of the opinion that 'Sanjay went beyond his mandate during the Emergency ... I feel in [the] course of time, Sanjay would
have been a threat to her [Mrs Gandhi's] power.'[30] By the end, his power
was, if anything, increasing. In the 1977 elections (which brought the
Emergency to an end), according to Ayub Syed (editor of *Current*), 'For the
first time in democratic India ... elections will be organized, dominated,
fought and won by the Youth Congress under the leadership of Sanjay

Gandhi'. It is said that he personally picked 150–200 of the 542 Congress candidates for the election.[31]

The communists may have been among the first to spot the implications of Sanjay's rise to power. In due course, they were referring to him and his supporters as 'the gang', 'the plotters', 'the reactionary gang in the ruling party'—but most often as 'the reactionary caucus'.[32] Initially however, they were cautious in their approach. Mohit Sen included, among a number of 'negative trends' in India in August 1976, 'the building up of certain personalities with anti-democratic and anti-Communist views'.[33] At the end of the year, *Link* noted:

> [T]he youth wing [of the Congress] has emerged as an important factor in Congress politics… . Some of the youth leaders have developed a contemptuous attitude towards the Congress leadership… . This is a disturbing factor.[34]

Just over a month later, the paper said that 'reactionary parties' had infiltrated the Youth Congress.[35] Communist publications, however, steadfastly refrained from naming Sanjay Gandhi in these and other attacks.[36]

What, in the CPI's view, was this caucus? It was, they said, based on lumpen and 'nouveau riche' elements which were contemptuous of the established upper classes. They noted, as we have, that these elements were zealously opposed to 'ideology'.[37] This made the caucus and the Youth Congress open to infiltration by decidedly ideological elements: 'RSS cadre, JP men and other such reactionary elements'. Furthermore, the caucus was being used as a tool to promote US interests in India.[38]

But what concerned the CPI most about the caucus was its growing anti-communism. Sanjay was intent on pursuing those in the Congress leadership whom he regarded as communist infiltrators—including Siddhartha Shankar Ray, Barooah and Chandrajit Yadav—and removing them from positions of influence.[39] At the same time, he maintained a steady barrage of anti-communist opinion. In early August 1975, Sanjay gave an extensive interview to Uma Vasudev, which was published in *Surge* on 27 August. At that time, what appeared to be the interview's most inflammatory section concerned the CPI.[40] He said:

> The communists may have a small cadre that actually works but if you take all the people in the Communist Party of India, the bigwigs—even

the not-so-bigwigs—I don't think you'd find a richer or more corrupt people anywhere.[41]

Now tension may have been rising between Congress and the communists, but recall that the CPI remained Mrs Gandhi's sole national political ally—one that she was not prepared to jettison just yet and certainly not on the basis of some ill thought-out remarks by Sanjay. She reacted swiftly. She wrote to her principal private secretary, P. N. Dhar:

> Sanjay has made an exceedingly stupid statement about the communists … . At a most crucial time we have not only grievously hurt those who have helped us and are now supporting us within the country but created serious problems with the entire Socialist Bloc… . Should we get Sanjay to say something … I'm quite frantic.[42]

By 28 August, Dhar had had the interview withdrawn and had made sure that no further comment would be made on it. As he wrote later, 'This was not very difficult at that time because of the press censorship rule.'[43] Sanjay was made to stumble through a 'clarification': 'I am not used to newspaper interviews and did not realise what meaning would be given to my words.'[44]

Despite this, in the context of the division, then opening up between the Congress and the CPI over the conduct of the Emergency, Sanjay's anti-communism did not cease. In fact, it was given new outlets and was eventually endorsed by his mother. In March 1976, David Selbourne quotes him as telling 'his cheering followers' in Calcutta that 'never again will the Red Flag fly in Bengal'. For good measure, he attacked the communists for provoking strikes, demanded an end to 'class politics' and denounced nationalisation.[45] After the Guwahati Youth Congress convention, he returned to the 'corruption' in the CPI, accused the communists of being in the pay of Moscow and alleged that they had betrayed the Quit India campaign against the British colonialists in 1942. Ayub Sayed crowed in support:

> The emergence of the Youth Congress as a militant force dedicated to the reconstruction of the country has unnerved the ageing, opportunistic and intellectually dishonest leaders of the Communist Party of India. They are unable to stomach a rejuvenated young India with Sanjay Gandhi as its charismatic leader.[46]

Sanjay continued his attacks till 1977. The communists were spreading rumours about the Youth Congress, following an imported ideology and weakening the national fabric.[47] There was now no restraining hand from the Prime Minister's Office (PMO) to halt the flow of wild anti-communist rhetoric. The Party could write with some justification of 'a campaign of vilification and slander' against its members, which included 'hoodlum demonstrations against our party'. The Party feared 'a general attack'.[48]

The CPI considered that the 5-Point Programme was a diversion from the more radical 20 points. The Party was disturbed when it found that, under the influence of the caucus, Congress was prioritising the former over the latter. Dange, the CPI chairman, said that the communists were not opposed to the 5-Point Programme, 'but [they] gave priority to quicker implementation of [the] 20-Point programme which aimed at giving a better deal to the working class and the rural poor.' The CEC resolved that 'this [5-Point] programme will not solve the problem of unemployment and poverty.'[49] The Party also objected to the campaign by Sanjay and his supporters to take down chief ministers, who would not sufficiently toe the Youth Congress line.[50]

The Party poured scorn on the 'efforts ... being made to push the Youth Congress to the fore under the harmful slogan of "youth power".'[51] The caucus, warned Rajeshwara Rao, sought to undermine parliamentary democracy on a permanent basis. Another CPI author related that 'a ministerial luminary of this constellation is very often heard declaring, "to hell with all these elections; what we need is four more years without such troubles".'[52] Rao concluded that, whereas before the main threat came from 'reaction and fascist forces outside the Congress':

> ... now it is coming from the reactionary caucus inside the ruling party, which has taken shape and has grown under the conditions of the Emergency ... the main thrust of reaction is now coming from inside the Congress. This is also because sections of reaction and fascism are also infiltrating into the Congress and Youth Congress to carry on their nefarious game.

He concluded: 'The struggle against the caucus has not ended, it has just begun.'[53] But how that struggle was to be carried out remained unclear.

The Sterilisation Campaign

Of all the excesses of the Emergency, perhaps the most egregious, in its scope and damage, was the campaign for 'family planning'—which turned into a widespread drive for forcible sterilisation. Once again, this campaign is tightly linked with Sanjay Gandhi and undoubtedly many of its worst aspects can be laid at his door. It should be remembered, however, that concerns about India's birth rate and efforts to reduce it preceded both Sanjay and the Emergency.

India's ever-vigilant economic observers, the World Bank, the International Monetary Fund and the Aid-India Consortium, for example, were keen for the introduction of a forced-pace sterilisation programme. When it appeared that this would be delivered, the World Bank president, Robert McNamara, noted that 'the authorities believe that some form of pressure (sterilization laws, loss of government jobs, increase in the marriage age, compulsory abortion) will be required'—without comment.[54] The Emergency, of course, opened up new vistas for authoritarian measures to be applied to the family planning campaign. The Minister of Health, Karan Singh, wrote to the Prime Minister in October 1975:

> … there seems to be no alternative but to think in terms of some element of compulsion in the larger national interest… . The present emergency, and the declaration of the 20-point programme by the Prime Minister, have provided an appropriate atmosphere for tackling the problem.[55]

Mrs Gandhi responded positively to the suggestion. She told the Association of Physicians the following January:

> We should not hesitate to take steps which might be described as drastic. Some personal rights have to be kept in abeyance, for the human rights of the nation, the right to live, the right to progress.[56]

The 75th session of the Indian National Congress (INC) duly resolved:

> Population control should become a mass movement and the number of acceptors [for sterilisation] increased from 17 million to 40 million within a period of three years. Bold and new measures covering incentives and disincentives will have to be devised to achieve this objective.[57]

The Health Ministry despatched a note to the cabinet in March 1976, agreeing that 'the introduction of stronger measures of State action for the adoption of fertility control by the people' was justified. The Ministry promised 'a judicious package of incentive and disincentive measures'.[58] A national target of 4.3 million sterilisations for 1976–77 was created by the central government and then allocated to the states. The targets were 'fairly high', wrote the Union Health Secretary to the states' chief secretaries, 'and can be achieved only by maintaining the tempo and enthusiasm shown in the closing months of last year'.[59] Sensing that the enthusiasm might wane, the chief censor ordered on 1 April: 'No criticism of the family planning programme. This includes letters to the editor.'[60]

It was at this point that Sanjay entered the sterilisation story. He was keen to make the family planning issue his own—and he succeeded in doing so, though not in any positive way.[61] Madhu Dandavate told the Oral History Project:

> It was a good programme, which they destroyed … by bad handling. Sanjay Gandhi was very ruthless. If by chance he were to become a Prime Minister, there would have been a greater problem in the country! He was ruthless to the hinge![62]

Sterilisation camps—at that point, on a volunteer basis—were set up in Delhi in March 1976. Given Sanjay's role in the administration of the Emergency in the capital, these were presumably under his supervision. But progress was slow and soon the volunteers turned into conscripts, and quotas of 'volunteers' were established for each camp. Sensing some political opposition, Sanjay warned 'so called leaders within and without the Congress' that 'any leader of any community or religion who opposes family planning … should be thrown out.'[63]

Haksar pointed out that one of the problems with the programme was that it offered only sterilisation (with all its associated folklore and rumour) as a method of birth control. Also, the programme was deficient in sensitive publicity and lacked essential infrastructure—qualified medical staff, after care, sterile areas and so forth.[64] Volunteers continued to refuse to volunteer, and forcible sterilisation began on a mass scale. Exacerbating this situation was the competition between chief ministers, vying for Sanjay's approval, that setting state targets had unleashed.[65] Once the national and state targets had been set for 1976–77, the authorities in nine states plus Delhi then *raised* their target figures.[66] The mere appearance of Sanjay was apt to set off a furious struggle for greater numbers of sterilisations. When he was due to visit Maharashtra in October 1976, government workers were told:

> ... the Chief Minister desires that before the visit of Shri Sanjay Gandhi, Maharashtra State must have completed 5 lakhs sterilisation ... though the task is stupendous, we shall have to leave no stone unturned to achieve this objective.[67]

This kind of misplaced effort led directly to the situation described by Madhu Dandavate:

> In my area one old man was put on the sterilisation table. He said: I am 70, how can I produce a child? They said: We are not concerned about your age— but our quota of sterilization is this. So, the operation was done like that.[68]

As it became increasingly difficult (though not, given sufficient police measures, impossible) to dragoon 'volunteers' into the sterilisation centres, more direct measures were adopted. *Link* reported that in Uttar Pradesh, the state government was 'depriving people with unplanned families [of] the supply of essential and controlled commodities, including Government built and controlled houses and car licences.'[69] Those of a suitable age (and that was a wide sector of the population) found that, without a sterilisation certificate, they were prevented from renewing driving, scooter, rickshaw and arms licences. Sometimes they were refused treatment at hospitals. Enclosed crowds—for example, in cinemas—were locked in, so that sterilisation certificates could be checked.[70]

With still not enough victims, the central and state governments fell back on an easier target: their own employees. The lieutenant-governor of Delhi, Kishen Chand, instructed the city's civil servants that all those with more than two children would have to be sterilised—otherwise 'no promotion, no confirmation, no increment, no entitlement to government housing, no loan advances, no leave.'[71] Civil servants were not only expected to be sterilised themselves, but to 'motivate' others to have the operation as well. The chief secretary of Uttar Pradesh instructed the state's district magistrates and divisional commissioners to 'inform everybody that failure to achieve monthly targets [of "motivations"] will not only result in stoppage of salary but also suspension and severest penalties.'[72] School teachers were expected to be sterilised and to motivate five other individuals for the operation. Janak Raj Jai reported, 'My wife Santal who was a teacher in a government school was forced to get herself sterilised; otherwise, her salary would not be released.'[73]

Fear of sterilisation was greater in the Muslim community—and thus it was insensitive, to say the least, for Sanjay to start his 'crash campaign' in the walled city of old Delhi, a predominantly Muslim area. Haksar noted that 'Muslims as a whole have come out in opposition to sterilisation' and were involved in resistance to it. Detailing some incidents he warned, 'If this goes on, the Congress runs the danger of losing support of Muslims, Harijans and poor people.'[74] Muslims were not the only resisters. The sterilisation programme, spreading from the urban centres to the countryside, had the effect of taking the Emergency's repressive features along with it. Previously, if Indian farmers identified the Emergency regime with anything, it was the relatively benign (if distant) prospect of land reform. Now they identified it with a harsh and authoritarian sterilisation regime. A major riot against forced sterilisation erupted in Muzaffarnagar (Uttar Pradesh) in October 1976, after the state's sterilisation quota was raised from 400,000 to 1,500,000 by the chief minister. Three days' rioting ensued, leaving 74 police injured—but the central government refused to acknowledge any civilian casualties. Disturbances spread to Haryana, Madhya Pradesh, Bihar, West Bengal, Punjab and Maharashtra.[75] Haksar again stated:

> These compulsions are creating a very unfavourable situation for the Government, at places leading to resistance against the Government and clashes with its law and order forces.[76]

Still, Sanjay and his acolytes pushed on. Neither he nor his mother was unaware of the brutal aspects of the campaign. K. K. Birla steeled himself to speak to Sanjay about a particular incident.

> He was, [reports the businessman] no doubt, sorry when he heard about the incident, but he said that when so many operations were being performed, some stray cases were bound to occur owing to the overzealousness of some people in the government.... When I informed [Indira Gandhi] about the reports which had come to my notice, she said that was not what she had heard.[77]

But eventually, Haksar's warning that '[t]he element of compulsion has to be eliminated if the Government decides to go in for elections' seems to have sunk in.[78] In late 1976, moves were made to wind back some of the repressive aspects of the campaign. Mrs Gandhi told a conference of chief ministers in January 1977:

… At lower levels unimaginative and ham-handed measures are sometimes adopted to achieve targets … it should be made clear that there should be no compulsion of any sort. Persons guilty of over-doing it should be severely taken to task.[79]

It is doubtful though, that the main person 'guilty of over-doing it' was ever 'taken to task'. Chandra comments that Mrs Gandhi's moderation came 'rather late in the day'.[80]

The communist approach to the sterilisation campaign was initially cautious, as it had been towards the reactionary caucus. When the national target for sterilisation was announced in April 1976 and passed on to the states for implementation, *Link* warned that '[g]iving the green signal to the states to go for compulsory sterilisation … may prove to be unwise.' The paper argued that a change in attitude was required, rather than legal enforcement.[81] In August, the paper drew an implicitly negative contrast between the central government's policy (persuasion rather than compulsion 'at this stage') and that of the Haryana government, busily campaigning against its own workers.[82] But it did not comment in September when 'a limit of three children is being fixed for every Central Government employee.'[83]

When the real nature of the campaign became clear, there was a steady flow of resolutions from the Party's CEC, condemning coercive methods, the involvement of the police and forced sterilisation. The communists appealed to the Prime Minister to intervene 'and save the situation from getting worse'—as did the National Federation of Indian Women in October 1976, which also 'warned that such moves will only defeat the very purpose of the programme.'[84] CPI students at Delhi University prevented a visit from Sanjay, intended to promote the sterilisation campaign.[85] In a major critique published in late 1976, the Party condemned 'the manner in which [the government] is pushing coercive sterilisation in the name of family planning… . This has led to mass resistance, resulting in both killing of police and other officials and police firings and deaths.' It drew attention to the fact that, just as Sanjay's 5 points were eclipsing the 20-Point Programme, sterilisation was overshadowing everything else. 'The whole administration in many states is engaged solely in the sterilisation programme'—while implementation of land ceiling laws 'has almost come to a halt.' This 'one-point programme' was of course being implemented by the bureaucracy 'with gusto'. For the CPI, forcible sterilisation was being used 'to shelve radical socio-economic policies and to curry favour with the World Bank and other neo-colonial agencies.'[86]

The communist protests had some impact, as did the fact that their leadership took up the question, directly with Mrs Gandhi herself. Prem Sagar Gupta of the CPI sent a report on the campaign to Dhar, who passed it on to the Prime Minister. She replied (according to Dhar) that 'all the allegations made in the report were found baseless and that we should not listen to motivated stories.' In early October 1976, she wrote to Rajeshwara Rao complaining at 'the manner in which your party is working against us in some districts ... Last time [she had written] also I specifically told you about the CPI's opposition to our family planning programme. This is now reaching limits which cannot coexist with cooperation with us.'[87] The Health Minister, Karan Singh, also wrote to Rao:

> The Prime Minister has repeatedly clarified the position in this regard, and apart from public pronouncements I have written personally to the chief ministers reiterating that there should be no coercion in the promotion of family planning and that only eligible persons should be motivated to undergo sterilisation.

He acknowledged the CPI's support for family planning, but noted that 'this has yet to be demonstrated in the field.'[88] Undeterred, Rajeshwara Rao fired off an 18-page report on forcible sterilisation to the health minister, 'alleging specific instances of coercion and use of force by authorities in the implementation of the family planning programme in Punjab, Uttar Pradesh, Haryana, Bihar, Rajasthan and Delhi.' Mrs Gandhi dismissed this (again, according to Dhar) as 'an orchestration of anti-Sanjay propaganda'.[89] In a CPI press statement, Rao wondered aloud as to how coercive methods could exist in Delhi and the surrounding area, 'when both the Prime Minister and the health minister repeatedly expressed themselves against any coercion in family planning'. He singled out 'the ghastly incident at Muzaffarnagar' for special mention.[90] As well as reporting on the excesses, the CPI claimed to have been involved in the resistance to them. 'It was out party comrades,' the 11th Congress was told, 'who were in the front line of popular resistance against the forced sterilisation drive in Muzaffarnagar' and also in instances of resistance in Uttar Pradesh, Madhya Pradesh, Haryana, Bihar 'and some other states'.[91]

Slum Clearance

Sanjay now turned to that part of his 5-Point Programme that concerned 'planting trees and cleaning the environment'. If trees were to be
planted and the environment cleaned in Delhi, space had to be cleared
which meant that Delhi's slums and 'unauthorised settlements', as well
as the people in them, had to be swept up and cleared away. Working
through a combination of Youth Congress cadre and the Delhi Municipal
Corporation, he set about doing just that. The Shah Commission found
that 'a majority of the operations were undertaken under the orders of
Shri Sanjay Gandhi.'[92] The Commission concluded:

> … [T]he actions taken were ill-conceived and in certain cases cruelly inhu-
> man. Thousands of people were uprooted after [being given] a few hours'
> notice, often without any warning and without remedy or compensation.
> The demolition activities were carried out ignoring the misery caused to
> men, women and children. Their lifelong abodes were demolished with the
> aid of bulldozers and their belongings were thrown and strewn all over the
> area cleared by such operations. They were forced to move to places where
> even the basic necessities of life like light, water and transport facilities
> were not immediately available.[93]

The CPI complained after only a few weeks of the Emergency rule, that
'[h]uts and wayside stalls are being bulldozed in the name of eradica-
tion of slums, widening streets and beautifying cities.'[94] In keeping with
Sanjay's usual approach, this was a crash programme, designed to be
implemented with maximum speed and with no aversion to the use of
maximum force.[95] Theoretically, those cleared out of the way were to be
relocated in 'resettlement colonies', outside the cities. According to Sanjay:

> In these colonies, about 50,000 plots, providing accommodation to about
> 2.5 lakh people, have been developed with all the basic, civil ameni-
> ties, drains, street lighting, public latrines, pure water supply, parks,
> playgrounds, schools, dispensaries, etc. In most of the new resettlement
> colonies even television and adult literary centres have been established.[96]

This might have been what Sanjay believed and what those around
him were reporting. But it appears to have been pure fantasy. Work on
the construction of these colonies (when it took place at all) generally

commenced only after the people had been relocated. In the meantime, they had to fend for themselves. The need for speed was evident in the removal, not the resettlement.[97] The CPI's National Committee protested again about the programme in February 1976. It considered Sanjay's campaign (unattributed at this stage) as an example of the Emergency powers being used 'in a highly arbitrary, authoritarian and vindictive manner against the common people and progressive forces'. The committee pointed out that this was aimed at the poorest sections—'stout supporters of the struggle against fascism and right reaction'—and could only lead to their 'demoralisation and alienation'.[98]

Worse was to come. The gaze of the beautifiers fell in April 1976 on the huge slum area surrounding the Turkman Gate in old Delhi. Here, Sanjay unleashed a combined campaign of shop and dwelling destruction, together with rigorous and forced sterilisation, both accompanied by generous numbers of armed police. The area was inhabited mainly by Muslims—which meant that Sanjay's actions were once again alienating an important source of Congress support.[99] The people attempted to stop the bulldozers on 19 April. Huge numbers of armed police and squads of the Central Reserve Police Force were mobilised to crush them. After lathi-charges and firing (in which six people died), they eventually succeeded. This was followed by a 45-day curfew, during which the demolition and clearance proceeded.[100] Sanjay regarded these events as a major achievement. When asked how he thought those resettled from Turkman Gate would vote in the 1977 election, he replied: 'I would say 95 to 99 per cent will vote in favour of Congress. Just now in Delhi I think that would be our most solid vote.'[101]

At their Congress after the Emergency, the communists maintained that they were among the first to actively protest against the slum clearances. They related:

> Our party in Delhi intervened in the Turkman Gate tragedy…. Despite the curfew and other difficult conditions, we carried out a house-to-house survey and prepared a factual note which exposed the patently anti-people and nakedly authoritarian direction the emergency was taking. We led the fight against the notorious Chawri Bazar demolition scheme and in fact prevented the caucus and its men from going ahead with it even during the darkest days of emergency excesses and of the rampage of the caucus in the capital. The brave example of our comrades inspired many congressmen to come forward to oppose such excesses.[102]

Unity and Struggle?

From the middle of 1976, the CPI believed that the progressive aspects of the Emergency were grinding to a halt. The 20-Point Programme was not being implemented and there was a little prospect of structures being created to ensure its implementation. Land reform was not taking place let alone workers' control. Prices were rising and wages were falling. There were increasing inroads on democratic rights. On 27 October, the CEC passed a resolution on 'Misuse of Emergency'. It condemned official 'high-handedness', harassment of the innocent and attacks on peasants, workers and the trade unions. It especially denounced the 'gruesome violence and coercion against weaker sections of the population by over-zealous officials seeking to fulfil sterilisation targets.' It demanded that these things should cease.[103] In November, the All-India Trade Union Congress (AITUC) started a campaign for the restoration of workers' rights and in January 1977, the Party organised national demonstrations against price rises.[104] One thing that particularly incensed the CPI was the arrest of its own members, which took place mostly under the strictures of the Maintenance of Internal Security Act (MISA).[105] The CEC reported that, in Uttar Pradesh alone, 400 CPI cadres campaigning against rising prices had been arrested. Arrests had also taken place in Punjab, Bihar, Haryana, Maharashtra and Madhya Pradesh.[106]

This grim picture darkened still further for the communists when, at the end of October 1976, the Congress leadership decided to postpone elections until March 1978.[107] This was done without consulting the CPI. They described it as 'the Emergency's politically most harmful and ill-advised step' as well as being a 'grave misuse' of the Emergency. Once again, they blamed the decision on 'a tiny handful of operators in the ruling party and bureaucracy who are alien to the ways of democracy', whose intention was to end parliamentary democracy and 'foist upon the nation an authoritarian rule'.[108]

India's constitutional system was to come under further threat from sections of the Congress leadership. The Congress session, in November 1975, appointed a committee under Swaran Singh to review the constitution. The committee's report, which was approved by the AICC in May 1976, recommended the retention of a parliamentary system with some adjustments in the relationship between the Indian state and the higher courts.[109] The CPI was in favour of constitutional change 'asserting the supremacy of parliament and safeguarding the vital interests of the toiling masses and other sections of the people.' It broadly supported the committee's recommendations—especially the committee's suggestion that 'socialist' and 'secular' should be added to the constitutional description of the state.[110]

Such lofty intentions, however, were not the project of Sanjay and his supporters. According to Dhar, they 'highjacked the idea of constitutional reform and organized a campaign for convening a new constitutional assembly. They had no thoughts on what the constitutional assembly should do beyond a single point programme of continuing the Emergency in one form or another.'[111] To this end, they pressured the Uttar Pradesh, Punjab and Haryana state assemblies to demand such a constitutional assembly.

The communists opposed any such move. Initially they admitted that '[w]hat has prompted the originators of this sinister move at this crucial moment is not yet clear'. Later, they correctly blamed it on 'the reactionary caucus in the ruling party' and said that it was aimed at stalling the election, subverting parliament and replacing it with 'the obnoxious idea of a presidential form of government'.[112] Rajeshwara Rao wrote to Indira Gandhi:

> A great responsibility rests on your shoulders at the critical moment. We hope you will oppose this suicidal move without any hesitation.[113]

With some hesitation, she did. Mrs Gandhi had effectively quashed the plan by late October.[114] But the issue of constitutional reform was a further bone of contention between the CPI and the Sanjay clique—and through the latter between the Party and the Prime Minister, whether she supported the matter in question or not.

Over Sanjay's role, over forced sterilisation and slum clearance, over the non-delivery of reform and over democracy, the communists had criticised, condemned and annoyed the government. Mrs Gandhi's counter-attack was not long in coming.[115] Following Sanjay's *Surge* interview, Mrs Gandhi justified his continuing anti-communist campaign. She insisted that, while he had made 'anti-communist remarks', he had not attacked 'communism'. The communists, she said, should have sat down and reasoned with him. 'But instead they launched a full-scale attack on him so naturally he again spoke once or twice more.'[116] She joined in. We have noted her warnings to the CPI over the family planning campaign. In early 1976, she accused the Party of 'running an international campaign against her government, against her personally and her family.'[117] Later in the year, when the CPI openly criticised Sanjay's attempts to destabilise the Orissa and West Bengal state governments (in order to replace them with his favoured candidates), it was warned not to interfere in Congress affairs.[118] Finally, in a speech to Congress workers in December 1976, Mrs Gandhi denounced the CPI by name. 'They [the CPI] say they support me,' she said, 'but there can be no greater insult than to say that I could be influenced by reactionaries or anybody else.' Since Sanjay was 'much too small a fry', it was clear that she was the main target of communist criticism: 'the attack on him is very definitely on me.'[119] Further, she returned to the question of the CPI's patriotism by harking back to the Party's non-participation (due to their support for the war against Nazism at that time) in the Congress 'Quit India' campaign of 1942.[120] Barooah joined in, asserting that the CPI 'certainly did not fight for national independence. This was a historic fact.'[121]

Mrs Gandhi clearly entertained some second thoughts on the wisdom of this approach in the ensuing weeks. 'I did not strongly attack the Communist Party of India,' she told an interviewer, 'I did not speak outside but only to our own workers in a training camp.' She blamed the conflict not on the issues involved but on communist manners: 'They did come to meet me, I think twice, but they came in a belligerent mood and shouted at me.'[122] She retracted somewhat, admitting that 'the CPI was in the struggle for independence, while other parties were siding openly with the British.'[123] But it was a half-hearted affair. Central News Service (CNS) reported 'the decision of the state youth congress to initiate an anti-communist campaign all over Bihar from December 18.'[124] The CPI leadership realised that her later statement 'has not persuaded the anti-Communists to give up their game' and that there remained, with 'a very small section of Congressmen', the demand that the Party should be banned.[125] The anti-communist campaign continued till the end of the Emergency, with the government news agency, Samachar, releasing a deliberately false account of the CPI's CEC meeting in January 1977:

> … Mr [Rajeshwara] Rao said party cadre must continue to sabotage the five-point programme and malign the Prime Minister's 20-point programme while the top leaders must adopt a soft line and speak openly in support of both the programmes … this policy would be in line with the CPI's infiltration into the ranks of the Congress. It would also ease the position of their supporters who were now in key positions and ran the risk of being exposed.[126]

This story appeared to threaten not only the communists, but also what remained of the Congress Left.

Conclusion

In this and the previous chapter, I have tried to demonstrate that despite the CPI's predictable support for the Emergency when it was first declared, the Party started to detach itself from the Emergency regime at a relatively early stage. The excesses and failures of the Emergency provoked a critical reaction from the communists. This, in turn, earned the Party a pasting from the Congress leadership—from Sanjay in the first instance, but soon supported by his mother and other Congress leaders. Nevertheless, as the Emergency neared its end the Party was preparing a national campaign against price rises.[127]

The more that the CPI took an independent and oppositional stance, the more the Party's strategy was torn asunder. Had the Emergency continued, we can be sure that the division between the CPI and the Congress leadership would have widened. Sanjay certainly saw the communists as an ongoing obstacle to his political schemes. When asked why he had 'permitted' Mrs Gandhi to call the 1977 election, he replied, 'I couldn't help it. She was too much influenced by the communists.'[128] By late 1976, the communist strategy towards the Congress, of unity and struggle—and remember that in the first few months of the Emergency, the emphasis had been very definitely on unity—was in tatters.

Two attempts were made to save it. The first was to heap the blame for the Emergency's failures and excesses on the 'reactionary caucus' in the Congress leadership—Sanjay and his supporters. If it could be shown that they were a rogue element, operating without the support of the Prime Minister and most Congress leaders, then the possibility existed of leading the Congress back to the path of righteousness. But this rather fell apart in the face of Mrs Gandhi's strong defence of her son and her warning that attacks on him would be interpreted as attacks on her. The second attempt was to take refuge in foreign policy. More and more emphasis was placed on the anti-imperialist, non-aligned and pro-Soviet aspects of the government's external outlook. True, the communists contrasted this with its inroads on the lives of workers, peasants and the poor. However, this was interpreted as reflecting the two faces of the national bourgeoisie—and, therefore, justifying the two aspects of communist policy: 'Because of this dual policy of the national bourgeoisie our party pursues the policy of unity and struggle.'[129] But it is doubtful whether the forcibly sterilised, the arbitrarily located, the worker with declining wages, the poor farmer still waiting for land reform and the citizen without rights, derived much comfort from the foreign policy of the Congress government.

There was much discussion of this problem in CPI circles from 1976 into early 1977. Again and again, it was stressed that there remained progressive elements among the Congress rank-and-file and that the communists had to leave no stone unturned in the search for any kind of unity or joint action with them—now against the government's 'anti-people' policies. In January 1977, the CEC decided that the policy of unity and struggle should continue.[130] *Link* reported, 'Despite the recent tensions, [the] CPI leadership came to the conclusion that its unity and struggle policy was "entirely correct". It had to be persisted [with] and pursued in the future as well.' This was based on the conclusion that the Congress still led 'India's struggle for radical economic advance'.[131]

Nearly a year before, the National Committee had resolved:

> We should support the firm anti-imperialist and antifeudal position of the Congress, while skilfully fighting the antipeople measures and negative features of the ruling party.[132]

But by then, the hour was getting late. And, as P. C. Joshi noted in the margin of his copy of the resolution: 'How?'

Notes

1. Aditya Mukherjee, ed., 'Introduction', in *A Centenary History of the Indian National Congress. Volume V: 1964–1984* (New Delhi: Academic Foundation, 2011).
2. Vinod Mehta, *The Sanjay Story* (New Delhi: Harper Collins Publishers, 2012 [1978]), 70–72. Mehta's book is, as far as I am aware, the only study of Sanjay that has been published. It has to be approached with some caution, however. It is littered with quotations, the majority of which are unattributed and unsourced. The only help in investigating Mehta's sources is in the two-page 'Bibliography (Books only)'.
3. See Krishna Kumar Birla, *Brushes with History: An Autobiography* (New Delhi: Penguin Viking, 2007), 164.
4. Bipan Chandra, *In the Name of Democracy: JP Movement and the Emergency* (New Delhi: Penguin Books, 2003), 23; Nayantara Sahgal, *Indira Gandhi: Her Road to Power*

(New York: Frederick Ungar Publishing Co. 1982), 54–55; Uma Vasudev, *Two Faces of Indira Gandhi* (New Delhi: Vikas Publishing House, 1977), 106. K. K. Birla relates that, according to Sanjay, Rajni Patel, Barooah and Siddhartha Shankar Ray (the chief minister of West Bengal) advised Mrs Gandhi that the Maruti affair was giving her a bad name. She asked Sanjay to close the business down, but Birla talked her out of the idea (Birla, *Brushes*, 165–66). Despite the scandal associated with the project, Tripathi and Jumani, in their *Concise Oxford History of Indian Business*, manage to portray the Maruti debacle as something of a success story undertaken by Mrs Gandhi's 'irrepressible' son (Dwijendra Tripathi and Jyoti Jumani, *The Concise Oxford History of Indian Business* [New Delhi: Oxford University Press, 2008], 203–4).

5.   See Vasudev, *Two Faces*, 145.

6.   According to C. P. Bhambri, 'Sanjay was a *goonda* [gangster]. He represented no one', Interview with the author 4 November 2014.

7.   Mehta, *Sanjay Story*, 92 and 110. The first quote from 'the papers', the second from Ashok Nigam.

8.   Interview with the *Tribune*, 3 January 1976 in Nehru Memorial Museum and Library (henceforward NMML): P. N. Haksar papers. Instalments I and II, V Press Clippings, File Number 5 ('Related to the various activities of Sanjay Gandhi'). Shaibal Gupta recently pointed out that 'the increasing clout of Sanjay ensured that "old hand" and "ideology-driven" leaders were marginalized, and businessmen, inheritors of princely states and persons of doubtful character were inducted into the party' ('End of Ideology', *Frontline*, XXXI, no. 9 (3–16 May 2014): 12).

9.   Christopher Andrew and Vasili Mitrokhin, *The Mitrokhin Archive II: The KGB and the World* (London: Allen Lane, 2005), 329; Chandra, *Name*, 198.

10.   Ferdinand E. Marcos, *The Democratic Revolution in the Philippines* (New Jersey: Prentice-Hall International, 1974), 2.

11.   Mehta, *Sanjay Story*, 136; Birla, *Brushes*, 178.

12.   P. N. Dhar, *Indira Gandhi, the 'Emergency', and Indian Democracy* (New Delhi: Oxford India Paperbacks, 2001), 317–8; see also Vernon Hewitt, *Political Mobilisation and Democracy in India: States of Emergency* (New York: Routledge, 2008), 97. Mehta says that the Prime Minister's House was 'a parallel government' (*Sanjay Story*, 123). Sumit Chakravartty (then a *Patriot* correspondent, today the editor of *Mainstream*) told the author:

>   'He was a very politically powerful figure, no doubt about it… . He was issuing orders, he was sitting in the PMO—though he never wanted to speak much, he was a man of few words … but he knew how to govern in this form, in an authoritarian form.' (Interview with the author, 8 November 2014)

13.   NMML Oral History project: Janak Raj Jai (interviewee), recorded by S. L. Manchanda and Usha Prasad (interviewers), 10 November 1994. Malhotra argues that 'Indira Gandhi's dynasty building and the Emergency went hand in hand. Sanjay's power was more than considerable even earlier. Behind the ramparts of the Emergency it became uncontestable' (Inder Malhotra, 'Indira Gandhi: An Overview', in *A Centenary History of the Indian National Congress. Volume V: 1964– 1984*, ed. Aditya Mukherjee (New Delhi: Academic Foundation, 2011), 53).

14.   NMML: P. N. Haksar papers. Instalments I and II, V Press Clippings, File Number 5. Haksar notes Sanjay's misbehaviour as early as 1967, on a visit to the Soviet Union

with Nehru and his mother. However, in a letter to the *New York Times* in April 1976, he denied 'the alleged escapades of the Prime Minister's son (Sanjay) and my alleged involvement in getting him out of situations' (NMML: P. N. Haksar papers. Instalment III. II: Subject Files. File Number 385).

15. Mehta, *Sanjay Story*, 107–10 (The first quotation is unattributed); Amarjit Kaur and Arjub Dev, interviews with the author, 15 January 2014. Chandra comments that these people 'had all the making of stormtroopers ... to be used to physically suppress his [Sanjay's] opponents, in or outside Congress' (Chandra, *Name*, 198).

16. Interview with *Tribune*, 3 January 1976 in Haksar's Sanjay Gandhi file (NMML: P. N. Haksar papers. Instalments I and II, V Press Clippings, File Number 5).

17. 'Emergency a boon to Youth Congress: Sanjay', *Hindustan Times*, 29 December 1975 in Haksar's Sanjay Gandhi file (NMML: P. N. Haksar papers. Instalments I and II, V Press Clippings, File Number 5).

18. Lloyd I. Rudolph and Susanne Hoeber Rudolph, *In Pursuit of Lakshmi: The Political Economy of the Indian State* (Hyderabad: Orient Longman, 1987), 140; Mehta, *Sanjay Story*, 113.

19. The exact points vary from author to author. This version is taken from an AICC circular of 23 July 1976 in Moin A. Zaidi, ed. *The Encyclopaedia of the Indian National Congress. Volume Twenty-four, 1976–1977: Amid Encircling Gloom*, (New Delhi: S. Chand and Company Ltd, 1984), 190–91. But see also Vasudev, *Two Faces*, 144; Ramachandra Guha, *India After Gandhi* (London: Picador, 2007), 511; Mehta, *Sanjay Story*, 112.

20. AICC circular, 23 July 1976 in *Encyclopaedia of the INC, Volume 24*, 190–91.

21. Indira Gandhi's speech to a conference of chief ministers, 18 January 1977 in Indira Gandhi, *Selected Speeches and Writings of Indira Gandhi. Volume III: September 1972– March 1977* (New Delhi: Ministry of Information and Broadcasting, Government of India, 1984), 396.

22. Indira Gandhi, *My Truth*, presented by Emmanuel Pouchpadass (New Delhi: Vision Books, 1981), 165. In all likelihood, the more personal (and, therefore, easier) nature of the five points initially came as something of a relief to many Congress officials.

23. Mehta, *Sanjay Story*, 104; Hewitt, *Political Mobilisation*, 141; Vasudev, *Two Faces*, 117.

24. Mehta, *Sanjay Story*, 103.

25. Ibid., 115.

26. The Youth Congress convention is covered in Mehta, *Sanjay Story*, 125–29, from which the following account and quotations are taken.

27. Chandra, *Name*, 195.

28. Mehta, *Sanjay Story*, 111.

29. 'Truth Will Prevail,' *Amrita Bazar Patrika*, 2 December 1975 in Haksar's Sanjay Gandhi file (NMML: P. N. Haksar papers. Instalments I and II, V Press Clippings, File Number 5).

30. NMML Oral History Project: Mandhu Dandavate (interviewee) recorded by Usha Prasad (interviewer) 12 December 2000, 270.

31. Ayub Syed quoted (but not referenced) in Mehta, *Sanjay Story*, 136–37; candidate numbers in Rudolph, *Lakshmi*, 141. Most of the 'Youth Congress' candidates were soundly defeated (Mehta, *Sanjay Story*, 137).

32. All in CPI, *Consembly Move and Democratic Fight-Back* (New Delhi: Communist Party Publication, 1976), 15–19.

33. Mohit Sen, 'Positive Trends Gaining the Upper Hand in India', *World Marxist Review* 19, no. 8 (August 1976): 31.

34.   'Congress Trends: Some Frank Views', *Link*, 28 November 1976, 10.

35.   'An Eventful and Portentous Year', *Link*, 2 January 1976, 9.

36.   The editors of *Link* and its associated paper *Patriot* refused to report on Sanjay's activities at all. *Patriot* was denied government advertising as punishment for this transgression (Chandra, *Name*, 159; Mohit Sen, *A Traveller and the Road: The Journey of an Indian Communist* (New Delhi: Rupa & Co., 2003), 355). Sumit Chakravartty told the author: 'Even I remember there was a photograph in which Sanjay Gandhi was most prominent but they somehow managed to arrange that he was not shown … After all, who is Sanjay Gandhi? Why should he be given this publicity?' (Interview with the author, 8 November 2014).

37.   Sen pointed out that 'Lack of ideology, and much more the making of a cult and fetish about nonideology, helps slippery customers to slip away' (Mohit Sen, *Congress Socialism: Appraisal and Appeal* (New Delhi: Communist Party Publication, December 1976), 5–7).

38.   CPI, *Consembly*, 10; Sen, *Traveller*, 354. The CPI was not alone in suspecting US support for Sanjay—see Dhar, *Indira Gandhi*, 322; Mehta, *Sanjay Story*, 88.

39.   Mehta, *Sanjay Story*, 131–34; Chandra, *Name*, 212.

40.   This section was certainly what caught the attention of his mother, the government and the Party itself. In fact, Sanjay's remarks on the economy were equally significant and will be examined in the next chapter.

41.   Vasudev, *Two Faces*, 207; this is taken from 'The entire, unexpurgated, original, tape-recorded interview' (109).

42.   Mrs Gandhi's Note in Dhar, *Indira Gandhi*, 326–28. Haksar was, as ever, keeping an eye on these events. His file on Sanjay reveals that he had the entire interview telexed to him (31 pages)—probably before it was published (Haksar's Sanjay Gandhi file, NMML: P. N. Haksar papers. Instalments I and II, V Press Clippings, File Number 5). See also Andrew and Mitrokhin, *KGB*, 329.

43.   Dhar, *Indira Gandhi*, 324.

44.   *Indian Express*, 29 August 1975 in Haksar's Sanjay Gandhi file (NMML: P. N. Haksar papers. Instalments I and II, V Press Clippings, File Number 5). The CPI's CNS also carried Sanjay's apology (CNS Number 429, 29 August 1975).

45.   David Selbourne, *Through the Indian Looking-glass* (London: Zed Press, 1992), 18.

46.   Mehta, *Sanjay Story*, 129–30.

47.   See Chandra, *Name*, 332 (note 12).

48.   CPI, Political Review Report, *Documents of the Eleventh Congress of the Communist Party of India, Bhakna Nagar, Bhatinda, 31 March to 7 April 1978* (New Delhi: Communist Party Publication, July 1978), 65. N. K. Krishnan wrote after the Emergency that the campaign was launched 'by Sanjay Gandhi and his coterie followed by Indira Gandhi herself and sections of sycophantic Congress Leaders' (N. K. Krishnan, 'Our Tasks in the Context of the New Situation in India', *World Marxist Review* XX, no. 11 (November 1977): 80). See also, Stanley A. Kochanek, 'The Coalition Strategies and Tactics of Indian Communism', in *Coalition Strategies of Marxist Parties*, ed. Trond Gilberg (Durham & London: Duke University Press, 1989), 224; Mohammed Yunus (senior civil servant) in Vasudev, *Two Faces*, 133.

49.   Dange in *Link*, 9 January 1977, 2; CEC resolution (16 January 1977) in P. C. Joshi Archive (JNU), Communism in India, 'Misuse of the Emergency', File Number 1977/909E. The CPI's 11th Congress declared that Mrs Gandhi 'brought consciously the so-called five-point program of Sanjay Gandhi, especially the compulsory

sterilization scheme, to the forefront to sidetrack implementation of the 20-point program. She thus finally fell in for the World Bank recipe for ending poverty' (CPI, *Documents of the Eleventh Congress*, 57.

50.   See CPI, *Consembly Move*, 23 and 29; Joseph Varkey, 'The CPI—Congress Alliance in India', *Asian Survey* 19, no. 9 (September 1979): 886. For the example of Chief Minister Nandini Satpathy in Orissa, see *Link*, 28 November 1976, 14; 26 December 1976, 1; 19 December 1976, 19.

51.   CPI, *Consembly Move*, 10.

52.   CPI, *Consembly Move*, 23 and 17.

53.   CPI, *Consembly Move*, 23 and 27.

54.   Devesh Kapur, John P. Lewis and Richard Webb, *The World Bank: Its First Half Century* (Washington: The Brookings Institution, 1997), 295; Mehta, *Sanjay Story*, 143–44. It was as part of the campaign in the pre-Emergency period that the famous offer of transistor radios in return for sterilisation was first made (Mehta, *Sanjay Story*, 141).

55.   Shah Commission of Inquiry, *Third and Final Report* (New Delhi: Government of India Press, 1978), 153.

56.   Mrs Gandhi cited in Shah Commission, *Third and Final Report*, 154. Her words were repeated in an AICC circular on 3 June 1976 (Encyclopaedia of the INC, Volume 23, 180).

57.   'Family Planning', Economic Policy Resolution, 75th session of the INC, 31 December 1975 to 1 January 1976 in Moin A. Zaidi, ed. *The Encyclopaedia of the Indian National Congress. Volume 23, 1974–1975: The Lengthening Shadows* (New Delhi: S. Chand and Company Ltd, 1984), 454.

58.   Shah Commission, *Third and Final Report*, 158.

59.   Ibid., 155.

60.   Mehta, *Sanjay Story*, 151.

61.   Dhar says that the issue was 'a turning point in Sanjay's political ascendancy' (Dhar, *Indira Gandhi*, 323).

62.   NMML Oral History Project: Madhu Dandavate, 226.

63.   Mehta, *Sanjay Story*, 150–51.

64.   NMML: P. N. Haksar papers, Subject File Number 57. Note to the Prime Minister as Principal Secretary, 1977, 16.

65.   Hewitt, *Political Mobilisation*, 140; Chandra, *Name*, 203; Mehta, *Sanjay Story*, 153.

66.   Shah Commission, *Third and Final Report*, 155.

67.   Maharashtra Joint Director of Family Planning circular, 30 September 1976 in Shah Commission, *Third and Final Report*, 164.

68.   NMML Oral History project: Madhu Dandavate, 225–26.

69.   'UP: Order on Family Planning', *Link*, 4 July1976, 4. This was reported without comment.

70.   Mehta, *Sanjay Story*, 158–59.

71.   Mehta's summary of the Lieutenant-Governor's statement (Ibid., 157–58).

72.   Shah Commission, *Third and Final Report*, 165.

73.   NMML Oral History project: Janak Raj Jai, 265.

74.   P. N. Haksar papers, Subject File Number 57. Note to the Prime Minister as Principal Secretary, 1977, 29–31.

75.   Mehta, *Sanjay Story*, 163–65.

76.   P. N. Haksar papers, Subject File Number 57. Note to the Prime Minister as Principal Secretary, 1977, 14.

77. Birla, *Brushes*, 177–78.
78. P. N. Haksar papers, Subject File Number 57. Note to the Prime Minister as Principal Secretary, 1977, 14.
79. Speech at chief ministers' conference in New Delhi, 18 January 1977 in Indira Gandhi, *Selected Speeches and Writings of Indira Gandhi. Volume III: September 1972– March 1977* (New Delhi: Ministry of Information and Broadcasting, Government of India, 1984), 398.
80. Chandra, *Name*, 211.
81. 'Strategy to Curb Population Growth', *Link*, 25 April 1976, 7.
82. 'Haryana: Family Planning Drive', *Link*, 22 August 1976, 21.
83. *Link*, 12 September 1976, 2.
84. CPI, *Report and Resolutions of the Meeting of the Central Executive Committee of the Communist Party of India, New Delhi 24–27 October 1976* (New Delhi: Communist Party Publication, November 1976), 23–24 and 39–40; 'Decade of Hope' (Report on the National Federation of Women 9th Congress), *Link*, 17 October 1976, 31; 'CPI's Hopes and Fears' (Report on CEC meeting), *Link*, 7 November 1976, 14; CEC Resolution, 16 January 1977 in P. C. Joshi Archive (JNU), Communism in India, 'Misuse of the Emergency', File Number 1977/909E.
85. Amarjit Kaur, interview with the author, 15 January 2014.
86. CPI, *Consembly Move*. Mohit Sen wrote at about the same time: 'One would like to ask whether anything like the present drive for family planning was or is being planned for the implementation of land reform, ending bonded labour, etc.' (Sen, *Congress Socialism*, 25).
87. Dhar, *Indira Gandhi*, 324. See also Chandra, *Name*, 211.
88. CNS, 4 November 1976.
89. Shah Commission, *Third and Final Report*, 169; Dhar, *Indira Gandhi*, 324–26.
90. CNS, 26 October 1976.
91. CPI, Political Review Report, *Documents of the Eleventh Congress*, 60. See also Anil Rajimwale, *Glimpses of CPI History through Party Congresses* (New Delhi: People's Publishing House, 2005), 106.
92. Shah Commission, *Third and Final Report*, 209. Janak Raj Jai confirms Sanjay's responsibility (NMML Oral History project: Janak Raj Jai, 263).
93. Shah Commission, *Third and Final Report*, 209.
94. CPI, *Resolutions and Report Adopted by the National Council of the Communist Party of India (New Delhi, August 1975)* (New Delhi: Communist Party Publication, September 1975), 26. See also Rajeshwara Rao, 'Duty of Patriotic Parties', *Link*, 26 January 1976, 25.
95. The authorities in Agra, for example, were told by Sanjay 'with immediate effect … to remove cattle from the streets, [as well as] unauthorized structures and beggars'—and to do it before the tourist season started (Shah Commission, *Third and Final Report*, 209).
96. Mehta, *Sanjay Story*, 121–2.
97. Mehta, *Sanjay Story*, 122. Although a more or less suitable relocation area was made ready for Mrs Thatcher's visit in September 1976 (Primila Lewis, *Reason Wounded: An Experience of India's Emergency* (London: George Allen & Unwin Ltd, 1978), 26–27).
98. CPI, *Report and Resolutions Adopted by the National Council of the Communist Party of India (Trivandrum, 7 to 11 February 1976)* (New Delhi: Communist Party Publication, 1976), 19.

99. Paul Brass, *The Politics of India since Independence* (New Cambridge History of India, Volume IV, Part 1) (Cambridge: Cambridge University Press, 1994), 42–43.

100. Chandra, *Name*, 208–9. See also Hewitt, *Political Mobilisation*, 139–40; Mehta, *Sanjay Story*, 116–23.

101. Mehta, *Sanjay Story*, 123 (undated, unsourced).

102. CPI, Political Review Report, *Documents of the Eleventh Congress*, 60.

103. CEC Resolution on Misuse of Emergency, 27 October 1976 in P. C. Joshi Archive (JNU), Communism in India, 'Misuse of the Emergency', File Number 1977/909E.

104. CEC Resolution, 16 January 1977 in JNU: P. C. Joshi Archive, File on 'Misuse of the Emergency', File Number 909E, 1977.

105. The Party opposed amendments to strengthen the MISA in the Lok Sabha in January 1976 (*Link*, 1 February 1976, 2).

106. CEC Resolution, 16 January 1977 in P. C. Joshi Archive (JNU), Communism in India, 'Misuse of the Emergency', File Number 1977/909E. See also CNS 15 January 1977; CPI, *Report and Resolutions of the Meeting*, 26 and 37; CPI, *Consembly Move*, 11; *Link*, 29 August 1976, 7.

107. According to his wife, Maneka, Sanjay wanted the elections put off until the economy 'stabilised' (Hewitt, *Political Mobilisation*, 146).

108. CPI, *Consembly Move*, 21 and 34–37.

109. Chandra, *Name*, 165–66.

110. CPI, *Report and Resolutions Adopted*, 13; CPI, *Reports and Resolution Adopted by the National Council of the Communist Party of India. Hyderabad, 4–8 August 1976* (New Delhi: Communist Party Publication, 1976), 25; 'Towards Major Reform of Constitution', *Link*, 18 July 1976, 8. *Link,* however, pointed out that the committee's recommendation 'to include agriculture in the list of subjects on which the Centre can have a say' (thus, breaking the hold of the states over land reform) had been 'quietly ditched' by Congress. The editorial concluded: 'It is of course nice to be a Socialist Republic without any commitments to socialism' (*Link*, 27 June 1976, 7).

111. Dhar, *Indira Gandhi*, 337.

112. CNS, 23 October 1976; CPI, *Consembly Move*, 5, 11, 18–19.

113. Rajeshwara Rao to Indira Gandhi, 23 October 1976 in Dhar, *Indira Gandhi*, 340. CNS noted at the end of October: 'The Communist Party of India has opposed the move to extend the life of the Lok Sabha by one year and called for elections to be held on schedule' (CNS, 30 October 1976).

114. The communists, not unnaturally, took some credit for this: 'The forthright position taken by the CPI had a salutary effect. The plotters now knew that they were not going to have an easy-go' (CPI, *Consembly Move*, 18).

115. The Central Executive Committee reported one day before the Emergency was to end: 'The CPI's attack on a section of the Congress leadership led to a counter-attack by the Congress leadership as a whole' (reported in 'Evolving Alignments', *Link*, 23 January 1977, 18).

116. Indira Gandhi, *My Truth*, 165.

117. Sen, *Traveller*, 356. This was after Mohit Sen had returned from visits to Moscow, Prague and East Berlin.

118. CPI, *Murder of Truth: Anti-CPI Barrage Exposed* (New Delhi: Communist Party Publication, 1976), 13–14.

119.   Mehta, *Sanjay Story*, 131. The speech lasted 100 minutes, according to Mehta. Varkey says that it was 'well-publicized' (Varkey, 'CPI Congress Alliance', 886).

120.   Kochanek, 'Coalition Strategies', 224; Francine R. Frankel, *India's Political Economy, 1947–1977: The Gradual Revolution* (Princeton: Princeton University Press, 1978), 567; Chandra, *Name*, 221. For a communist reply to the Quit India charges, see M. Basavapunnaiah, *Quit India Call and the Role of the Communists* (New Delhi: National Book Centre, 1984).

121.   *Hindustan Times*, 24 December 1976 reported by CNS, 10 January 1977.

122.   Indira Gandhi, *My Truth*, 164–65.

123.   *Indian Express*, 5 January 1977.

124.   CNS, 18 December 1976.

125.   CEC Resolution, 15 January 1977 in P. C. Joshi Archive (JNU), 'Misuse of the Emergency', Communism in India, File Number 1977/909E.

126.   The story was dutifully reported nationally by *The Hindu* and *The Indian Express* (CNS, 13 January 1977).

127.   CNS, 17 January 1977.

128.   Mehta, *Sanjay Story*, 136. While Sanjay's assertion is certainly untrue—the communists did not exercise that kind of influence on his mother—it indicates his opinion of their attitude.

129.   CPI, *Consembly Move*, 13 and 32. See also CPI, *Report and Resolutions Adopted*, 15–17.

130.   CPI, *Reports and Resolution Adopted*, 24 and 30; CPI, *Report and Resolutions of the Meeting*; CEC Resolution, 16 January 1977 in P. C. Joshi Archive (JNU), Communism in India, 'Misuse of the Emergency', File Number 1977/909E; Varkey, 'CPI Congress Alliance', 886–87.

131.   'Evolving Alignments', *Link*, 23 January 1977, 18.

132.   CPI, *Report and Resolutions Adopted*, 45 (copy in P. C. Joshi Archive (JNU), Communism in India, File Number 1976/880).

6

Aftermath

In the elections of March 1977, which brought the Emergency to an end, the CPI supported neither the Congress nor the newly formed Janata party (hastily cobbled together from elements of the opposition). No electoral arrangements were made with either party. The attitude towards the Congress was in part explained by the fact that the CPI was still demanding the release of some hundreds of its members, arrested under Maintenance of Internal Security Act (MISA) and the Defence of India Rule (DIR).[1] The Party's election manifesto supported the lifting of all repression associated with the Emergency, the extension of democracy, the establishment of popular committees to implement land reform and 'other democratic measures'. It urged voters to 'cast their votes for the candidates of the CPI and other progressive and democratic forces.' But the Congress was no longer listed among these forces.[2]

In the turbulent debate into which the Party now entered, simply leaving out the Congress was now no longer a sufficiently critical attitude towards its erstwhile ally for some members of the NC. Biswanath Mukherjee, Geeta Mukherjee and Kanai Bhowmik wrote later:

> The party supported the emergency not only while it lasted, but even when it was for the time being withdrawn and election declared. We did not come out full-throated against the emergency and against Indira Gandhi who had imposed it. On the contrary, we decided to have [an] electoral adjustment with the Congress led by her.[3]

But there was little that could deliver the CPI from a crushing electoral defeat at this stage. In 1971, the Party received 4.73 per cent of the national vote, which gave it 23 Lok Sabha seats. In 1977, its vote was reduced to 2.8 per cent and seven seats. The Congress was roundly defeated and thrown out of office to be replaced by a Janata party government. At this point, according to Mohit Sen, from his position within the CPI leadership:

> Gloom and panic descended on Ajoy Bhavan [the CPI's headquarters in Delhi]. It was as if it was the end of the world.... The whole mood of

the majority of the leaders was one, of how to escape responsibility for the setback, the CPI had suffered. Who was to be made the scapegoat?[4]

Sen contends that that honour was to go to the advocates of Congress/CPI unity, and in particular to the venerable, but now largely honorary Party chairman, Shripad Amit Dange. This was certainly going to be the case, but not yet awhile. The first resolution of the NC, after the election, combined some self-criticism with the main elements of the Party's critique of Congress and the Emergency, which had been in place before the election was called. The resolution drew some comfort from the 'massive mandate' the election represented against 'the distortions and departures from democratic processes and institutions by the leadership of Smt Indira Gandhi' as well as the 'stunning blow' delivered to 'the extra-constitutional centre of personal power' (that is, Sanjay). The result was not a verdict against progressive policies, the communists argued. The Janata Party—which was certainly opposed to those policies—had won due to the absence of a national Left and democratic alternative. The CPI's prospects had also been damaged by the 'vicious campaign of slanders and abuse launched . . . by Sanjay Gandhi and his caucus, followed by Smt Indira Gandhi and ... sycophantic Congress leaders' and by the fact that 'in the mind of large sections of the masses our demarcation from the Congress became blurred.'[5]

The NC identified further errors. Once the negative features of the Emergency had become clear, it was a mistake not to call for its end. Leaving 'vast emergency powers' with the state was dangerous and it was wrong to think that the Emergency could be used 'to bring about progressive shifts in the state power in a national democratic direction'. The progressive nature of the national bourgeoisie and the Congress leadership had been overestimated. Finally, the Party had tried 'to avoid confrontation with the Indira Gandhi government'.[6]

After the election, the CPI was faced with a Right-wing government in which, according to Krishnan, 'the objectives of socialism, planning, industrialisation, of giving the public sector the commanding heights in the economy and radical agrarian reforms are all being denigrated.'[7] Yet, the Party's most pressing task was an analysis of its role in the Emergency and the recalibration of its relationship with the Congress. The first CEC after the Emergency, despite being subject to 'tirades against Indira Gandhi by almost everybody', produced three positions on the question.[8] The main leadership under Rajeshwara Rao argued that support for the

Emergency should have ended in mid-1976, but remained silent on the Party's initial support for it and on the future of an alliance with Congress. A group around Dange reiterated that the Emergency was a regrettable necessity—but that the alliance with Congress was still necessary and should remain. A third group around Biswanath Mukherjee, Satyapal Dang and A. P. Bardhan, which had earlier criticised the Party's support of the Emergency, declared that the support had been wrong from the start and had turned the Party into an 'appendage' of Congress. The Congress/CPI alliance should therefore end. Sen comments that 'this extreme view at that time received no support'. There seemed to be consensus that the Party should certainly have withdrawn its support in early 1976—at the time when Sanjay was settling into positions of power.[9]

Appeals to progressives in the Congress continued at an official level, despite the fact that the communists regarded the Congress as still dominated by 'the reactionary caucus' around Sanjay.[10] Rajeshwara Rao said that 'there are democratic forces inside the Congress and democratic elements within the Janata Party'—though he warned that 'the main components of reaction are united in the Janata party.' Congress remained a special case—and it was 'a good sign that a struggle is taking place inside the Congress for liberating [it] from authoritarian tendencies which brought disaster on it.'[11] Subsequent NC meetings endorsed these positions. Writing after the April NC, Krishnan noted that it acknowledged its mistakes but also recognised the struggle of 'the Congress Party Left and democratic forces' against 'the Sanjay Gandhi caucus and its reactionary policies.' Joint work between the CPI and the Congress therefore 'assumed tremendous importance'.[12] The July NC meeting also referred to the struggle of the Left against the caucus and instructed that 'unity with the left and democratic forces inside the Congress and the masses supporting it has to be maintained and extended.'[13]

But things were not proceeding smoothly within the leadership. The Party leaders called a national congress for March–April 1978 in Bhatinda (now Bathinda) in Punjab. It had been three years since the last congress in early 1975—before the Emergency was declared. The General Secretary wrote the traditional 'Political Review Report', along the consensual lines outlined above.[14] Party leader, Bhupesh Gupta presented an alternative report premised on the argument that support for the Emergency had been wrong from the start and that this was the source of all subsequent errors. After vigorous discussion between supporters of Rao and those of Gupta in the Party Secretariat, the Political Review Report was altered to conform to Gupta's version. Sen says, 'The Emergency and the entire episode of the CPI's cooperation with the Congress was condemned bell, book and candle.' He continues:

> The discussion in the Party in the run up to the Party Congress saw the balance tilt increasingly in favour of the strategy to use denunciation of the Emergency to repudiate the strategy of collaboration with Congress and shift to a strategy of anti-Congressism and unity with other parties of the Left, in particular with [the] CPI(M).[15]

The 11th CPI Congress gathered in Bhatinda at the end of March 1978. The Party membership was recorded as 546,343. At the previous Congress, in early 1975, it had been 355,525.[16] The revised Political Review Report, covering the period from February 1975 to December 1977 was presented. The Party's activities during the Emergency dominated the proceedings in a debate that lasted for three days.[17] The main thrust of the Report was now that it had been wrong in its analysis of the Congress, of the 1969 Congress split and of Indira Gandhi. The view that the split was one 'between the anti-imperialist, democratic sections of the bourgeoisie and the pro-imperialist, anti-communist sections' was mistaken. Far from representing the former, Mrs Gandhi 'was trying to salvage bourgeois rule, Congress power and her own position'. She had 'built up a caucus with some unscrupulous junior ministers and officers to assist her in running the government'. It was she who promoted Sanjay, who 'soon became the centre of the reactionary anti-communist caucus, some members of which maintained close links with US agencies.'[18] The Party had become mesmerised by the Congress government's progressive foreign policy and had forgotten that 'a progressive foreign policy cannot eventually be safeguarded without progressive internal policies.'[19]

For these two reasons—the overestimation of Mrs Gandhi's Congress and of its foreign policy—as well as the 'fear of giving a handle to the extreme reactionary forces', the Party entered a period of non-confrontation with the government in 1975.

> The above understanding was our main mistake and as a result of this wrong understanding, we supported the emergency. Hence our support to the emergency was wrong from the beginning.[20]

In the 'turbulent and complicated situation in 1975', the Report declared 'it would have been prudent on our part to have waited to grasp the full implications of the emergency, instead of rushing to support it.'[21]

Furthermore, the opportunities to use the Emergency—and the Congress state machine—to implement progressive policies (the 20-Point programme, for example) had been greatly exaggerated. The leadership had ignored the warning signs:

> Though our entire party supported the emergency at its onset, comrades at various levels began to express doubts about the things which were developing. Instead of taking these things seriously and taking an objective view of changing developments, the central leadership continued the wrong course in a dogmatic way.[22]

The Party congress resolved that it was opposed to both the continuation of Janata Party rule and the restoration to government of the Congress. Instead, the Party would promote a 'Left and democratic alternative'—in which moves towards unity with the CPI (M) would assume a 'special importance'. However, the communists did not *equate* the Congress with Janata. This was clear in their criticism of the CPI (M), 'which takes the Janata party as its ally while painting the [Congress] as the main enemy'. The CPI's attitude to Congress, though modified, remained distinct. Despite the fact that the Congress remained dominated by Mrs Gandhi's personality cult, personal power and 'members of the old caucus', 'there are Left and Democratic sections in [the Congress] which continue to be allies of our movement'. It was necessary to adopt a positive attitude to these sections—and if this was done from 'the class point of view and in the interests of the democratic advance of the nation', past mistakes could be avoided.[23]

Emergency Events

The Congress was preceded by an intense debate, both at Party meetings and in print. NC members who had voted against the Political Review Report were given the opportunity to have their views circulated in print.[24]

We will deal with the deeper theoretical questions raised in the debate further. At the level of events in and around the Emergency period, the leadership's opponents were divided between those who wanted to take a more critical stand on the Party's activities on the one hand, and those around Dange on the other, who defended the Party's former stand against both critics and the leadership. One of the more hotly contested assertions of the leadership was that the Party pursued 'a broadly correct policy up to August 1974, that is, up to the time when JP's so-called total revolution got a setback in Bihar.' Before that, from 1969 there had been a 'glorious period for the party ... a period of great achievements.'[25] For that reason, the Political Resolution now advocated a return to the policy of 'left and democratic unity' and a 'left and democratic government' (co-operation with the Left), rather than a 'national democratic government' (co-operation with Congress).[26] The rot had set in, in August 1974, leading to the Party's support for the Emergency. Dange commented:

> The contradictions in the situation facing us and the fast-changing or unstable attitudes taken by the national bourgeoisie, and particularly by Indira Gandhi have been baffling our party leadership for a long time and more so since the emergency. In the present document itself [the Political Review Report] the confusion is seen very vividly until it culminates in the all-embracing and all-absolving formulation that everything went wrong with us when we committed 'the main mistake' of supporting the emergency as soon as it was declared. Then the resulting minor mistakes inevitably follow the logic of the main mistake.[27]

Mohit Sen, supporting Dange, told Rajeshwara Rao that the leadership's new position would turn the Party into a 'clone' of the CPI (M)—which had maintained a constant anti-Congress stance: 'I added that while there could be more than one Communist Party in the country, there was no room for two CPI (M)s.'[28]

The leadership's Report conceded that the Party's position on the national bourgeoisie, the Congress and Indira Gandhi had been 'a serious deviation from the understanding of our party program,' placing too much confidence in the national bourgeoisie and in Indira Gandhi as its representative.[29] Satyapal Dang accused the Party of remaining silent on the activities of Sanjay Gandhi because it had 'built up a theory about the necessity of not injuring the sentiments of his mother ... we refused to see the obvious hand of Indira Gandhi behind her son'.[30] Dange however remained steadfast, telling his comrades, 'in the anti-Indira hate campaign we need not ignore or distort what was good for the country in her policies and exhibit our subjective anger at our setback.'[31] Ajoy Das Gupta argued that once the government began its 'slide-back' towards World Bank-type economic policies in 1974, the Party should have been campaigning for a Left and Democratic Front to replace Congress in government. Fear of Right-reaction stopped it from doing so: 'We accordingly gave up the struggle for the overthrow of the government and [the] setting up of the alternative government of Left and Democratic unity.'[32] Biswanath Mukherjee and his co-writers maintained that the fear of the Right was exaggerated and played into the government's hands:

[T]hat a fascist coup was about to take place was a bogy raised by Indira Gandhi for her own ends. And we actually fell a prey to that, and exaggerated the apprehension to the point of blindness.[33]

Dange expresses some hesitation on the extent to which the Party should have opposed the Congress before 1975. On the question of whether it should have joined the pre-JP movement against the state government in Gujarat (led by Morarji Desai), he wrote, 'I am not sure whether we could have joined in these demands ... I am not sure.'[34] But Prakash Roy was certain that the 1977 election debacle resulted from the Party's non-confrontation policy with Congress from before 1975.[35]

The debate moved on to the Emergency itself. Dange castigated the confusion over its purpose in the Political Review Report:

The political report admits that this [the civil disobedience planned from 29 June 1975 onwards] was a right-reactionary uprising, that it was fascist in character, though everyone in it was not fascist. Even then we are advised that we should have waited to grasp the full implications of the Emergency, that is, the full implications of a mainly fascist uprising to suppress which the Emergency was supposed to have been declared.[36]

The Political Review Report argued that the Emergency was designed to curb the Left, solve the capitalist crisis at the expense of the people and subvert parliamentary democracy. Therefore, it should never have been supported.[37] Dange, as a supporter of Congress/CPI unity and of the initial stages of the Emergency, naturally had quite a different view. He maintained that the Emergency was necessary to thwart an imperialist-backed plot to overthrow the government. As the Emergency continued however, it enabled the emergence of another centre of power: 'the finance, commerce and home ministries, with their economic, political and financial links with US imperialist circles and their tentacles in the vital internal spheres of monopoly capital.' The policies of this powerful grouping were executed by the 'corrupt bureaucracy led by Sanjay Gandhi'. It was soon beyond Mrs Gandhi's control. Later it drew her in—and she became its 'public shield' for 'World Bank recipes on population, inflation and economic growth.'[38] '[T]he caucuses ... came into the open to attack the masses and in reality, to provoke them into revolt so as to pave the way for a Right-wing takeover'—at that point, support for the Emergency should have been withdrawn.[39]

Along with Dange, most of the other NC critics argued that the initial support for the Emergency was justified, but should have been withdrawn well before its official end—'at the CEC meeting of December 1975 or, at the latest, [at] the national council meeting of February 1976', according to Dange.[40] Mukherjee and his comrades were, at this stage, the exception: 'In our opinion, we should have opposed the very declaration of the Emergency from the start.'[41] As already noted, this was to be the eventual position of the leadership and of the Eleventh Congress' Political Review Report.

Theoretical Debate

Dange quickly identified the question at the heart of the whole theoretical debate.

> Our old controversies [around the 1964 CPI split] in essence were the same as we have them today. Can the national bourgeoisie really become independent of imperialism even if its own class-interests demand it? . . . Was it really interested in industrialisation which gives birth not only to profit but to the working class, which it fears? And in those days, the same question ... was put [:] whether a split has taken place in the national bourgeoisie [by which he means the Indian bourgeoisie] between its pro-imperialist and anti-imperialist sections. The question is as old as the 1948 party congress, if not earlier ... . And the 'curse' of that question comes up again and again.[42]

Dange said that the Party had usually responded in a 'left sectarian and negative' way, 'and so it is in 1978.' He added, 'but we also had short spells of Right-reformism as exceptions. And so on it goes.'[43] *Link*'s report on the Congress said: 'Differences over the "dual" role of the bourgeoisie, in a way reflect the complexity of the Indian situation. Therefore, any over-simplified and one-sided assessment of this factor leads to mistakes.' But the paper was clear. There was no split between the pro- and anti-imperialist bourgeoisie.[44]

Since the CPI had always conflated the Indian bourgeoisie and the Congress (see Chapter 1), the question of a theoretical split in the former could be quickly identified with an actual split in the latter (the split of 1969). Was the 1969 split one between the forces of Right-reaction and progressive forces? Did this in turn, reflect a split between the monopoly bourgeoisie and the national bourgeoisie? Whether the CPI had been correct to support Indira Gandhi's Congress and to include the national bourgeoisie in the ranks of the national democratic revolution, depended on the answer to these questions—as did whether it would do so in the future.

In the pre-Congress debate, those most critical of the leadership's mistakes argued that the differences within the bourgeoisie (and therefore within Congress) had been systematically over-emphasised. The progressive nature of the national bourgeoisie and Indira Gandhi's Congress had been similarly misjudged.[45] Agarwal dates this from the 1969 split. After this, the Party 'trailed behind the Congress or, in class terms, behind the national bourgeoisie represented by the Congress led by Indira Gandhi'.[46] Ghosh and Gupta pointed out that the Party consequently redefined 'Left and democratic unity' as unity between the CPI and Congress.[47] The over-estimation of the progressive character of the Congress (R) continued at the Ninth Party Congress in Cochin (in 1971). According to Satyapal Dang: 'the Cochin resolution made an incorrect assessment of the sharp differences which were emerging amongst the bourgeoisie'.[48] And again at the Tenth Congress, which urged the Party not to dwell on 'the negative side of the Indira Gandhi government'.[49] Ghosh and Gupta conclude: 'It [was] as if the differentiation within the ruling bourgeoisie would be the main axis around which the struggle for the non-capitalist path would evolve.'[50]

Dange, on the other hand, attacked the leadership for abandoning the old positions on the national bourgeoisie and the Congress. On the 1969 Congress split, he demanded, 'if this was not a split in the national [i.e. Indian] bourgeoisie what else was it?' The Congress (R), he wrote, produced nationalisation, state-built heavy industry, scientific development (including nuclear energy) and increasing friendship with the Soviet bloc. 'There is no doubt,' he concluded, 'that this split in the Congress was in a *progressive direction*.'[51] Dange was especially keen to place events in India in a global context of US imperialist aggression, which produced the attempt (through the JP Movement) to overthrow the Congress government.[52] Ghosh and Gupta countered this argument:

It would be a serious methodological error to judge the role of the national bourgeoisie with reference to almost exclusively its anti-imperialism, for this would mean identifying anti-imperialism with revolutionary potentiality, and this would lead to overestimation of the role of the national bourgeoisie.[53]

As indeed it had done. According to Ghosh and Gupta, the contradiction between the two sections of the Indian bourgeoisie 'has been pushed forward to such an absolute point that the non-monopoly national bourgeoisie is made even a constituent of the leadership of the national democratic revolution'[54]—which, it will be remembered, was, for the CPI, the current stage of the Indian revolution. The 10th Congress in early 1975 had indicated that differentiation within the bourgeoisie could 'pave the way for transition to the non-capitalist path and to national-democratic power.'[55] Various Party leaders had endorsed the leading role of the non-monopoly bourgeoisie in the national democratic revolution at the time.[56] This was why, wrote Prakash Roy, the aim of Left and democratic unity and a government of Left and democratic forces had been replaced with national-democratic unity and a government of the national-democratic front.[57] 'The idea,' said Mukherjee and his co-writers, 'that the correlation of forces can be pushed [in a] national-democratic direction under the leadership of [the] national bourgeoisie is sheer tailism and a gross violation of the party program.'[58]

What can be said about the foregoing debate on the theoretical foundations of the Party's position at this time?

Conclusion

Clearly, what was at stake here was the question that we have found the communists asking themselves since 1947: what was the current nature and stage of the Indian revolution? As I have indicated at several stages in this account, in Marxist terms, India was still going through the process of the bourgeois revolution. As was pointed out in the Introduction, historically (and again, in Marxist terms), the bourgeois revolution:

- Lays the basis for the (further) development of capitalism.
- Has often been initiated and carried through by the state.
- Is a process, not an insurrectionary act.

- Establishes the conditions, both objective (economic development) and subjective (a politically conscious and majoritarian working class), for socialism.

Furthermore, it has a dual aspect. In the first place, it allows the level of the development of the productive forces to rise, as it allows the capitalist relations of production to be fully established and developed. In the second place, it increases the size and political maturity of the working class—and this can be conducive to providing the conditions for mass democracy and lay the foundations for socialism. Whether these conditions and foundations emerge, depends on the strength of the working class movement. In the course of the bourgeois revolution, the task of that movement is to establish the strongest possible position for itself within capitalism—with regard to democracy, trade union organisation, decision-making processes, culture and so on. Karl Kautsky, the German Marxist, can give us some authority here, both from his observations of the Russian revolutions before 1917 and his participation in the German one of 1918–19. In 1904, he wrote:

> A revolution in Russia could not, for the present, establish a socialist regime. The country's economic conditions are too immature for that. Initially, it would be able only to bring into being a democratic regime, behind which, however, a strong and impetuous proletariat would stand, pressing forward. Through its efforts, this proletariat would be able to achieve considerable concessions.[59]

The CPI's 'national democratic revolution' can be seen as an attempt to campaign for and establish these 'considerable concessions' within the framework of post-independence India—which had not the material basis for socialism and remained in the midst of its bourgeois revolution. That is to say, the national democratic revolution aimed at establishing the most Left-wing version of the bourgeois revolution—with the workers' and peasants' movements occupying positions of considerable power in a democratic framework—that was possible at the time.[60]

Back in the inner-Party debates of 1955–56, the Rightists (such as Bhowani Sen, P. C. Joshi and Ravi Narayan Reddy) argued that 'the basic tasks of the Indian revolution were anti-imperialism and anti-feudalism and not anti-capitalism; and India was still in the stage of completing the bourgeois democratic revolution.'[61] That revolution would have the support of workers, peasants, the middle classes and the national bourgeoisie.

According to Sen and Reddy, 'Nehru represented and was the leader of the progressive sections of the big bourgeoisie, which was interested in independent capitalist development and which was no longer collaborating with imperialism.'[62] Despite its compromises with the reactionary sections of the bourgeoisie, as well as pro-imperialist and pro-feudal sections of the ruling class, the Nehru government was not the main enemy, as it had made a positive turn in economic policy (planning, etc.) and was asserting India's national independence.[63] The CPI Right wanted to form a united front with the national bourgeoisie (represented by Nehru and progressive Congress leaders) to bring about a united front and a 'national democratic' government.[64] That was the national democratic revolution—a bourgeois revolution in which the Left contributed to the establishment of a progressive capitalism. This concept was faithfully reflected in the 1964 Programme—the programme adopted after the split with the CPI (M).[65] Sumit Chakravartty contrasted the CPI position with that of the CPM in this way:

> On the one hand, the CPM was [advocating] a people's democratic revolution led by the working class. The CPI's position was [for] a national democratic revolution in which the working class and the bourgeoisie will co-exist—or share power. This was countered by the CPM saying this was reformist. But the CPI said no, it is Marxist. Why? Because neither the bourgeoisie nor the working class would accept the hegemony or leadership of the other side.[66]

In a pamphlet explaining the Programme, P. C. Joshi wrote:

> The N[ational] D[emocratic] F[ront] relies upon the planned and skilful combination of parliamentary initiative and intervention along with a rising militant mass movement to influence the course of existing Government policies … the task of the NDF is to unrelentingly organize parliamentary and mass pressure to push all the Rightist elements outside the Government and render impossible any weakening or sabotage in the implementation of national policies … A full-fledged National [Democratic Front] Government … will rely overwhelmingly on the Left progressive forces inside Parliament and on the resurgent popular mass kept constantly mobilized and organized outside, ready to give it all possible support.[67]

Whether this second aspect of the bourgeois revolution is achieved or not, its first aspect—the development of capitalism—continues regardless. Bearing in mind Marx's injunction that:

No social order is ever destroyed before all the productive forces for which it is sufficient have been developed, and new superior relations of production never replace older ones before the material conditions for their existence have matured within the framework of the old society.[68]

I would argue that the bourgeois revolution is completed when it has established the material basis (sufficient abundance) for socialism.[69] As I pointed out in the Introduction, bourgeois revolutions from the late nineteenth century were often kick-started by the national state. They then proceeded in the common—but contingent—interests of the state and the bourgeoisie (defence of the state for the former and accumulation of capital for the latter). But in the final stages of the bourgeois revolution (when sufficient abundance is being achieved), the interests of the state and capital diverge. Under the pressures of globalisation, states strive to protect what remains of their national economies. Capital strains to escape the national priorities of the state.[70]

At this point, the Left-wing aspect of the bourgeois revolution—the CPI's national democratic revolution, for example—becomes both impossible and irrelevant. It is no longer possible to steer the bourgeois revolution in a progressive direction, or to establish positions of power for the workers' and peasants' movements. It is too late.

This is what was happening in 1975. The year and its events mark the beginnings of the final stages of the bourgeois revolution in India: the possibility of material abundance (albeit chronically unequally distributed) and the initial globalisation of India's capital. It was the beginning of a messy and confusing transition from a state-run to an open economy in which it was extremely difficult to correctly identify the forces in play.

If this is accepted, then it is immediately obvious that in and after 1975, the CPI's theoretical premises, its strategy, its tactical decisions and the positions taken in the debate that ensued around them were mostly wrong. The party identified a division within the bourgeoisie and the Congress between the national bourgeoisie, along with its political representatives on the one hand, and the monopoly bourgeoisie and Right-reaction on the other. For part of the period, I have examined the division was non-existent and for part of it, misplaced. During the freedom struggle and for the first 20 years or so of free India, the Indian bourgeoisie was clearly in favour of, and working towards the completion of the bourgeois revolution. Sections of the bourgeoisie, that were beholden to foreign capital ('compradors') and therefore, indifferent to India's bourgeois revolution—were insignificant. Obviously, the bourgeoisie's primary aim was to achieve what I have described as the first aspect of the bourgeois revolution—the full establishment of capitalist relations of production. But it was content, by and large, to do this under Congress tutelage—and if that meant accepting elements of the second aspect (increasing the strength of the working class movement), so be it. The division and conflict between monopoly and non-monopoly elements of the bourgeoisie did not exist, nor was it manifested politically in division within the Congress. The division that was lying dormant in both the bourgeoisie and the Congress was one between those who were invested in the maintenance of the state economy and those who were not. Big business, at least until the early 1990s, tended to stick with the state—albeit, suitably 'internally liberalised' (with state regulation relaxed).[71] The new industries wanted to get away from the state model. In the Congress, the Left identified itself with the defence of the state economy, the Right did not. Globalisation brings this division into the open because it threatens the state economy on the one hand, and makes possible, a break from that economy into the world market for the new industries on the other. The catalyst was the economic and political crisis leading up to the Emergency in 1975. The division that emerged was one between the Congress state, together with elements of big business (and the CPI on its left flank), in opposition to the Right and the new industrialists, together with elements around Sanjay. The two sides lined up, in defence of the national economy, in the case of the former and in favour of globalisation (external liberalisation), in the case of the latter. The events of the Emergency were played out against this background.

In retrospect, it was undoubtedly correct for the communists to orient towards India's mass social-democratic formation (which is what Congress—as a political movement rather than a state—was) and to fight Right-reaction. But continuing to promote the national democratic revolution when it was no longer a possibility, produced an alliance with the Congress *state*—and thus, continuing support for the Emergency and the expectation that the state itself would enact 'national democratic' reforms.

Notes

1.   CNS, 22 January 1977.
2.   *Election Manifesto of the Communist Party of India*, P. C. Joshi Archive (JNU), Communism in India, Pamphlet 897A.

3. Biswanath Mukherjee, Geeta Mukherjee and Kanai Bhowmik, *A Critical Note on the National Committee's Draft Review Report for the Eleventh Party Congress* (New Delhi: Communist Party of India, February 1978), 12–13. This last point, according to the NC, was not true (CPI National Council, *Resolution on Lok Sabha Elections*, 3–6 April 1977. P. C. Joshi Archive (JNU), Communism in India, Pamphlet 901, 11).

4. Mohit Sen, *A Traveller and the Road: The Journey of an Indian Communist* (New Delhi: Rupa & Co., 2003), 365. In this atmosphere, the Party's CNS could not even bring itself to report that the Emergency had been ended and seems to have ceased publication at the end of January 1977. Meanwhile, no issue of *Link* appeared between 23 January and 26 June 1977.

5. CPI National Council, *Resolution on Lok Sabha Elections*, 4–6, 10.

6. CPI National Council, *Resolution on Lok Sabha Elections*, 9–10.

7. N. K. Krishnan, 'Our Tasks in the Context of the New Situation in India', *World Marxist Review*, XX, no. 11 (November 1977): 80–82.

8. Sen, *Traveller*, 368. The only account of the internal politics of the CPI after the Emergency is Sen's—on which the following section is based.

9. Sen, *Traveller*, 367–71. The differing positions will be further elaborated later in the chapter.

10. 'The Third Alternative', *Link*, 26 June 1977, 10; 'Caucus Rules Congress', *Link*, 10 July 1977, 10.

11. C. Rajeshwara Rao, 'Left and Democratic Unity the Need', *Link*, 15 August 1977, 16. In the same article, Rao criticises the CP (Marxist) for demanding that 'the CPI should … sever all connections with the progressive sections of the Congress'.

12. Krishnan, 'Our Tasks', 85.

13. This meeting also noted that 'the vast masses … have voted for the Janata Party' and that 'democratic elements within the Janata Party itself' should also be approached (CPI, *Resolutions of the National Council of Communist Party of India, New Delhi, 9–12 July 1977* (New Delhi: Communist Party Publication, July 1977), 7 and 9.

14. Again, Sen's is the only available account.

15. Sen, *Traveller*, 369–71. Sen acidly remarks 'Their remorse for their misguidance of the Party did not extend, however, to surrendering their leadership.'

16. CPI, Organisation Report, *Documents of the Eleventh Congress of the Communist Party of India, Bhakna Nagar, Bhatinda, 31 March to 7 April, 1978* (New Delhi: Communist Party Publication, July 1978), 128.

17. Anil Rajimwale, *Glimpses of CPI History through Party Congresses* (New Delhi: People's Publishing House, 2005), 104.

18. CPI, Political Review Report (henceforward PRR), Documents of the 11th Congress, 53–54, 57–58, 66–67.

19. PRR, Documents of the 11th Congress, 67.

20. Ibid.

21. Ibid., 66. Bhupesh Gupta illustrated this more prudent approach on the part of the Party leadership. According to Sen, 'He held up the forefinger of his right hand and almost shrieked that he wanted to cut it off as that was the finger that pressed the button in the Rajya Sabha supporting the resolution approving the declaration of the Emergency!' (Sen, *Traveller*, 372). This account was confirmed to the author by Sumit Chakravartty in an interview with the author on 8 November 2014.

22. PRR, Documents of the 11th Congress, 68. Gargi Chakravartty adds: 'They realised within six months the excesses and within the Party there was a lot of dissatisfaction and a kind of simmering that something needs to be done. But why did they not take

up a position? Individuals among the communists did' (Interview with the author, 6 November 2014).

23.   PRR, Documents of the 11th Congress, 36–67 and 40.

24.   See for example, the contributions of S. A. Dange, Prakash Roy, Ajoy Das Gupta and Ramanand Agarwal among others—all in P. C. Joshi Archives (JNU), Communism in India, Pamphlets.

25.   PRR, Documents of the 11th Congress, 71.

26.   CPI, Political Resolution, Documents of the 11th Congress, 36. Satyapal Dang argued that it was wrong 'to consider Congress as a force without which socialism could not be built in India' (Ramanand Agarwal and Satyapal Dang, *Critical Notes on the Draft Political Review Report for the Eleventh Congress* (New Delhi: Communist Party of India, February 1978), 20).

27.   S. A. Dange (Chairman, CPI National Council), *Some Observations on the Political Review Report* (New Delhi: Communist Party of India, March 1978 [written in February 1978]), 7. Kochanek notes 'strong opposition [to the leadership position] from a pro-Indira faction led by S. A. Dange'—which as the reader will discover below, hardly does Dange's position justice (Stanley A. Kochanek, 'The Coalition Strategies and Tactics of Indian Communism', in *Coalition Strategies of Marxist Parties*, ed. Trond Gilberg (Durham & London: Duke University Press, 1989), 225). Dange was removed from the chairmanship of the Party in 1980 and expelled in 1981. He went on to be associated with the All-India Communist Party and then the United Communist Party, both of which advocated an alliance of communists and Congress members.

28.   Sen, *Traveller*, 370.

29.   PRR, Documents of the 11th Congress, 71.

30.   Agarwal and Dang, *Critical Note*, 20.

31.   For example, Dange believed that during the Emergency 'the state sector grew stronger and wider'. Congress rhetoric aside, this was, in fact, not true (Dange, *Some Observations*, 5).

32.   Prakash Roy and Ajoy Das Gupta, *Critical Notes for the Eleventh Party Congress* (New Delhi: Communist Party of India, February 1978), 28–29.

33.   Mukherjee, Mukherjee and Bhowmik, *A Critical Note*, 4–5.

34.   Dange, *Some Observations*, 23.

35.   Roy and Das Gupta, *Critical Notes*, 22.

36.   Dange, *Some Observations*, 9.

37.   PRR, Documents of the 11th Congress, 55.

38.   Dange, *Some Observations*, 12 and 22. Mohit Sen largely agrees with Dange's version (*Traveller*, 354). The theory does rather depend on accepting that the forces against whom the Emergency was apparently aimed—forces backed by US imperialism—were then able to use the Emergency to their own ends, employing its architects (Sanjay and his mother) as their agents. As I have tried to make clear, I do not think that the Congress was beholden to either business or imperialist interests.

39.   Dange, *Some Observations*, 22.

40.   Ibid., 13. See also Roy and Das Gupta, *Critical Notes*, 18; Roy and Das Gupta, *Critical Notes*, 27.

41.   Mukherjee, Mukherjee and Bhowmik, *Critical Note*, 3. They also note 'we had been pressing for [this position] for a long time' (2). Satyapal Dang confirms that during the Emergency period, 'At least one member of the CEC more than once opined that the party must demand withdrawal of the Emergency' (Agarwal and Dang, *Critical Notes*, 23).

42.   Dange, *Some Observations*, 16.

43.   Dange, *Some Observations*, 16.

44.   'A Left Alternative,' *Link*, 9 April 1978, 10.

45.   Parimal Chandra Ghosh and Sobhanlal Datta Gupta, *A Note on the Theoretical Roots of the Mistakes in Our Party's Line: Some Comments on the Draft Review Report for the Eleventh Party Congress* (New Delhi: cyclostyled, 7 March 1978), 1; Agarwal and Dang, *Critical Notes*, 7. Sumit Chakravartty agreed, telling the author,

> some of the CPI leaders went absolutely overboard in the sense of trying to distinguish between monopoly sections of the bourgeoisie and non-monopoly sections and Mrs Gandhi was considered to be representative of the non-monopoly sections which is, I think, a bit too much. That was not the case. Some of us also supported it but this was not borne out by reality. (Interview with the author, 8 November 2014)

46.   Agarwal and Dang, *Critical Notes*, 5.

47.   Ghosh and Gupta, *A Note*, 1.

48.   Agarwal and Dang, *Critical Notes*, 15.

49.   CPI, Political Resolution, *Documents of the Tenth Congress of the Communist Party of India, Bhowanisennagar, 27 January to 2 February 1975* (New Delhi: Communist Party Publication, 1975), 185.

50.   Ghosh and Gupta, *A Note*, 8.

51.   Dange, *Some Observations*, 18.

52.   Dange, *Some Observations*, 10 and 12–13. He was critical of the Political Review Report's lack of comment on this.

> It is considered enough if the report makes us understand our complicated home situation and mainly the sins of Indira Gandhi and our mistakes…. But one might object that once you start on international events you cannot then limit them to one or two only … the discussion of our home worries will leave our delegates very little energy or time for an international review. (pp. 6–7)

53.   Ghosh and Gupta, *A Note*, 7.

54.   Ibid., 12.

55.   CPI, Political Resolution, *Documents of the 10th Congress*, 184.

56.   See for example M. Farooqui and Mohit Sen in *Party Life* X, no. 6 (7 April 1974): 25–26 and 28; M. Farooqui, *Party Life* XI, no. 1 (7 January 1975): 15.

57.   Roy and Das Gupta, *Critical Notes*, 17.

58.   Mukherjee, Mukherjee and Bhowmik, *Critical Note*, 5. Ghosh and Gupta added, 'the national bourgeoisie cannot be the leader of the national democratic revolution in the second stage of the national liberation struggle' (*A Note*, 7).

59.   Kautsky cites this 1904 article in his *The Road to Power* (Alameda: Center for Socialist History, 2007 [1909]), 13.

60.   'A left perspective, to be effective, would have had to accept the "national programme" historically evolved within the national movement but seek to accomplish a radical people's democracy and impart to the programme of industrialization a socialist direction' (Shashi Joshi, *Struggle for Hegemony in India, 1920–47. The Colonial State, the Left and the National Movement. Volume I: 1920–34* (New Delhi: SAGE Publications, 1992), 27).

61. Paraphrased by Bipan Chandra, 'A Strategy in Crisis: The CPI Debate 1955–56', *Studies in History*, Volume III, no. 1 and 2 (1981): 300.
62. Chandra, 'Strategy in Crisis', 290 and 296.
63. Ibid., 292–93.
64. Ibid., 298–99.
65. See CPI, *The Programme of the Communist Party of India. As adopted by the Seventh Congress of the Communist Party of India, Bombay 13–23 December 1964* (New Delhi: Communist Party of India, 1965). In fact, a version of it survives to this day. The current *Draft of the Party Programme* envisages 'the democratic revolution … preparing the transition to socialism. The democratic revolution has to be anti-feudal, anti-imperialist and anti-monopolist.' However: 'It will be a type of new democratic revolution, not the old type of bourgeois democratic revolution.' (CPI, *Draft of the Party Programme* [New Delhi: CPI National Council, 2012], 52.)
66. Sumit Chakravartty, interview with the author, 8 November 2014.
67. Puran Chand Joshi, *People's 'Warrior': Words and Worlds of P.C. Joshi*, ed. Gargi Chakravartty (New Delhi: Tulika Books, 2014), 250.
68. Karl Marx, Preface, *A Contribution to the Critique of Political Economy* (New Delhi: People's Publishing House, 2010 [1859]), 21.
69. There is considerable debate in orthodox Marxist circles whether this stage—in which *all* the productive forces have been developed to their maximum potential—can ever actually be reached before a change in the relations of production becomes necessary.
70. See Nigel Harris, *Of Bread and Guns: The World Economy in Crisis* (Harmondsworth: Penguin, 1983); Nigel Harris, *The Return of Cosmopolitan Capital: Globalization, the State and War* (London: IB Tauris, 2003); David Lockwood, *The Destruction of the Soviet Union: A Study in Globalization* (Houndmills: Macmillan Press Ltd, 2000).
71. See Oswald Pereira, Arindam Mukherjee and Shekhar Ghosh, 'The Ghost of the Bombay Club', *Outlook* 10 April 1996, www.outlookindia.com/printarticle.aspx?201149; Pragya Singh, 'The Home Alone Boys', *Outlook* 10 January 2011, www.outlookindia.com/printarticle.aspx?269748. Big business was forced to accede to globalisation in the 1980s and 1990s. There followed, according to Chandrasekhar and Ghosh, 'a shift in the relative balance away from established big capitalists in favour of smaller but sizeable capitalist groups or even in favour of altogether new entrants into business' (C. P. Chandrasekhar and Jayati Ghosh, *The Market That Failed: Neoliberal Economic Reform in India* (New Delhi: LeftWord Books, 2004), 33).

7

Globalisation and the Emergency

We have examined the aims, effects and excesses of the Emergency and the role that India's communists played in it. In this final chapter, I want to further illuminate the Emergency's context: the crisis of the Indian economy in the 1960s and 1970s. This will involve setting aside the issues that traditionally accompany (and sometimes obscure) the Emergency—the intent of dictatorship, the accusation of conspiracy, the aspiration to social reform and the actuality of repression. The Emergency was invoked to combat the JP movement. But the context in which it took place made it something more than an attempt to suppress a disruptive and potentially violent opposition movement. That movement resulted from an economic crisis. The economic crisis was due, in part, to the pressures of the world market bearing down on a statist economy. I will re-examine the nature of the Indian crisis and consider possible responses to it, in order to review the forces at play and their actions at the time.

As I argued in Chapter 2, the crisis in India was not unique. The state-run economy was stagnating by the late 1960s. The Indian state's refusal to open up to the world market and the bureaucratic obstacles to the expansion of private industry it had erected, indicated that the Indian economy was a standard-bearer of the national economies of the post-war era—and not of the new era of globalisation. But India was by no means alone in this respect. Globalisation weakened the capacity of national states to make national economic decisions, or decisions in 'the national interest'. The pressure on states to 'liberalise' their economies—often manifest in the advice, decisions and instructions of the World Bank and the IMF—was relentless. Some states, especially those with state-controlled or heavily state-invested economies, resisted. But resistance was expensive, damaging and dangerous. The once-mighty Soviet bloc, for example, believed it could remain isolated. Then it allowed in 'limited' market forces—and then it collapsed. Others eventually acquiesced. The process took a number of decades and its course can today be more or less clearly discerned. In 1975, it was not clear what the process was, what forces were driving it, or what its effects would be. The undermining and ultimate deconstruction of state-run economies was not foreseen. No one therefore, in India or anywhere else, had a worked-out strategy for dealing with globalisation—or even the realisation that this was the phenomenon they were facing. Most national governments, particularly in state-run economies, believed that small doses of liberalisation, which left them in control, would suffice.

The beginnings of world market pressure gave rise to the beginnings of liberalisation under Lal Bahadur Shastri, including the devaluation of the rupee. This was soon abandoned due to an electoral backlash. After electoral defeats and in battle with the Syndicate, Mrs Gandhi's wing of the Congress returned to statism. But by 1974, India was once again in economic difficulties. The war for Bangladesh in 1971 had ended in victory—but it had pushed 10 million refugees onto the Indian economy and produced a substantial budget deficit. In 1972 and again in 1973, the monsoon failed, producing not only drought but a shortage of food and an increase in its price. Power generation declined, as did agricultural production and the demand for manufactured goods. Unemployment followed. Finally, the decision of the Arab oil producers to raise prices in 1973 drained India's foreign reserves and deepened what was now a serious recession. Once again, as in the mid-1960s, the siren voices of the world market were heard—the World Bank and the IMF—serenading India with promises of aid, but simultaneously demanding changes in Indian economic policy. According to Jeremiah Novack in the *Times of India*:

> … the aid-to-India consortium, in part because of prodding by [US ambassador to India] Mr Daniel Moynihan, proved to be insistent that Mrs Gandhi give up her quasi-socialist policies … and turn to more 'western policies'—policies more in keeping with the make-up of the members of the consortium, all of whom were western oriented.[1]

In a rapid about-face, the Congress government appears to have once again abandoned Leftism in the face of the recession. The wholesale trade in food grains, which had only recently been nationalised (at the behest of the Congress Working Committee), was denationalised in February 1974.[2] In return for the IMF's agreement to help with the balance of payments deficit, the Government accepted the IMF's suggested economic policies. Wages were cut, government spending reduced and compulsory savings policies imposed on all wage earners and tax payers.

> By 1974, [Mrs Gandhi] was clearly moving away from progressive policies; that year her anti-inflationary package was based on the primacy of the free market mechanism as an instrument for stabilizing the economy.... . By 1974–1975, the socialist model of development, embryonic though it was, had been abandoned in favor of the World Bank model.[3]

It was, however, unclear whether these policies represented a permanent turn in the Gandhi administration's economic thinking, or a one-off response to a temporary setback—along the same lines as the 'mini-liberalisation' around the 1966 devaluation. There was certainly reaction against the new policies in and around the Congress Left.[4] Overall, despite six years of Leftism, when 1975 dawned, Congress economic policy presented something of a confused picture.

This was the Indian economic crisis—though it was not recognised in these terms. What were the possible responses to it?

Strengthening the State Politically

The reaction of many states under pressure from external forces was to strengthen themselves politically. This was obviously an ultimately ineffective defence against economic forces—but it created a pleasing sense of a state still in control and was a preparation for the instability that a weakening state-run economy might produce.[5] If some liberalisation was found to be absolutely necessary, a strengthened state would be in a better position to cope with the fall-out.[6] The Indian state was strengthening its powers before the Emergency. Carras, conscious of world market pressures, argues that, during the Railway strike of 1974:

> ... the government was prepared to stand firm to protect the economy from further inflationary pressures and to demonstrate to the IMF and the World Bank that the Indian government was worthy of the international bankers' trust. A similar motivation accounts, in part, for the Emergency proclamation and the sterilization program embarked upon during Emergency rule.[7]

After the strikes, confronted with the JP Movement, the Indian state strengthened its powers still further with the Emergency.

Strengthening the State Economically

Another response to globalisation on the part of national states, sometimes combined with political self-strengthening, was to confront it head-on by strengthening the economic power of the state. We had seen India move in this direction after Mrs Gandhi's accession to power, and in response to the Congress electoral losses following partial liberalisation. Nationalisation, planning and curbs on business were the order of the day from 1967 to 1974. The rhetoric that accompanied those years was of one voice. Malaviya wrote on the effect of the extension of state intervention:

> It is the growth of the State sector resulting from co-operation with the Soviet Union and Socialist countries which the monopolists in India and the Right reactionaries of the political parties detest and hate most... . State intervention, State 'meddling', 'Statism' as it has been put, is the great bugbear, almost like the red rag before the bull.[8]

Mrs Gandhi warned the Federation of Indian Chambers of Commerce and Industries (FICCI's) 48th session, two months before the Emergency, that '[t]here can be no general liberalisation'—and further, 'the key to the revival of the economy lies in augmenting public investment.'[9] This rhetorical statism was continued into the Emergency. Mrs Gandhi extolled the virtues of self-reliance (the polar opposite of globalisation) in August 1975:

> When we raise this slogan, it is not merely from the point of view of national pride ... . It is because it is [a] dire and urgent necessity for us that we must stand on our feet.[10]

In fact, real measures to strengthen the state's role in the economy had ground to a halt in 1974, when India once again confronted serious economic problems. According to Lucas, before the Emergency, Mrs Gandhi had instructed the Finance and Industry Ministers (Chidambra Subramaniam and T. A. Pai) 'to loosen constraints on private industry, encourage the big companies, liberalize terms for foreign private, and crack down hard on labor unrest.'[11]

From 1974, the Indian government's response to globalisation was not to increase the state's role in the economy. That strategy had failed. Rhetoric aside, the Emergency was not used to revive it.

Liberalisation

The third possible response to globalisation by national states was to accede to it. Most states did this only gradually.[12] In doing so, they did not generally recognise that opening up and deregulating an economy would necessarily weaken central direction and planning. In this respect, the Indian experience presents us with a paradox. While the regime had staked its popularity on statist measures up to 1974 and while statist rhetoric remained its hallmark thereafter, it was liberalisation that was implemented after 1975. During the years of the Emergency, there was not a single measure taken to strengthen the state's economic power. Its political power, of course, increased immensely. But in terms of state economic intervention, quite the contrary process was at work. As Shaibal Gupta observed recently, 'the opening up of the Indian economy started in the days of the Emergency itself.'[13] This is not to argue that liberalisation was the *purpose* of the Emergency.[14] The Emergency was essentially a political project designed to strengthen the state in the face of mass opposition. However, it provided a platform and an opportunity for measures of economic liberalisation, which had previously proved impossible due to electoral pressure. Lukas concluded, 'the Emergency is profoundly schizoid. The left has been given control of the rhetoric. The Right has been granted most of the tangible benefits.'[15] The global proponents of liberalisation and the role of world market forces seem to have recognised this and been satisfied with the results. The World Bank's Robert McNamara visited India in November 1976 and noted 'a disciplined, realistic approach to development programs and a willingness to find practical solutions to economic problems rather than an attitude of falling back on "socialist ideologies" and didactic debate.'[16]

How did the forces at work in Indian society respond to globalisation? Which—if any—of these strategies did they advocate?

The Congress State

In 1975, the Congress state was faced with world market pressures, economic crisis and the JP Movement. In response to the last, it invoked the Emergency. During the Emergency, while strengthening the state politically, Congress began the liberalisation of the Indian economy. In Chapter 2, it was noted that liberalisation comes in two forms—internal (the relaxation of state controls on the private sector) and external (the relaxation of controls on the entry of foreign capital). Congress was more inclined to the former than the latter. Internal liberalisation encroached somewhat on the state's powers (by giving more economic power to the private sector)—but, given the strength of the state and its close ties with big business, it was thought that this could be tolerated. External liberalisation was a more dangerous prospect and, in view of the power of global capital, a more powerful force.[17] In line with internal liberalisation, the Emergency was not used to attack the private sector. Mrs Gandhi assured her listeners the day after the Emergency was announced, 'wild conjectures are circulating about impending nationalisation of industries ... and drastic new controls. We have no such plans.'[18] Erdman wrote in February 1976, 'there has been no menacing, radically Left-wing posture on the part of the government ... the captains of industry have been left relatively unscathed.' According to Toye, 'the government ... treated the industrial capitalists with noticeable benevolence.'[19] Bhargava concludes:

> The Congress government of Indira Gandhi redirected economic policy during the Emergency from a planned economy of the Soviet type working towards supremacy of the public sector to one in which planning was mainly of the indicative variety and the private sector was to be the major partner, or at least the senior partner in an equal partnership.[20]

The 20-Point Programme itself was business-friendly, reserving most of its radicalism for the rich farmers.[21] The 14th point of the Programme announced: 'Liberalisation of investment procedures'. This meant a relaxation of state controls (licencing) in 21 major industries, allowing undertakings to use unlicensed industrial capacity (engineering industries, for example, were allowed to automatically increase capacity by 25 per cent over a five-year period), encouraging (rather than attempting to restrict) diversification, simplifying and lessening regulatory procedures, reviewing price controls, liberalising import and export policies and creating a more positive investment climate.[22] In her broadcast to the nation after the Emergency was declared, the Prime Minister said:

Licensing procedures have come in the way of new investment, causing delay. These will be simplified. The investment limit of those industries which need no imports or governmental held will be raised. At the same time, I must point out that licences are being misused. Import-export regulations are being amended. There will be speedy trials, and penalties for breaking rules will included the confiscation of goods.[23]

The finance minister (C. Subramaniam) told the Rajya Sabah at the end of July that the government was 'actively considering further proposals for streamlining the system of industrial licences.'[24]

When the relaxation of state controls allowed sackings, the AICC warned that 'the management of the private sector would have to function in accordance with national priorities and government policies' and declared itself against 'unjustified retrenchments, lockouts and layoffs.'[25] But the labour minister told the Lok Sabha that the government could not stop big business using the Emergency to restructure itself.[26]

Further largesse was to follow. Price controls were relaxed in order to improve profits for new private investment. Restrictions on foreign investment were reduced 'after candid talks between the government and business representatives from the US and West Germany'. Tax evaders were offered the chance to confess without prosecution. 'Depressed' luxury industries were offered relief, while the tax on luxury items (like cars) was reduced.[27]

Big Business

As we know, India's leading business houses were strong supporters of the general thrust of Congress economic policy—that is, of ISI. There was an argument over the detail of the policy—over the suitability of state intervention, the rigour (or not) of planning, the size and influence of the state sector. But overall, the support remained more or less steady. So much so, that in the very midst of Mrs Gandhi's pre-Emergency Leftist policies, no less a person than J. R. D. Tata felt able to advise the government on economic policy *within the framework* of the Congress approach (see Chapter 2). Business support for Congress was not a one-way affair.

Sahgal suggests that from 1966 to 1975, 'the total assets of the twenty largest industrial houses increased by 150 percent'.[28]

Thus, the approach of big business in 1975 to the twin economic and political crises was very similar to that of the Congress leadership: strengthening the political power of the state while pursuing opportunities thereby unleashed for the internal liberalisation of the economy. Big business declared immediate support for the Emergency.[29] Tata told journalists:

> Things had gone too far. You can't imagine what we have been through here—strikes, boycotts, demonstrations. Why, there were days I couldn't walk out of my office onto the street.[30]

FICCI welcomed both the Emergency and the 20-Point Programme, describing the latter as a 'sensitive and realistic programme of action which must be supported by all responsible sections of the public.'[31] Venkata points out that 'the Emergency gave industrialists what all along eluded them—industrial peace.'[32]

Strengthening the state, then, was one aspect of the industrialists' response. But the Emergency gave them much more than that. As *Link* suggested ironically, 'now that there is peace in the country and the labour-force is doing its best, all that is necessary to boost growth is to provide as many facilities as possible to private industry.'[33] As we have seen, those facilities—in the shape of internal liberalisation—were soon being provided. The *Link* article maintained:

> The private sector has never had it so good. In fact the captains of private industry and trade are apparently so taken aback by the bonanza of concessions that they have received in the short span of about six months that they really do not seem to know how to express their gratitude.[34]

Nevertheless, it was not long before big business was asking for more.[35] According to FICCI's official history, the industrialists were desperate to increase exports and wanted government assistance to this end.[36] Those exports were to be directed at Western markets. More concessions were demanded: lower taxes, further licencing deregulation, lifting the restrictions on the growth of big business—a general reversal of priorities with regard to the state and private sectors.[37]

Some industrialists also wanted a further political strengthening of the state. Tata had declared (in the interview cited above) that 'the parliamentary system is not suited to our needs.' Both he and G. D. Birla were said to favour 'a presidential form of democracy', since the Westminster system was too unstable.[38] It seemed unlikely that many business leaders, having enjoyed the Emergency conditions so much, would want to return to the pre-Emergency system of chaotic democracy.[39]

There were two connected factors that gave the big industrialists food for thought, as the Emergency continued. The first concerned the forces that the Emergency had unleashed (which will be considered more fully in the next section); the second concerned the question of *external* liberalisation.

In the first place, big business considered the authoritarianism of the period to be all very well in its place—and that place was primarily in disciplining the labour force and ensuring order. Any further extension of state authority was met with some apprehension. Strong states, however, have an inbuilt desire to expand their powers. Thus Hewitt relates:

> ... an all-pervading fear soon began to affect the morale of the business communities, no matter how much they had appeared to benefit from price deregulation and an atmosphere conducive to shedding excess labour.[40]

One of the main sources of that fear was 'the behaviour of the Youth Congress towards party funding and the general defence of property from arbitrary interference by people claiming to represent the state.'[41]

In the second place—and partly from the same source—arose the demand for external liberalisation; opening the economy to imports and foreign capital. To this, both big business and the Congress were opposed. As Patnaik put it, 'the established monopoly capitalists would be in favour of selective "liberalisation" and averse to any blanket "liberalisation" especially import liberalisation.'[42] Internal liberalisation allowed big business to 'move into the space occupied by the public sector or smaller capitalists ... hence they demand an opening of that space.' According to Chandrasekhar and Ghosh, internal liberalisation could include 'the elimination of anti-monopoly legislation, the removal of legislation "reserving" certain sectors for small capitalists, a regime of high interest rates that squeezes small capitalists, the privatization of profitable public sector units, and the delinking of the public sector from budgetary support of any kind.'[43] This partially coincided with the globalisation reforms, envisaged by the World Bank and the IMF. Thus, big business extended 'qualified support' to internal liberalisation—'no matter how uneasy it feels about some other aspects of such programmes.'[44] The latter referred to external liberalisation. Big business opposed 'encroachments by metropolitan capital upon their own empires.'[45]

New Industries—and their Supporters

The existence of a different wing of Indian capital—newer industrial groups rather than traditional big business—has been noted in Chapter 2. Chandrasekhar and Ghosh declare baldly that 'a schism developed within the ranks of Indian capital'.[46] The Australian government's East Asia Analytical Unit noted the features that separated them from big business.

> The new breed of entrepreneurs is more flexible than larger and older Indian companies, who operate with the constraints of over-manning, outdated plant and equipment and rigid corporate bureaucracies ... many of these new start-up firms are absorbing new technology into India [and] taking up the export challenge.[47]

Patnaik identifies them as both new industries and 'a new upstart group of Indian capitalists, many of whom are non-resident but many resident with large assets abroad.'[48]

The reaction of these groups to the political and economic crisis was to endorse the authoritarian political system (the Emergency) as well as measures to deregulate the economy (internal liberalisation)—but to call for external liberalisation as well. Chandrasekhar and Ghosh comment:

> Such groups were interested in the abolition of state regulations which offered protection to traditional oligopoly and wanted to use foreign collaboration as a means of entry into the industrial sector. Such groups therefore became vocal supporters of policies towards liberalization and globalization.[49]

The new industries had emerged, perhaps unexpectedly, under Nehru and Indira Gandhi—during the 'Licence-Permit Raj'. One of them was the Reliance Group, led by Dhirubhai Ambani.

It is widely believed, [say Tripathi and Jumani] that the Ambanis' success was to a large extent due to Dhirubhai's ability to manipulate, using fair and foul means alike, the government machinery to his advantage ... no one can accuse Dhirubhai and his associates of failing to appreciate the opportunities inherent in the environment during the license-permit raj and to exploit them to the maximum possible extent.[50]

This experience made the new industries aware that there were ways around regulation. But it also made them realise how very inconvenient those ways were—and gave rise to the thought that state controls impeded their progress and should be removed.[51] The new industries were interested in diversification and the imports that it required. They realised that the protected nature of the Indian economy impeded experiment, innovation and technological advance, for which exposure to, and integration with, the world market was necessary. The new industries, therefore, had a material interest in external liberalisation. They are described, somewhat disparagingly, by Chandrasekhar and Ghosh as 'those who were more in the nature of upstarts, international racketeers, fixers, middlemen, often of NRI origin or having NRI links, often linked to smuggling and the arms trade ... their parasitic intermediary status as well as the international value of their operations naturally inclined then towards an "open economy".'[52] McDonald says of Ambani: 'Dhirubhai also played on the perception that he was an outsider and an "upstart" who deserved help to break through the glass ceilings of vested interest and privilege in the business community.'[53] Thus, the new businessmen were often seen, in contrast to the more staid big business houses, as 'entrepreneurs-on-the-make, who see in the Emergency the kind of political and moral climate in which they can amass millions.'[54]

Which brings us back to Sanjay Gandhi.

There is little doubt that Sanjay saw himself as one of the new entrepreneurs, straining against the monopolies of big business and the restrictions of the state-regulated economy.[55] Despite his foray into business being of a relatively limited duration, the self-image seemed to stick and when he entered the political realm he became a loud spokesman for the new industries. He carried their message of authoritarianism, linked to internal and external liberalisation and a vision of dismantling the state sector into the heart of the administration. In this, he was supported by 'lumpen capitalists, entrepreneurs on the make who expected Sanjay to shift government licences, quotas, and credit in their direction.'[56] These people and these policies were also carried into the Youth Congress, which called for more government incentives for the private sector, further liberalisation and the deprioritisation of planning.[57]

Sanjay attacked the state-controlled economy and big business—and, especially, the nexus between the two.[58] In his interview with *Surge* (noted in the previous chapter for its anti-communist content), he declared that the public sector could never produce 'the expertise and the hard work' that private enterprise produced. Singling out a state-owned power generation unit in Uttar Pradesh, he exclaimed, 'I think the managers there should be taken out and shot!' The public sector, he said, 'should function only in competition with the private sector, and where it cannot function in competition with the private sector, it should be allowed to die a natural death.' In nationalised industries—the coal industry, for example—'it is the bureaucracy which gets all the advantage,' said Sanjay. He complained, 'I think the totally controlled sector of the economy is what we're pouring all our taxes into to keep it running somehow or other.'[59]

It was big business that was the special object of Sanjay's wrath—and here again, we can feel the irate frustration of the failed entrepreneur.[60] He believed (correctly) that big business had helped to create the state-regulated economy and that it survived and grew because of the advantages it conferred on them.

> ... everybody thinks we have controls to control the big businessmen. Well, in the past twenty years who [has] grown, the big businessmen, or the small businessmen? So what are the controls doing? They're just consolidating the big businessmen. Publicly they argue for less control and privately they finance for more control.[61]

As far as Sanjay and the interests he represented were concerned, the state bureaucracy and big business were in lock-step in their economic attitudes.

> Well, in a controlled economy actually, it is only the big business houses that expand because they are the people who have the resources and the capacity of getting around all the controls. I would say if you remove all the controls it would virtually finish off the big businessmen. They are the ones who create this lobby to keep the controls. It's partly the big businessmen and partly the bureaucracy because this is what gives the bureaucracy patronage and money.[62]

He compared big business in India with those in Singapore, Hong Kong and South Korea and found it wanting.[63] And he saw the hand of big business behind the pre-Emergency campaigns against Congress: 'It was these people who were providing the finance to back the agitations which had been launched against the lawfully established Government,' he added.[64]

Sanjay's economic ideas are sometimes portrayed as part of a conspiracy involving the US and American multinationals. Dhar, for example, contends that Sanjay's *Surge* interview was 'a calculated attempt to please the Americans'; and that '[one] of his cronies was reported to regularly meet a US embassy official in a very suspicious manner'.[65] Mayer notes 'the very close ties which were said by competent observers to exist between the US Embassy and Sanjay Gandhi.'[66] Sunil Chakravartty suggested to the author:

> He had connections with dubious people, with foreigners also, who were egging him on. Because he didn't have any ideology there was a possibility that he could be drawn into the Western camp and that kind of thing.[67]

Mehta actually names two 'foreign multinationals' (International Harvester and Piper Aircraft), for whom Sanjay was supposedly 'an agent'.[68] There was also concern in Moscow at his 'pro-Western' attitudes.[69]

Sanjay may or may not have had contact with foreign embassies and multinational capital. But the only thing he was an 'agent'—or, more accurately, a voice – for, was that stratum of Indian capital which I have described as the new industries, which wanted the Emergency (for as long as possible), liberalisation and the dismantling of state regulation. This was not an American plot—it was acquiescence to globalisation. But we should recall that this was a confused time. Well into the 1980s, globalisation was often mistaken for the expansion of US state power—that is, 'US imperialism'.

The CPI

The CPI's reactions to the political crisis—the threat from the Right, the JP Movement and the Emergency—have been studied in the previous chapters. What was the Party's response to the wider crisis—globalisation and the forces undermining the economic power of the national state?

At the outset, we should be clear that the Party did not recognise this greater crisis in these terms—virtually no one did. India's communists believed that what was occurring was a crisis in the capitalist path of development. Two paths lay open: some kind of non-capitalist system on the one hand, or subservience to imperialism on the other. Mohit Sen wrote in 1975:

> But now the contradictions of this mixed economy have burst out and an intense struggle is now being waged to change the mixture drastically— either in the direction of export-oriented dependent capitalism or in that of a self-reliant internal-market oriented, public-sector based, democratic, planned economy.[70]

Very broadly, this was an accurate description of the choices on offer. Sen's 'export-oriented dependent capitalism' was the direction in which world market forces were pushing (decreasingly) national economies. 'Self-reliance' (with its attendant descriptors) was the time-honoured strategy of states, seeking to protect their economic sovereignty. Their ability to do this was declining—but the method was clear: the state had to be strengthened, economically in the first place and politically if necessary.

This was the CPI's response. The Party's working assumption was that an economically strong state was automatically progressive. Politically, it focused on the Indian national bourgeoisie—which, it will be remembered, was thought to be represented by the Congress. Thus, the Emergency was given the communist seal of approval by the CPI. To be sure, the communists demanded genuine reform and popular mobilisation. But in the initial stages, they fastened on to the Congress' statist rhetoric and endorsed it as a path to the 'self-reliant' economy.

The Emergency regime's concessions to business, throughout the period therefore, were a major blow. *Link* pointed out that economically the government was continuing 'to follow a capitalist path of development'— just when politically, India was going to become 'a socialist, secular and democratic republic'. Some measure of the uncertainty that was beginning to set in is indicated in the article's conclusion: 'This is a striking illustration of the complexity of the Indian politico-economic situation.'[71] By late 1976, the communists and their supporters had identified a full-scale retreat in government policy on regulating business: 'the Government was persuaded to "streamline"—[a] euphemism for relaxation—the licencing procedures… . Amazingly, what was a crime a few days ago suddenly became a virtue.' The CPI appealed to Congress members to stem the tide. Mohit Sen wrote in December 1976, 'patriotic and progressive Congressmen have to ask themselves whether socialism and the drive to socialism is at all compatible with the pampering and strengthening of the monopolies and big business.'[72]

At the same time, any indication of a reversal in Congress' pro-business policy was seized upon. *Link* reported in July 1976:

> The days of concessions [to business] appear to be over. If the mood of the Government is any indication, the private sector, which received a bonanza of concessions in the last few months, is unlikely to get any more.[73]

But it was a false dawn. In December, the paper would complain that 'never before has the private sector of Indian industry got so many concessions and privileges as in the past three and [a] half years [dated from the first major relaxation of licensing regulations in February 1973].'[74] The Party convinced itself that these were merely mistaken policies—in much the same way that Sanjay was merely a rogue element—in a basically progressive Congress. If this were true, then Congress could be convinced of the error of its pro-business ways and the march to self-reliance could be resumed. But it could not be—because these were not simply errors, they were part and parcel of the Congress state's response to the greater crisis. The Congress state was not the tool of either wing of Indian capital. It was a force with its own interests and its own methods of defence. One of those was its political strength, expressed in the Emergency. Another was its close relationship with big business and its willingness to allow some measures of internal economic liberalisation. The CPI misinterpreted both of these—the first as a progressive initiative of the national bourgeoisie, later drawn along a deviant path by Sanjay; the second as an imperialist conspiracy.

It may be argued that the Party's approach was at cross-purposes with reality. But so were those of most of the social forces involved. During the Emergency, the Congress believed it was defending itself and India's sovereignty; big business believed that it was endorsing a controlled liberalisation; the new industries believed that the economy was being opened up; while the CPI was marching towards self-reliance. In reality, they were doing none of these things—instead, things were being done to them. The parameters for economic action were ceasing to be set in India—increasingly, they were being set by forces outside. The fact that the period we have been examining was the beginning of a rather messy transition from statism to an open economy (not only in India) accounts for the confusion.

The purpose of my account of the CPI in the Indian Emergency has not been to demonstrate that the Party got everything wrong. The situation in the world in 1975 was not a simple one. The problem was that many in the Left did not realise that it was not.

Despite this, the CPI achieved some positive things. Its position towards the Congress was a plausible one, of 'unity and struggle', even though it was based on an identification of the Congress with the Indian bourgeoisie and on an entirely fanciful division within that bourgeoisie. It attacked anti-people measures by the Congress government but defended that government against Right-reaction. Its support for the Emergency was unwise—but, as I have tried to show, that support soon turned to criticism of the excesses and of the 'Sanjay brigade' and eventually of his mother's role (all before the Emergency was ended). Its attempts to actually implement land reform and other radical measures in the 20-Point Programme, its resistance to Sanjay and its persistence in these efforts were laudable.

There were two things that the CPI could not have been expected to have factored into its analysis.

The first concerned the nature of the state. In the Introduction to this book, I set forth the idea that the state is not, as most Marxists (and certainly the CPI) believe, part of the 'superstructure', the nature of which is determined by the economic 'base'. I argued that the state is a production relation—a part of the base—itself. An obscure point, the reader may have concluded at the time. But if the Indian state was part of the superstructure, as the CPI argued, it followed that its nature was determined by India's economic base—that is, by a capitalist economic system. That worked for the communists when the state acted clearly in the interests of the monopolists or the imperialists. A problem for the analysis arose when the state acted against them—controlling the economy, for example, or attempting to steer a non-aligned course in foreign policy.

As we know, the communists resolved this dilemma by dividing the bourgeoisie between 'the monopolists' and the 'national bourgeoisie'. The latter was a progressive force and when its representatives (Nehru, Indira

Gandhi) were in power, progress took place. I have tried to show that this division was a false one—and in any case, was not the determining factor in state actions. The Congress state was not a part of the superstructure, controlled by Indian capitalism. The state remained itself—a production relation dominating the economic base. It was primarily interested in self-preservation—which could mean increasing its own power, leaning to the Left or dallying with economic liberalisation. At times, the state carried out progressive measures. The problem for the CPI was that, driven by the need to identify the state and the bourgeoisie, progressive measures had to mean that the state was in progressive hands—that is, those of the progressive national bourgeoisie. This led to the Party's belief that the state could, in the conditions of the Emergency, be trusted to carry out radical reforms.

The second thing that the Party could not have been expected to factor in was globalisation and the effects that it would have on national economic units. By the mid-1970s, globalisation had started to push national economies—even state-controlled ones—in the direction of opening up. But it was not recognised for what it was—and if the effects were recognised, they were generally blamed on something else (Thatcher and Reagan in the advanced economies, 'imperialism' everywhere else.). The CPI was no blinder in this respect than others. The lack of understanding of globalisation meant that the real pressure on the Indian economy and the real division within the Indian bourgeoisie was obscured.[75]

It would be easy to pronounce a simplistic judgement on the Emergency. It was the state defending itself; it was a power-grab by the Congress leadership; it was necessary to avert internal chaos; it had the potential to become a dictatorship. It was, in part, all of these things. But the economic context, in which it took place, gave rise to its inner contradictions—running in two directions, towards increased statism and away from it, at the same time. This is what made it unique—a marker of the transitional period in India from a state-managed to a globalised economy.

Finally though, there was one factor that the CPI should have recognised and acted upon. The state in India—whether part of the super-structure or part of the base—could not be relied upon to be consistently progressive. The interests of that state were its own. They were not determined by either 'the monopolies' or by 'the national bourgeoisie'. They were not those of the Indian people—although at times, the two may have temporarily intersected. Thus, the attempt to use that state—in the belief that the national bourgeoisie controlled it—to bring about mass-based radical reform was delusional.

For the most part, we can judge these events only after the event. Marxism provides us with some tools to help us in that judgement. It is always harder on the spot. We can conclude with Marx:

> Just as one does not judge an individual by what he thinks about himself, so one cannot judge such a period of transformation by its consciousness, but, on the contrary, this consciousness must be explained from the contradictions of material life, from the conflict existing between the social forces of production and the relations of production.[76]

Notes

1.   *Times of India*, 1 July 1977, cited in Uma Vasudev, *Two Faces of Indira Gandhi* (New Delhi: Vikas Publishing House, 1977), 76.
2.   P. N. Dhar, *Indira Gandhi, the 'Emergency', and Indian Democracy* (New Delhi: Oxford India Paperbacks, 2001), 234.
3.   Mary C. Carras, *Indira Gandhi: In the Crucible of Leadership* (Bombay: Jaico Press Private Ltd, 1980), 171 and 209. P. N. Dhar comments:

> 'All these steps went against earlier policy pronouncements of the government, which aimed at less dependence on foreign aid, the decentralization of economic power, the promotion of distributive justice through nationalization, an expansion of the public sector, and a stricter regulation of the private sector.' (Dhar, *Indira Gandhi*, 234)

4.   See Dhar, *Indira Gandhi*, 265 and 306.
5.   With a good deal of hindsight, we can see such a defence at work in the USSR under Brezhnev and Andropov (see David Lockwood, *The Destruction of the Soviet Union: A Study in Globalization* (Houndmills: Macmillan Press Ltd, 2000), Chapter 4.
6.   With the same kind of hindsight, we can see this process unfolding in China after 1978.
7.   Carras, *Indira Gandhi*, 173.
8.   Harsh Dev Malaviya, *The Danger of Right Reaction* (New Delhi: Socialist Congressman Publications, 1965), 230.
9.   Indira Gandhi, *Selected Speeches and Writings of Indira Gandhi. Volume III: September 1972–March 1977*, 25 April 1975 (New Delhi: Ministry of Information and Broadcasting, Government of India, 1984), 353–4.
10.   Indira Gandhi, Speech to Chairmen of Port Trusts and labour leaders, 6 August 1975 in Indira Gandhi, *Democracy and Discipline: Speeches of Shrimati Indira Gandhi* [1975] (New Delhi: Ministry of Information and Broadcasting, Government of India, n.d.), 68.

11. J. Anthony Lukas, 'India is as Indira does', *New York Times Magazine*, 4 April 1976. See www.nytimes.com/section/magazine/archives (last accessed on 02 September 2015).

12. Hewitt suggests that liberalisation 'was not so much a decisive shift in strategy underlying the class interests of state action, but the easiest option by the state to take when confronted with powerful societal interests it did not seem to be able to either influence or intimidate' (Vernon Hewitt, *Political Mobilisation and Democracy in India: States of Emergency* [New York: Routledge, 2008], 130).

13. Shaibal Gupta, 'End of ideology', *Frontline* XXXI, no. 9 (3–16 May 2014): 13.

14. As, for example, Jeremiah Novack does: 'Mrs Gandhi had to go in for the Emergency to be able to carry out India's economic resurgence' (cited in Vasudev, *Two Faces*, 76).

15. Lukas, 'India is as Indira does'.

16. Devesh Kapur, John P. Lewis and Richard Webb, *The World Bank: Its First Half Century* (Washington, D.C.: The Brookings Institution, 1997), 478. Kapur et al do point out though that during the period, the Bank's internal papers and memoranda were 'remarkably free of all traces of India's "Emergency"'.

17. There is no sturdy wall between internal and external liberalisation—either side can edge towards the other. Measures that approached external liberalisation were taken. Toye argues that the acceptance of large amounts of foreign aid during the Emergency 'indicates unambiguously that [the government] has abandoned its policy of self-reliance' (J. F. J. Toye, 'Economic Trends and Policies in India during the Emergency', *World Development* 5, no. 4 (1977): 308). Hewitt likewise: 'the Emergency was used to encourage foreign industrial corporations to enter the Indian economy and dismantle government regulations within the state sector' (Hewitt, *Political Mobilisation*, 130). *Link* stated baldly, 'the infrastructure is being built to increase India's capacity to absorb the western technology and, thus, tie it more closely to the capitalist world' ('Revised Plan Targets', *Link*, 3 October 1976, 14). See also Primila Lewis, *Reason Wounded: An Experience of India's Emergency* (London: George Allen & Unwin Ltd, 1978), 25; P. N. Haksar, *Premonitions* (Bombay: Interpress, 1979), 240.

18. Indira Gandhi, 27 June 1975, *Democracy and Discipline*, 4. See also Bhabani Sen Gupta, 'Communism Further Divided', in *Indira Gandhi's India: A Political System Reappraised*, ed. Henry C. Hart (Boulder: Westview Press, 1976), 171 and 178. On the proposition that nothing was done during the Emergency to strengthen the state economy, Sumit Chakravartty countered: 'Nothing was done to undermine it as well … But yes, that is true, no steps were taken' (interview with the author, 8 November 2014).

19. Howard L. Erdman, 'The Industrialists', in *Indira Gandhi's India: A Political System Reappraised*, ed. Henry C. Hart (Boulder: Westview Press, 1976), 138; Toye, 'Economic trends', 314.

20. Ashok Bhargava and Gopalan Balachandaran, 'Economic Changes during the Indian Emergency', *Bulletin of Concerned Asian Scholars* 9, no. 4 (October–December 1977): 57. See also Dhar, *Indira Gandhi*, 306; Bipan Chandra, *In the Name of Democracy: JP Movement and the Emergency* (New Delhi: Penguin Books, 2003), 224.

21. '… the drift of the twenty-point program with its ad hoc modifications is very favorable to the large-scale private sector industrialists' (Erdman, 'Industrialists', 140).

22. AICC meeting 29–30 May 1976 in Moin A. Zaidi, ed., *The Encyclopaedia of the Indian National Congress, Volume 24, 1976–1977: Amid Encircling Gloom* (New Delhi: S. Chand and Company Ltd, 1984), 85–86. See also Erdman, 'Industrialists', 138.

23. Indira Gandhi, Broadcast 1 July 1975, *Selected Speeches III 1972–77*, 357.

208 The Communist Party of India and the Indian Emergency

24. C. Subramaniam to Rajya Sabah, 28 July 1975 in D. V. Gandhi, ed., *Era of Discipline: Documents on Contemporary Reality* (New Delhi: Samachar Bharati, 1976), 56.
25. AICC Resolution on the Economic Situation, 22 November 1976, *Encyclopaedia of the INC Volume 24*, 136.
26. Hewitt, *Political Mobilisation*, 130.
27. Toye, 'Economic Trends', 307–11; Bhargava and Balachandaran, 'Economic Changes', 54–55.
28. Nayantara Sahgal, *Indira Gandhi: Her Road to Power* (New York: Frederick Ungar Publishing Co., 1982), 173.
29. Erdman, 'Industrialists', 125–26 and 140.
30. Cited in Tariq Ali, 'The Fall of Congress in India', *New Left Review* I/103, May–June 1977.
31. Cited in Erdman, 'Industrialists', 140. Erdman says that the programme was 'very favourable to the large-scale private sector industrialists' (140). See also Harish Mahindra (FICCI President) in H. Venkatasubbiah, *Enterprise and Economic Change: 50 Years of FICCI* (New Delhi: Vikas Publishing House, 1977), 161; 'Correspondent', 'The Emergency in India,' *Bulletin of Concerned Asian Scholars*, 7, no. 4 (October–December 1975): 2; Lewis, *Reason*, 25.
32. Venkata, 'Enterprise', 161.
33. 'Idle Capital, Soaring Profits', *Link*, 9 May 1976, 9.
34. Ibid. See also *Link* editorials, 12 September 1976, 5; 26 September 1976, 5; Harry W. Blair. 'Mrs Gandhi's Emergency, The Indian Elections of 1977, Pluralism and Marxism: Problems with Paradigms', *Modern Asian Studies* 14, no. 2 (1980): 257.
35. Reporting on the FICCI annual session in May 1976: 'the private sector started asking for more, this time with greater boldness … [w]hile praising the Emergency, the 20-point programme and all other measures taken by the Government' (*Link*, 9 May 1976, 9).
36. Venkata, 'Enterprise', 161.
37. See 'Tactics of Big Business', *Link*, 2 May 1976, 6; 'Idle Capital, Soaring Profits', *Link*, 9 May 1976, 10; 'FICCI Attempts', *Link*, 25 July 1976, 6.
38. Ali, 'Fall of Congress'; Dhar, *Indira Gandhi*, 334.
39. Erdman, 'Industrialists', 146.
40. Hewitt, *Political Mobilisation*, 144.
41. Ibid., 145.
42. Prabhat Patnaik, 'On the Political Economy of Economic "Liberalisation"', *Social Scientist* XIII, no. 146–7 (July–August 1985): 13.
43. C. P. Chandrasekhar and Jayati Ghosh, *The Market that Failed: Neoliberal Economic Reform in India* (New Delhi: LeftWord Books, 2004), 36.
44. Ibid., 36.
45. Ibid., 37.
46. Ibid., 32.
47. East Asia Analytical Unit, Department of Foreign Affairs and Trade, *India's Economy at the Midnight Hour: Australia's India Strategy* (Canberra: Australian Government Publishing Service, 1994), 37.
48. Patnaik, 'Political Economy', 13. Patnaik draws attention to historical precedents of 'The phenomenon of two distinct sections within big business and the association between the emergence of "new" big business to power and the institution of authoritarian political regimes.'
49. Chandrasekhar and Ghosh, *Market that failed*, 34.

50. Dwijendra Tripathi and Jyoti Jumani, *The Concise Oxford History of Indian Business* (New Delhi: Oxford University Press, 2008), 191. The Ambani case is comprehensively covered by Hamish McDonald in *The Polyester Prince: The Rise of Dhirubhai Ambani* (St Leonards: Allen & Unwin, 1998). He comments, 'Dhirubhai was not a law breaker but had a creative attitude towards regulation' (42).

51. See Vivek Chibber, *Locked in Place: State-Building and Late Industrialization in India* (Princeton: Princeton University Press, 2006), 253.

52. Chandrasekhar and Ghosh, *Market that Failed*, 37.

53. McDonald, *Polyester Prince*, 39.

54. Lukas, 'India is as Indira does'. Lukas recognises the group, but then describes them as 'Mrs Gandhi's closest business allies'. This is well wide of the mark, but illustrates the confused nature of the period. More accurately he says, 'of late a gaggle of aspiring tycoons have also begun to pay court to Sanjay'.

55. In the *Surge* interview, for example, he contrasted Maruti's difficulties in obtaining materials with those of the 'large industrialists' (Telexed typescript of *Surge* interview in Nehru Memorial Museum and Library: P. N. Haksar papers. Instalments I and II, V Press Clippings, File Number 5 ('Related to the various activities of Sanjay Gandhi').

56. Lloyd I. Rudolph and Susanne Hoeber Rudolph, *In Pursuit of Lakshmi: The Political Economy of the Indian State* (Hyderabad: Orient Longman, 1987), 141.

57. Hewitt, *Political Mobilisation*, 144. Hewitt points out, however, that 'there was, by 1976, no sign of a coherent anti-communist, free market ideology emerging with the Youth Congress. Indeed there was little sign of any coherence at all.' The operative word here is 'coherent'. The thrust of Sanjay's politics—with the Youth Congress and the new industries behind him—was clear. In India's transitional crisis, coherence was too much to expect—least of all from Sanjay.

58. In this, he was unwittingly reproducing a classic position of fascism. See Chandra's critique of the JP Movement on this score—which could just as easily be applied to Sanjay and his Youth Congress followers: Chandra, *Name*, 153.

59. *Surge* interview in Vasudev, *Two Faces*, 202–04. See also 'Sanjay Gandhi is against concept of controlled economy', *Indian Express*, 28 August 1975 in Haksar's Sanjay Gandhi file.

60. Initially, it appears that there was some support from big business circles for Sanjay and his supporters (see Hewitt, *Political Mobilisation*, 144; David Selbourne, *An Eye to India: the Unmasking of a Tyranny* [Harmondsworth: Penguin, 1977], 305). But this faded when his attitude to big business became clearer.

61. *Surge* interview in Vasudev, *Two Faces*, 202.

62. Telexed typescript of *Surge* interview in Haksar's Sanjay file. It is possible that Sanjay had received some of this wisdom from his apparent mentor, Ferdinand Marcos, who had written:

> In the old society [i.e., before Marcos' militarily-enforced "New Society"] how-ever, it was not unusual for certain businessmen to be in politics and certain politicians to be in business…. . Eventually we found that [this system] was only working for the few oligarchs, who were capitalists in the old style when business was good but who demanded assistance from the government when business was in distress. (Ferdinand E. Marcos, *Notes on the New Society of the Philippines* [Manila: Marcis Foundation, 1974], 123)

63.   David Selbourne, *An Eye to India*, 304.
64.   'Sanjay's call to youth', *Indian Express*, 3 January 1976 in Haksar's Sanjay Gandhi file.
65.   Dhar, *Indira Gandhi*, 325 and 329.
66.   Peter Mayer 'Congress (I), Emergency (I): Interpreting Indira Gandhi's India', in *India: Rebellion to Republic*, eds. Robin Jeffrey, Lance Brennan, Jim Masselos, Peter Mayer and Peter Reeves (New Delhi: Sterling Publishers, 1991), 404.
67.   Sumit Chakravartty, interview with the author, 8 November 2014.
68.   Vinod Mehta, *The Sanjay Story* (New Delhi: Harper Collins Publishers, 2012 [1978]), 88.
69.   Vojtech Mastny, 'The Soviet Union's Partnership with India', *Journal of Cold War Studies* 12, no. 3 (Summer 2010): 74; Christopher Andrew and Vasili Mitrokhin, *The Mitrokhin Archive II: The KGB and the World* (London: Allen Lane, 2005), 329.
70.   Mohit Sen, *Congress Socialism: Appraisal and Appeal* (New Delhi: Communist Party Publication, December 1976), 22.
71.   'Revised Plan Targets', *Link*, 3 October 1976, 14.
72.   Sen, *Congress Socialism*, 25.
73.   'No More Concessions', *Link*, 4 July 1976, 6.
74.   'Retreat on Policies', *Link*, 5 December 1976, 20. Rather in contrast with its editorial line, *Link* ran a full page advertisement for the Bihar Finance Corporation on 3 October 1976: 'Attention ENTREPRENEURS. Bihar offers bagfuls of ready money for your use' (22). On the CPI's attitude to the government's pro-business policies, see also: CPI, *Consembly Move and Democratic Fight-Back* (New Delhi: Communist Party Publication, 1976), 9; Gupta, 'Communists Divided', 171; Hewitt, *Political Mobilisation*, 130; Erdman, 'Industrialists', 140–42.
75.   One of the reasons that we can recognise globalisation today is because it is still with us. The pressures on national economies still persist. In the Indian case, as early as 1980, when Mrs Gandhi was returned to power, she started a serious process of economic liberalisation (see Mitu Sengupta, 'Making the State Change Its Mind—the IMF, the World Bank and the Politics of India's Market Reforms', *New Political Economy* 14, no. 2 [June 2009]: 188).
76.   Karl Marx, *A Contribution to the Critique of Political Economy*, (New Delhi: People's Publishing House, 2010 [1859]), 21.

Bibliography

Adhikari, Gangadhar (general editor). *Documents of the History of the Communist Party of India. Volume VII: 1948–1950.* New Delhi: People's Publishing House, 1976.

———— (general editor). *Documents of the History of the Communist Party of India. Volume VIII: 1951–1956.* New Delhi: People's Publishing House, 1977.

Agarwal, Ramanand, and Satyopal Dang. *Critical Notes on the Draft Political Review Report for the Eleventh Congress.* New Delhi: Communist Party of India, February 1978.

Alavi, Hamza. 'The State in Post-Colonial Societies: Pakistan and Bangladesh'. *New Left Review* I, no. 74, 1972. www.hamzaalavi.com.

Ali, Tariq. 'The Fall of Congress in India'. *New Left Review* I, no. 103, May–June 1977.

All India Congress Committee. *Congress Marches Ahead—VII, September 1972–December 1972.* New Delhi: All India Congress Committee, 1972.

Amin-Khan, Tariq. *The Post-colonial State in the Era of Capitalist Globalization: Historical, Political and Theoretical Approaches to State Formation.* New York: Routledge, 2011.

Andrew, Christopher and Vasili Mitrokhin. *The Mitrokhin Archive II: The KGB and the World.* London: Allen Lane, 2005.

Arora, Arjun. 'Planning Without Direction'. *Indian Left Review* 2, no. 1 (March 1973): 44–47.

————. 'Congress Left: A Pathetic Tale'. *Indian Left Review* 2, no. 7 (September 1973): 5–10.

Awana, Ram Singh. *Pressure Politics in Congress Party: A Study of the Congress Forum for Socialist Action.* New Delhi: Northern Book Centre, 1988.

Balaram, N. E. *Three Years of UF Government Headed by C. Achutha Menon.* New Delhi: Communist Party Publication, 1973.

Bardhan, Pranab. *The Political Economy of Development in India.* Oxford: Basil Blackwell Ltd, 1984.

Basavapunnaiah, M. *Quit India Call and the Role of the Communists.* New Delhi: National Book Centre, 1984.

Basu, Jyoti, (ed.). *Documents of the Communist Movement in India. Volume 5: 1944–1948.* Calcutta: National Book Agency, 1997.

———— (ed.). *Documents of the Communist Movement in India. Volume 6: 1949–1951.* Calcutta: National Book Agency, 1997.

———— (ed.). *Documents of the Communist Movement in India. Volume 13: 1969.* Calcutta: National Book Agency, 1998.

———— (ed.). *Documents of the Communist Movement in India. Volume 17: 1975–1977.* Calcutta: National Book Agency, 1998.

Benediktov, Ivan A. 'Russian Foreign Ministry Documents on Soviet-Indian Relations'. In *Cold War International History Project.* www.wilsoncenter.org.

Bell, Bernard R. (ed.). *Report to the President of the International Bank for Reconstruction and Development and the International Development Association on India's Economic Development Effort. Volume 1.* Main Report, 1 October 1965. At www-wds.worldbank.org.

————. *A Conversation with Bernard Bell, Part 1.* Interviewed by Robert W. Oliver. Washington D.C.: California Institute of techinology, 1985. http://go.worldbank.org/ASNT3Q5DE0.

Bhagwati, Jagdish N., and Padma Desai. *India: Planning for Industrialization*. London: OECD & Oxford University Press, 1970.

Bhagawati, B. C. *Presidential Address, Indian National Trade Union Congress*. 20th Session, Bombay, 28 December 1974. New Delhi: INTUC, 1975.

Bhargava, Ashok and Gopalan Balachandaran. 'Economic Changes during the Indian Emergency'. *Bulletin of Concerned Asian Scholars* 9, no. 4 (October–December 1977): 50–58.

Birla, Krishna Kumar. *Brushes with History: An Autobiography*. New Delhi: Penguin Viking, 2007.

Blair, Harry W. 'Mrs Gandhi's Emergency, The Indian Elections of 1977, Pluralism and Marxism: Problems with Paradigms'. *Modern Asian Studies* 14, no. 2 (1980): 237–71.

Brass, Paul. *The Politics of India since Independence*. New Cambridge History of India, vol. IV, part 1. Cambridge: Cambridge University Press, 1994.

Brenner, Robert. 'The Social Basis of Economic Development'. In *Analytical Marxism*, edited by John Roemer. Cambridge: Cambridge University Press, 1986.

Bhushan, Shashi. 'The Only Answer'. *Indian Left Review* 3, no. 1 (March 1974): 8–11.

Callaghan, John. *Rajani Palme Dutt: A Study in British Stalinism*. London: Lawrence & Wishart, 1993.

Callinicos, Alex. 'Bourgeois Revolutions and Historical Materialism'. *International Socialism*, no. 43 (1989): 113–71.

Carras, Mary C. *Indira Gandhi: In the Crucible of Leadership*. Bombay: Jaico Press Private Ltd, 1980.

Chakravarty, Nikhil. 'Indira Gandhi: Moment of Truth'. *Mainstream*, 21 June 1975. www. mainstreamweekly.net/article2869.html.

Chandavarkar, Rajnarayan. 'From Communism to Social Democracy: the Rise and Resilience of Communist Parties in India, 1920–1995'. *Science and Society* 61, no. 1 (Spring 1997): 99–106.

Chandra, Bipan. 'Total Rectification'. *Seminar* 178, (June 1974): 24–37.

———. 'A Strategy in Crisis: The CPI Debate 1955–1956'. *Studies in History* III, no. 1 and 2 (1981): 259–400.

———. 'S. A. Dange—An Interview'. In *Indian Communism: Life and Work of S. A. Dange*, edited by Mohit Sen. New Delhi: Patriot Publishers, 1992.

———. *In the Name of Democracy: JP Movement and the Emergency*. New Delhi: Penguin Books, 2003.

———. 'P. C. Joshi: A Political Journey'. *Mainstream* XLVI, no. 1 (2007). www.mainstreamweekly.net/article503.html.

———. *The Writings of Bipan Chandra: The Making of Modern India from Marx to Gandhi*, edited by Aditya Mukherjee. Hyderabad: Orient Blackswan Private Ltd, 2012.

Chandra, Bipan, Mridula Mukherjee and Aditya Mukherjee. *India Since Independence*. New Delhi: Penguin, 2008.

Chandrasekhar, C. P. 'Crony Capitalism and State Capture'. *Frontline*, 21 March 2014: 35–37.

Chandrasekhar, C. P. and Jayati Ghosh. *The Market That Failed: Neoliberal Economic Reform in India*. New Delhi: LeftWord Books, 2004.

Chaudhry, Praveen K., Vijay L. Kelkar, and Vikash Yadav. 'The Evolution of "Homegrown Conditionality" in India/IMF Relations'. *Journal of Development Studies* 40, no. 6 (August 2004): 59–81.

Chattopadhyaya, Gautam. 'Behind Bangladesh Coup'. *Indian Left Review* 3, no. 12 (September 1975): 15–29.

Chibber, Vivek. *Locked in Place: State-building and Late Industrialization in India*. Princeton: Princeton University Press, 2006.

Cliff, Tony. *Deflected Permanent Revolution*. London: Socialist Workers Party, 1990 [1963].

Cohen, G.A. *Karl Marx's Theory of History*. Oxford: Clarendon Press, 1991.

Communist Party of India. *Third Congress of the Communist Party of India, Madurai 27 December 1953–4 January 1954: Political Resolution*. Delhi: Communist Party of India, 1954.

———. *Resolutions of the National Council of the Communist Party of India, Hyderabad 14–20 August 1962*. New Delhi: Communist Party of India, 1962.

———. *The Programme of the Communist Party of India. As adopted by the Seventh Congress of the Communist Party of India, Bombay 13–23 December 1964*. New Delhi: Communist Party of India, 1965.

———. *The Present Political Situation. Resolution of the National Council of the Communist Party of India, Hyderabad 9–15 June 1966*. New Delhi: Communist Party of India, 1966.

———. *Election Manifesto of the Communist Party of India*. New Delhi: Communist Party of India, 1966.

———. *Political Resolutions Adopted by Eighth Congress of the Communist Party of India, Patna 7-15 February 1968*. New Delhi: Communist Party of India, 1968.

———. *Programme of the Communist Party of India. Adopted by Eighth Congress of the Communist Party of India, Patna 7–15 February 1968*. New Delhi: Communist Party of India, 1968.

———. *Report and Resolutions. Adopted by the National Council of the Communist Party of India*. New Delhi: Communist Party of India, 1968.

———. *Resolutions of the National Council of the Communist Party of India*. New Delhi: Communist Party of India, 1970.

———. *On the General Election of March 1971. Resolutions and Review report of the National Council of the Communist Party of India, New Delhi 23–28 April 1971*. New Delhi: Communist Party of India, 1971.

———. *Documents of the Ninth Congress of the Communist Party of India, Cochin 3–10 October 1971*. New Delhi: Communist Party of India, 1972.

———. *Review of Elections to State Assemblies (1972) and Resolutions Adopted by the National Council, New Delhi 14–18 April 1972*. New Delhi: Communist Party of India, 1972.

———. *Party Education Series: Preliminary Course*. New Delhi: Communist Party of India, 1972.

———. *Party Education Series: Grade I Course*. New Delhi: Communist Party of India, 1972.

———. *Party Education Series: Grade II Course*. New Delhi: Communist Party of India, 1972.

———. *Documents of the Tenth Congress of the Communist Party of India, Bhowanisennagar, 27 January to 2 February 1975*. New Delhi: Communist Party Publication, 1975.

———. *Resolutions and Documents Adopted by the National Council of the Communist Party of India, New Delhi, 1 to 5 April 1975*. New Delhi: Communist Party Publication, May 1975.

———. *National Emergency and Our Tasks: Resolution Adopted by the Central Executive Committee, Communist Party of India, New Delhi, 30 June to 2 July 1975*. New Delhi: Communist Party Publication, July 1975.

———. *Resolutions and Report Adopted by the National Council of the Communist Party of India (New Delhi, August 1975)*. New Delhi: Communist Party Publication, September 1975.

———. *Report and Resolutions Adopted by the National Council of the Communist Party of India (Trivandrum, 7 to 11 February 1976)*. New Delhi: Communist Party Publication, 1976.

———. *Reports and Resolution Adopted by the National Council of the Communist Party of India. Hyderabad, 4–8 August 1976*. New Delhi: Communist Party Publication, 1976.

Communist Party of India. *Report and Resolutions of the Meeting of the Central Executive Committee of the Communist Party of India, New Delhi 24–27 October 1976.* New Delhi: Communist Party Publication, November 1976. (Reprinted as *On the Misuse of the Emergency by the CPI in January 1977.*)

———. *Murder of Truth: Anti-CPI Barrage Exposed.* New Delhi: Communist Party Publication, 1976.

———. *Consembly Move and Democratic Fight-Back.* New Delhi: Communist Party Publication, 1976.

———. *Resolutions of the National Council of Communist Party of India, New Delhi, 9–12 July 1977.* New Delhi: Communist Party Publication, July 1977.

———. *Documents of the Eleventh Congress of the Communist Party of India, Bhakna Nagar, Bhatinda, 31 March to 7 April, 1978.* New Delhi: Communist Party Publication, July 1978.

———. *Draft of the Party Programme.* New Delhi: CPI National Council, 2012.

——— (National Council). *Draft Political Resolution for Tenth Party Congress.* New Delhi: New Age Printing Press, 1974.

——— (National Council). *Some Problems Concerning the Agrarian Movement and Our Tasks.* New Delhi: Communist Party Publication, 1975.

Correspondent. 'The Emergency in India'. *Bulletin of Concerned Asian Scholars* 7, no. 4 (October–December 1975): 2–16.

Dang, Satyapal. 'Not Dictatorship but a Revolutionary Government'. *Indian Left Review* 3, no. 1 (March 1974): 15–17.

Dange, S. A. *Defeat Government—Monopolist Offensive with United Struggles.* New Delhi: AITUC Publication, 1972.

———. *Some Observations on the Political Review Report.* New Delhi: Communist Party of India, March 1978. (Written in February 1978.)

Democratic Research Service. *Communist Conspiracy in India: An Analysis of the Private Proceedings of the Third Congress of the CPI with Full Text of Secret Documents.* Bombay: Popular Book Depot, 1954.

Denoon, David B. H. 'Cycles in Indian Economic Liberalization, 1966–1996'. *Comparative Politics* 31, no. 1 (October 1998): 43–60.

Dhar, P. N. *Indira Gandhi, the 'Emergency', and Indian Democracy.* New Delhi: Oxford India Paperbacks, 2001.

Dongre, Anil P. 'Policy Changes in the Wake of Globalization and Its Impact on Indian Industries'. *Journal of Policy Modeling* 34 (2012): 476–96.

Drieberg, Trevor, and Sarala Jag Mohan. *Emergency in India.* New Delhi: Manas Publications, 1975.

Dutt, V. P. 'The Emergency in India: Background and Rationale'. *Asian Survey* 16, no. 12 (December 1976): 1124–38.

East Asia Analytical Unit, Department of Foreign Affairs and Trade. *India's Economy at the Midnight Hour: Australia's India Strategy.* Canberra: Australian Government Publishing Service, 1994.

Engels, Frederick. 'Socialism: Utopian and Scientific'. In *Selected Works*, edited by Karl Marx and Frederick Engels. Moscow : Progress Publishers, 1970.

———. 'The Origin of the Family, Private Property and the State'. In *Selected Works*, edited by Karl Marx and Frederick Engels. Moscow: Progress Publishers, 1970 [1884].

Epstein, Simon. 'District Officers in Decline: The Erosion of British Authority in the Bombay Countryside, 1919 to 1947'. *Modern Asian Studies* 16, no. 3 (1982): 493–518.

Erdman, Howard L. 'The Industrialists'. In *Indira Gandhi's India: A Political System Reappraised*, edited by Henry C. Hart. Boulder: Westview Press, 1976.

Fic, Victor M. *Kerala: Yenan of India*. Bombay: Nachiketa Publications, 1970.

Frankel, Francine R. *India's Political Economy, 1947–1977: The Gradual Revolution*. Princeton: Princeton University Press, 1978.

Gandhi, D. V. (ed.). *Era of Discipline: Documents on Contemporary Reality*. New Delhi: Samachar Bharati, 1976.

Gandhi, Indira. *Democracy and Discipline: Speeches of Shrimati Indira Gandhi [1975]*. New Delhi: Ministry of Information and Broadcasting, Government of India, n.d.

———. *My Truth, presented by Emmanuel Pouchpadass*. New Delhi: Vision Books, 1981.

———. *Selected Speeches and Writings of Indira Gandhi. Volume III: September 1972–March 1977*. New Delhi: Ministry of Information and Broadcasting, Government of India, 1984.

Ghosh, A. K. and S. A. Dange. 'Concerning the Question of Partisan Struggle'. *Revolutionary Democracy* XVI, no. 1 (April 2010). www.revolutionarydemocracy.org.

Ghosh, Parimal Chandra and Sobhanlal Datta Gupta. *A Note on the Theoretical Roots of the Mistakes in Our Party's Line: Some Comments on the Draft Review Report for the Eleventh Party Congress*. New Delhi: cyclostyled, 7 March 1978.

Ghose, Sankar (ed.). *The March towards Socialism (souvenir of the 74th Congress Session, 26–29 December 1972, Calcutta)*. Calcutta: H. Chakravorty, 1972.

Ghose, Sankar (ed.). 'Editorial' and 'The Congress and Democratic Socialism'. In *The March towards Socialism (souvenir of the 74th Congress Session, 26–29 December 1972, Calcutta)*. Calcutta: H. Chakravorty, 1972.

Gilberg, Trond (ed.). *Coalition Strategies of Marxist Parties*. Durham and London: Duke University Press, 1989.

Gilmartin, William B. 'A Conversation with William Gilmartin'. Conducted by Robert W. Oliver, Washington, D.C., November 14 1985. World Bank Archives, Oral History: web.worldbank.org.

Gour, Raj Bahadur. *Working Class under Congress Raj*. New Delhi: Communist Party Publication, 1961.

Gramsci, Antonio. *Selections from the Prison Notebooks of Antonio Gramsci*. Edited and translated by Quintin Hoare and Geffrey Nowell Smith. New York: International Publishers, 1971.

Guha, Ramachandra. *India After Gandhi*. London: Picador, 2007.

Gupta, Amit Kumar (ed.). *Myth and Reality: The Struggle for Freedom in India, 1945–1947*. New Delhi: Manohar, 1987.

Sen Gupta, Bhabani. *Communism in Indian Politics*. New York: Columbia University Press, 1972.

———. 'Communism Further Divided'. In *Indira Gandhi's India: A Political System Reappraised*, edited by Henry C. Hart. Boulder: Westview Press, 1976.

Gupta, Bupesh. *The Big Loot: A Brief Study of Foreign Exploitation in India*. New Delhi: Communist Party of India, 1962.

———. *Right-Reaction Bids for Power*. New Delhi: Communist Party Publication, 1971.

Gupta, D. N. *Communism and Nationalism in Colonial India, 1939–45*. New Delhi: SAGE Publications India, 2008.

Gupta, Partha Sarathi. 'Imperial Strategy and the Transfer of Power, 1939–51'. In *Myth and Reality: The Struggle for Freedom in India, 1945–1947*, edited by Amit Kumar Gupta. New Delhi: Manohar, 1987.

Gupta, Shaibal, 'End of ideology'. *Frontline* 31, no. 9 (3–16 May 2014). www.frontline.in.

Sen Gupta, Sukhomoy. 'The Task Ahead'. In *The March towards Socialism (souvenir of the 74th Congress Session, 26–29 December 1972, Calcutta)* edited by Sankar Ghose. Calcutta: H. Chakravorty, 1972.

Haksar, P. N. *Premonitions*. Bombay: Interpress, 1979.

Hankla, Charles R. 'Party Linkages and Economic Policy: An Examination of Indira Gandhi's India'. *Business and Politics* 8, no. 3 (2006). www.basc.berkeley.edu/bap/archive.html

Harris, Nigel. 'India: Part One'. *International Socialism* (1st series), no. 17 (Summer 1964): 4–14. www.marxists.org/history/etol/writers/harris/1964/xx/india3.htm.

———. 'India: A First Approximation II'. *International Socialism* (1st series), no. 18 (Autumn 1964): 19–21. www.marxists.org/history/etol/writers/harris/1964/xx/india2.htm.

———. *Of Bread and Guns: The World Economy in Crisis*. Harmondsworth: Penguin, 1983.

Harris, Nigel. *The Return of Cosmopolitan Capital: Globalization, the State and War*. London: IB Tauris, 2003.

Hart, Henry C. (ed.). *Indira Gandhi's India: A Political System Reappraised*. Boulder: Westview Press, 1976.

———. 'Introduction.' In *Indira Gandhi's India: A Political System Reappraised*, edited by Henry C. Hart. Boulder: Westview Press, 1976.

Hewitt, Vernon. *Political Mobilisation and Democracy in India: States of Emergency*. New York: Routledge, 2008.

Jha, Bhogendra. 'Birth and Growth of Communists in Bihar'. *Indian Left Review* 4, no. 4 (February 1976): 8–16.

Josh, Bhagwan. *Struggle for Hegemony in India, 1920–47. The Colonial State, the Left and the National Movement. Volume II: 1934–41*. New Delhi: SAGE Publications, 1992.

Joshi, Puran Chand. *Congress and Communists*. Bombay: People's Publishing House, 1940.

———. *A Free Happy India: Election Policy of Indian Communists*. Bombay: People's Publishing House, 1944.

———. *For the Final Bid for Power! Freedom Project of Indian Communists*. Bombay: People's Publishing House, 1946.

———. 'Possibilities and Constraints of Intermediate Classes'. *Indian Left Review* 3, no. 3 (May 1974).

———. *People's 'Warrior': Words and Worlds of P. C. Joshi*. Edited by Gargi Chakravartty. New Delhi: Tulika Books, 2014.

Joshi, Shashi. *Struggle for Hegemony in India, 1920–47. The Colonial State, the Left and the National Movement. Volume I: 1920–34*. New Delhi: SAGE Publications, 1992.

Kalugin, Oleg. *Spymaster*. London: Smith Gryphon Ltd, 1994.

Kapur, Devesh, John P. Lewis and Richard Webb. *The World Bank: Its First Half Century*. Washington: The Brookings Institution, 1997.

Kautsky, Karl. *The Road to Power: Political Reflections on Growing into the Revolution*. Edited by John H. Kautsky. Alameda: Center for Socialist History, 2007.

Khrushchev, N. S. *Special Report to the 20th Congress of the Communist Party of the Soviet Union*. New York: New Leader, 1962.

Khrushchov, Nikita S. *Report of the Central Committee of the Communist of the Soviet Union to the 20th Party Congress*. Moscow: Foreign Languages Publishing House, 1956.

Kochanek, Stanley A. *The Congress Party of India: The Dynamics of One-Party Democracy*. Princeton: Princeton University Press, 1968.

———. *Business and Politics in India*. Berkeley: University of California Press, 1974.

———. 'Mrs. Gandhi's Pyramid: The New Congress'. In *Indira Gandhi's India: A Political System Reappraised*, edited by Henry C. Hart. Boulder: Westview Press, 1976.

Kochanek, Stanley A. 'Briefcase Politics in India: the Congress Party and the business elite'. *Asian Survey* 27, no. 12 (December 1987): 1278–301.

———. 'The Coalition Strategies and Tactics of Indian Communism'. In *Coalition Strategies of Marxist Parties*, edited by Trond Gilberg. Durham and London: Duke University Press, 1989.

Kohli, Atul. 'Politics of Economic Liberalization in India'. *World Development* 17, no. 3 (1989): 305–28.

———. *State-Directed Development: Political Power and Industrialization in the Global Periphery*. Cambridge: Cambridge University Press, 2004.

Krishnan, N. K. 'The Situation in India and the Tasks of the CPI'. *World Marxist Review* XV, no. 8 (August 1972): 33–35.

———. 'The Initiative is in the Hands of the Left and Democratic Forces'. *World Marxist Review* XVI, no. 4 (April 1973): 18–21.

——— (compiler). *Political Role of the Army in Developing Countries*. New Delhi: Communist Party of India, 1974.

———. 'A Sharp Turn'. *World Marxist Review* XVIII, no. 10 (October 1975): 10–13.

———. 'Our Tasks in the Context of the New Situation in India'. *World Marxist Review* XX, no. 11 (November 1977): 80–88.

Krishnan, N. K., Raj Bahadur Gour and T. N. Siddhanta. *Working Class and the Emergency*. New Delhi: Communist Party Publication, August 1975.

Kudaisya, Medha M. '"Reforms by Stealth": Indian Economic Policy, Big Business and the Promise of the Shastri Years, 1964–1966'. *South Asia: Journal of South Asian Studies* 25, no. 2 (2002): 205–29.

———. *The Life and Times of G.D. Birla*. New Delhi: Oxford University Press, 2003.

Kumaramangalam, S. Mohan. *Communists in Congress: Kumaramangalam's Thesis*. Edited and Introduced by Satindra Singh. Delhi: D. K. Publishing House, 1973 [1964].

Lal, Bansi. 'Haryana Enters its Seventh Year'. In *The March towards Socialism (souvenir of the 74th Congress Session, 26–29 December 1972, Calcutta)*, edited by Sankar Ghose. Calcutta: H. Chakravorty, 1972.

Lewis, Primila. *Reason Wounded: An Experience of India's Emergency*. London: George Allen & Unwin Ltd., 1978.

Leys, Colin. 'The "Overdeveloped" Post Colonial State: A Re-evaluation'. *Review of African Political Economy*. www.roape.org.

Shao-Ch'i, Liu. *The Collected Works of Liu Shao-Ch'i: 1945–1957*. 19XX: Union Research Institute, Hong Kong.

Lockwood, David. *The Destruction of the Soviet Union: A Study in Globalization*. Houndmills: Macmillan Press Ltd, 2000.

———. 'Historical Materialism and the State'. *Critique* 34, no. 2 (August 2006): 163–78.

———. 'War, the State and the Bourgeois Revolution'. *War and Society* 25, no. 2 (October 2006): 53–79.

———. *The Indian Bourgeoisie: A Political History of the Indian Capitalist Class in the Early Twentieth Century*. London: Tauris Academic Studies, 2012.

———. 'Was the Bombay Plan a Capitalist Plot?' *Studies in History* 28, no. 1 (2012): 99–116.

Lukas, J. Anthony 'India is as Indira Does'. *New York Times Magazine*, 4 April 1976. www.nytimes.com/section/magazine/archives

Mahendra, K. L. *Defeat the RSS Fascist Designs*. New Delhi: Communist Party Publication, December 1973.

Mahajan, Sucheta. 'British Policy, Nationalist Strategy and Popular National Upsurge, 1945–46'. In *Myth and Reality: The Struggle for Freedom in India, 1945–1947*, edited by Amit Kumar Gupta. New Delhi: Manohar, 1987.

Majumdar, Sumit K. *India's Late, Late Industrial Revolution: Democratizing Entrepreneurship*. Cambridge: Cambridge University Press, 2012.

Malaviya, Harsh Dev. *The Danger of Right Reaction*. New Delhi: Socialist Congressman Publications, 1965.

———. *Socialist Ideology of Congress: A Study in its Evolution*. New Delhi: Socialist Congressman Publications, 1966.

———. 'Congress Left is Alive and Kicking'. *Indian Left Review* 2, no. 7 (September 1973): 13–21.

———. 'Nationalisation for Economic Advance'. *Indian Left Review* 2, no. 11 (January 1974): 20–31.

———. 'Implementation and the Party (Part 1)'. *Indian Left Review* 3, no. 11 (August 1975): 27–29.

Malaviya, Harsh Dev. 'Implementation and the Party (Part 2)'. *Indian Left Review* 3, no. 12 (September 1975): 7–12.

———. *International Conference against Fascism (Patna: December 4–7, 1975): Western Aid, Multinationals and the CIA*. Delhi: Everest Press, 1975.

Malhotra, Inder. 'Indira Gandhi: An Overview'. In *A Centenary History of the Indian National Congress. Volume V: 1964–1984*, edited by Aditya Mukherjee. New Delhi: Academic Foundation, 2011.

Marcos, Ferdinand E. *The Democratic Revolution in the Philippines*. New Jersey: Prentice-Hall International, 1974.

Marcos, Ferdinand E. *Notes on the New Society of the Philippines*. Manila: Marcis Foundation, 1974.

Martin, Briton. *New India 1885: British Official Policy and the Emergence of the Indian National Congress*. Berkeley: University of California Press, 1969.

Marx, Karl. *A Contribution to the Critique of Political Economy*. New Delhi: People's Publishing House, 2010 [1859].

Marx, Karl and Frederick Engels. *Manifesto of the Communist Party*. Moscow: Progress Publishers, 1966 [1848].

———. *Selected Works*. Moscow : Progress Publishers, 1970.

Mason, Edward S. and Robert E. Asher. *The World Bank since Bretton Woods*. Washington: Brookings Institution, 1973.

Mastny, Vojtech. 'The Soviet Union's Partnership with India'. *Journal of Cold War Studies* 12, no. 3 (Summer 2010): 50–90.

Mayer, Peter. 'Congress (I), Emergency (I): Interpreting Indira Gandhi's India'. In *India: Rebellion to Republic* edited by Robin Jeffrey, Lance Brennan, Jim Masselos, Peter Mayer and Peter Reeves. New Delhi: Sterling Publishers, 1991.

Mazumdar, Surajit. 'The State, Industrialisation and Competition: A Reassessment of India's Leading Business Enterprises under Dirigisme'. *Economic History of Developing Regions* 26, no. 2 (2011): 33–54.

McDonald, Hamish. *The Polyester Prince: The Rise of Dhirubhai Ambani*. St Leonards: Allen & Unwin, 1998.

Mehta, Vinod. *The Sanjay Story*. New Delhi: Harper Collins Publishers, 2012 [1978].

Mukherjee, Aditya (ed.). *A Centenary History of the Indian National Congress. Volume V: 1964–1984*. New Delhi: Academic Foundation, 2011.

Mukherjee, Aditya (ed.). 'Introduction'. In *A Centenary History of the Indian National Congress. Volume V: 1964–1984*, edited by Aditya Mukherjee. New Delhi: Academic Foundation, 2011.

Mukherjee, Biswanath, Geeta Mukherjee and Kanai Bhowmik. *A Critical Note on the National Committee's Draft Review Report for the Eleventh Party Congress.* New Delhi: Communist Party of India, February 1978.

Mukherji, Rahul. 'India's Aborted Liberalization—1966'. *Pacific Affairs* 73, no. 3 (Autumn 2000): 375–92.

Nagy, L. and C. Unni Raja. 'Confidence in the Party's Strength'. *World Marxist Review* XV, no. 2 (February 1972): 14–16.

Nahata, Amrit. 'Now, Or Never'. *Indian Left Review* 3, no. 11 (August 1975): 12–23.

Nanda, Gulzari Lal. 'Introduction'. In *Congressman's Primer for Socialism by Jawaharlal Nehru.* Compiled by H. D. Malaviya. New Delhi: A Socialist Congressman Publication, 1965.

Nayar, Baldev R. *The Modernisation Imperative and Indian Planning.* Delhi: Vikas Publications, 1972.

Nehru, Jawaharlal. *Congressman's Primer for Socialism.* Compiled by H.D. Malaviya. New Delhi: A Socialist Congressman Publication, 1965.

———. *Selected Works. Volume XXXI: 18 November 1955–31 January 1956.* New Delhi: Jawaharlal Nehru Memorial Fund, 1984-2012.

Office of the Economic Adviser to the Government of India, Ministry of Commerce and Industry. *Handbook of Industrial Policy and Statistics, 2008–2009.* www.eaindustry.nic.in/handbook_200809/Chapter%201.pdf.

Overstreet, Gene D., and Marshall Windmiller. *Communism in India.* Berkeley: University of California Press, 1960.

Pandey, Sarjoo. 'The Rightist Threat'. *Indian Left Review* 3, no. 2 (April 1974): 15–16.

Parakal, Panly V. *Prices, Monopolies and Government Policies.* New Delhi: Communist Party Publication, September 1972.

Pereira, Oswald, Arindam Mukherjee and Shekhar Ghosh. 'The Ghost of the Bombay Club'. *Outlook,* 10 April 1996. www.outlookindia.com/printarticle.aspx?201149.

Patnaik, Ila. 'Turn the Clock Back'. openlibrary.org/home/ila/MEDIA/2005/turn_clock.html.

Patnaik, Prabhat. 'On the Political Economy of Economic "Liberalisation"'. *Social Scientist* XIII, no. 146–47 (July–August 1985): 3–17.

Pedersen, Jorgen Dige. 'Explaining Economic Liberalization in India: State and Society Perspectives'. *World Development* 28, no. 2 (2000): 265–82.

Pomeroy, William. 'Martial Law and the National Democratic Struggle in the Phillippines'. *Indian Left Review* 3, no. 11 (August 1975): 30–42.

Potter, David C. 'Manpower Shortage and the End of Colonialism: the Case of the Indian Civil Service'. *Modern Asian Studies* 7, no. 1 (1973): 47–73.

Poulantzas, Nicos. *Political Power and Social Classes.* London: NLB, 1975.

Rahman, Mohammed Mahafoozur. *The Congress Crisis.* New Delhi: Associated Publishing House, 1970.

Rajimwale, Anil. *Glimpses of CPI History through Party Congresses.* New Delhi: People's Publishing House, 2005.

———. *Life and Works of P.C. Joshi.* New Delhi: People's Publishing House, 2007.

———. 'Ajoy Ghosh: the Creative Marxist'. *Mainstream,* no. 1, 26 December 2009.

Ram, Mohan. *Indian Communism: Split within a Split.* Delhi: Vikas Publications, 1969.

Rao, C. Rajeshwara. *RSS and Jana Sangh.* New Delhi: Communist Party Publication, January 1969.

Rao, C. Rajeshwara. 'Left and Democratic Unity against the Right Threat'. *World Marxist Review* XVI, no. 8 (August 1973): 15–17.

———. *Lenin's Teachings and Our Tactics*. New Delhi: Communist Party Publication, November 1974.

———. 'Awareness of Historical Responsibility'. *World Marxist Review* XVIII, no. 5 (May 1975): 21–24.

Rao, C. Rajeshwara, Pauly V. Parakal, Sadhan Mukherjee and Shamim Faizee. *Parties of Right Reaction*. New Delhi: Communist Party Publication, August 1975.

Rao, C. Rajeshwara. 'RSS-Janasangh—Spearhead of JP's Counterevolution'. In *Parties of Right Reaction*, edited by C. Rajeshwara Rao, Pauly V. Parakal, Sadhan Mukherjee and Shamim Faizee. New Delhi: Communist Party Publication, August 1975.

Rao, C. Rajeshwara, Bhupesh Gupta and Mohit Sen. *Emergency and the Communist Party*. New Delhi: Communist Party Publication, August 1975.

Rao, M. B. (ed.). *Documents of the History of the Communist Party of India. Volume VII: 1948–1950*. New Delhi: People's Publishing House, 1976.

Rao, N. Prasada. *Land Reforms under Congress Raj*. New Delhi: Communist Party of India, 1961.

Reddy, Arutla Ramachandra. *Telangana Memoirs*. New Delhi: People's Publishing House, 1984.

Reddy, N. Rajsekhar. *What Is CPIs Programme?* New Delhi: Communist Party Publication, 1975.

Reich, Robert. *The Work of Nations*. New York: Knopf, 1991.

Roy, Prakash and Ajoy Das Gupta. *Critical Notes for the Eleventh Party Congress*. New Delhi: Communist Party of India, February 1978.

Rudolph, Lloyd I. and Susanne Hoeber Rudolph. In *Pursuit of Lakshmi: The Political Economy of the Indian State*. Hyderabad: Orient Longman, 1987.

Sahgal, Nayantara. *Indira Gandhi: Her Road to Power*. New York: Frederick Ungar Publishing Co., 1982.

Sangal, O. P. 'The March to Delhi—and What Next?' *Indian Left Review* 2, no. 2 (April 1973): 3–6.

———. 'Rightist Threat Persists'. *Indian Left Review* 3, no. 1 (March 1974): 3–5.

———. 'The Left's Dilemma'. *Indian Left Review* 3, no. 2 (April 1974): 3–5.

———. 'People's Mood'. *Indian Left Review* 3, no. 6 (August–September 1974): 3–5.

———. 'The Fiftieth Anniversary'. *Indian Left Review* 4, no. 3 (January 1976): 3–5.

———. '30th Year of Independence'. *Indian Left Review* 4, no. 10 (August 1976): 3–5.

Sardesai, Srinivas. *Devaluation: The Great Betrayal*. New Delhi: Communist Party Publication, 1966.

———. *Fascist Menace and Democratic Unity*. New Delhi: People's Publishing House, August 1970.

———. 'Hold the Economy, Before You Plan'. *Indian Left Review* 2, no. 1 (March 1973): 35–39.

———. 'The Future of the Congress Left'. *Indian Left Review* 2, no. 7 (September 1973): 28–33.

———. 'Positive Mass Action, Not Search for a Saviour'. *Indian Left Review* 3, no. 1 (March 1974): 11–14.

———. *Student Upsurge and Indian Revolution*. New Delhi: Youth Life Publication, June 1974.

———. 'Unholy Alliance of India's Right and "Left"'. *World Marxist Review* 19, no. 4 (April 1976): 27–31.

———. 'The Path Ahead'. *Indian Left Review* 3, no. 11 (August 1975): 24–26.

Sarkar, Jagannath. 'Bankruptcy of Centrism'. *Indian Left Review* 2, no. 7 (September 1973).

Sathe, V. P. 'National Crisis and the Role of the Left'. *Indian Left Review* 3, no. 2 (April 1974): 12–15.

Sathyamurthy, T. V. (ed.). *State and Nation in the Context of Social Change*. Delhi: Oxford India Paperbacks, 1997.

Saul, John S. 'The State in Post-Colonial Societies: Tanzania'. *The Socialist Register, 1974*. London: Merlin Press, 1974.

Selbourne, David. *An Eye to India: the Unmasking of a Tyranny*. Harmondsworth: Penguin, 1977.

———. *Through the Indian Looking-glass*. London: Zed Press, 1992.

Sen, Bhowani. *The Truth About CPM. A Critique of the Ideological-political Line of the Communist Party of India (Marxist)*. New Delhi: Communist Party of India, 1972.

Sen, Mohit. *The Indian Revolution: Review and Perspectives*. New Delhi: People's Publishing House, 1970.

———. 'Question and Answer: CPI and the United-Front Tactics'. *Party Life* (Inner-Party Journal of the Organization Department), 1971 (no other date provided).

———. *The People's March to Delhi*. New Delhi: Communist Party Publication, January 1973.

———. 'Forward from Plan Approach'. *Indian Left Review* 2, no. 1 (March 1973): 33–35.

———. 'Anti-Rightist Counter-Attack'. *Indian Left Review* 2, no. 2 (April 1973): 6–8.

———. 'Skirmishes and Confrontations'. *Indian Left Review* 2, no. 3 (May 1973): 3–6.

———. 'Revolutionary Process in India'. *Indian Left Review* 2, no. 4 (June 1973): 11–15.

———. 'Our Wonderful People'. *Indian Left Review* 2, no. 6 (August 1973).

———. 'Immense Potential'. *Indian Left Review* 2, no. 7 (September 1973): 21–23.

———. 'Radical Turn, Not Limited Dictatorship'. *Indian Left Review* 2, no. 12 (February 1974): 3–5.

———. 'The Perspective of Struggle'. *Indian Left Review* 3, no. 2 (April 1974): 9–12.

———. 'New Confrontation'. *Indian Left Review* 3, no. 3 (May 1974): 3–6.

———. 'Confrontation'. *Indian Left Review* 3, no. 8 (November 1974–March 1975): 3–5.

———. 'Implementation and Power'. *Indian Left Review* 3, no. 11 (August 1975): 9–11.

———. 'Spring-board for Democratic Advance'. *Indian Left Review* 3, no. 12 (September 1975): 3–6.

———. 'Emergency Balance Sheet'. *Indian Left Review* 4, no. 1 (October 1975): 3–5.

———. 'Positive Trends Gaining the Upper Hand in India'. *World Marxist Review* 19, no. 8 (August 1976): 11–15.

———. *Congress Socialism: Appraisal and Appeal*. New Delhi: Communist Party Publication, December 1976.

——— (ed.). *Documents of the History of the Communist Party of India, Volume VIII 1951–1956*. New Delhi: People's Publishing House, 1977.

——— (ed.). *Indian Communism: Life and Work of S.A. Dange*. New Delhi: Patriot Publishers, 1992.

———. *A Traveller and the Road: The Journey of an Indian Communist*. New Delhi: Rupa & Co., 2003.

Sengupta, Mitu. 'Making the State Change Its Mind—the IMF, the World Bank and the Politics of India's Market Reforms'. *New Political Economy* 14, no. 2 (June 2009): 181–210.

Shah, Ghanshyam. *Protest Movements in Two Indian States: A Study of the Gujarat and Bihar Movements*. Delhi: Ajanta Publications, 1977.

Shah Commission of Inquiry. *Third and Final Report*. New Delhi: Government of India Press, 1978.

Shekhar, Chandra. *Presidential Address: Congressmen's National Convention for Implementation of 10 Point Programme*. New Delhi: Congress Forum for Socialist Action, 1969.

———. *A Peep into Birla House*. New Delhi: Shashi Bushan, M.P., April 1969.

Sherlock, Stephen. *The Indian Railways Strike of 1974: A Study of Power and Organised Labour*. New Delhi: Rupa & Co., 2001.

Shourie, Arun. 'Growth, Poverty and Inequalities'. *Foreign Affairs* 51, no. 2 (January 1973): 340–52.

Shukla, Vidya Charan. 'The Crisis Ahead'. In *Era of Discipline: Documents on Contemporary Reality*, edited by D. V. Gandhi. New Delhi: Samachar Bharati, 1976.

Singh, Mahendra Prasad. *Split in a Predominant Party: the Indian National Congress in 1969*. New Delhi: Abhinav Publications, 1981.

———. *Split in a Predominant Party: the Indian National Congress in 1969*. New Delhi: Abhinav Publications, 1981.

Singh, Pragya. 'The Home Alone Boys'. *Outlook*, 10 January 2011. www.outlookindia.com/printarticle.aspx?269748.

Singh, Satindra. 'Introduction'. In S. Mohan Kumaramangalam, *Communists in Congress: Kumaramangalam's Thesis*, edited by Satindra Singh. Delhi: D.K. Publishing House, 1973 [1964].

Singh, Vijay, comp. 'The Discussions of S.A. Dange with the C.P.S.U. (b) (July–September 1947)'. *Revolutionary Democracy* 7, no. 1 (April 2001). www.revolutionarydemocracy.org/rdv7n1/Dange.htm.

———. 'Stenographic Record of the Discussion of the Members of the CC A-UCP(B) with the representatives of the CC Communist Party of India on 4th and 6th February 1951'. *Revolutionary Democracy* 12, no. 2 (September 2006). www.revolutionarydemocracy.org/rdv12n2/cpi1.htm.

Singh, Vijay, comp. 'Record of the Discussions of J.V. Stalin with the Representatives of the C.C. of the Communist Party of India Comrades, Rao, Dange, Ghosh and Punnaiah'. *Revolutionary Democracy* 12, no. 2 (September 2006). www.revolutionarydemocracy.org/rdv12n2/cpi1.htm.

———. 'Record of the Discussions of Comrades G.M. Malenkov and M.A. Suslov with the Representatives of the Central Committee of the Communist Party of India Comrades Rao, Dange, Ghosh and Punnaiah'. *Revolutionary Democracy* 12, no. 2 (September 2006). www.revolutionarydemocracy.org/rdv12n2/cpi1.html.

Sinha, Indradeep. *Real Face of JP's 'Total Revolution'*. New Delhi: CPI Publication, 1974.

Sivadasan, Jagadeesh. 'Regulatory Regime in India: 1947 to 1998'. webuser.bus.umich.edu/jagadees/other/indmfg_data/Reg_history_india.pdf.

Skocpol, Theda. *States and Social Revolutions: A Comparative Analysis of France, Russia and China*. Cambridge: Cambridge University Press, 1979.

Srivastava, Ravi S. 'Bonded Labor in India: Its Incidence and Pattern'. 4 January 2005. www.digitalcommons.ilr.cornell.edu.

Stalin, Joseph. *Marxism and the National Question*. Moscow: Foreign Languages Publishing House, 1945 [1913].

Strange, Susan. 'New World Order: Conflict and Co-operation'. *Marxism Today* (January 1991): 30–33.

———. *States and Markets*. London: Pinter, 1994.

Talwar, Sadar Nand. *Under the Banyan Tree: The Communist Movement in India, 1920–1964*. New Delhi: Allied Publishers, 1985.

Tiwari, Lalan. *Democracy and Dissent: A Case Study of the Bihar Movement, 1974–75*. Delhi: Mittal Publications, 1987.

Torri, Michelguglielmo. 'Factional Politics and Economic Policy: The Case of India's Bank Nationalization'. *Asian Survey* 15, no. 12 (December 1975).

Toye, J. F. J. 'Economic Trends and Policies in India during the Emergency'. *World Development* 5, no. 4 (1977): 303–16.

Tripathi, Dwijendra and Jyoti Jumani. *The Concise Oxford History of Indian Business*. New Delhi: Oxford University Press, 2008.

Vanaik, Achin. *The Painful Transition: Bourgeois Democracy in India*. London: Verso, 1990.

Varkey, Joseph. 'The CPI—Congress Alliance in India'. *Asian Survey* 19, no. 9 (September 1979): 881–95.

Vasudev, Uma. *Two Faces of Indira Gandhi*. New Delhi, Vikas Publishing House, 1977.

Venkatasubbiah, H. *Enterprise and Economic Change: 50 Years of FICCI*. New Delhi: Vikas Publishing House, 1977.

Vyas, H. K. *Communist Reply to Tata Memorandum*. New Delhi: Communist Party Publication, September 1972.

Wilson, Kalpana. 'Class Alliances and the Nature of Hegemony: The Post-Independence Indian State in Marxist Writing'. In *State and Nation in the Context of Social Change*, edited by T. V. Sathyamurthy. Delhi: Oxford India Paperbacks, 1997.

Windmiller, Marshall. 'Indian Communism and the New Soviet Line'. *Pacific Affairs* 29, no. 4 (December 1956): 347–66.

Wood, John B. 'Observations on the Indian Communist Party Split'. *Pacific Affairs* 38, no. 1 (Spring 1965): 47–63.

Yadav, Chandrajeet. 'On Socialism'. In *The March towards Socialism (souvenir of the 74th Congress Session, 26–29 December 1972, Calcutta)* edited by Sankar Ghose. Calcutta: H. Chakravorty, 1972.

Zaidi, Moin A. *Full Circle 1972–1975. The Dynamics of a Social Revolution: The National Emergency*. New Delhi: Michiko & Panjathan, 1975.

——— (ed.). *The Encyclopaedia of the Indian National Congress. Volume 20, 1968–1969: Facing the City Bosses*. New Delhi: S. Chand and Company Ltd, 1983.

——— (ed.). *The Encyclopaedia of the Indian National Congress. Volume 22, 1972–1973: At War with Poverty*. New Delhi: S. Chand and Company Ltd, 1984.

——— (ed.). *The Encyclopaedia of the Indian National Congress. Volume 23, 1974–1975: The Lengthening Shadows*. New Delhi: S. Chand and Company Ltd, 1984.

——— (ed.). *The Encyclopaedia of the Indian National Congress. Volume 24, 1976–1977: Amid Encircling Gloom*. New Delhi: S. Chand and Company Ltd, 1984.

Zhdanov, Andrei A. *The International Situation (Speech at the Cominform Conference, September 1947)*. Place of printing unknown: no publisher, no date.

Ziemann, W. and M. Lanzendorfer. 'The State in Peripheral Societies'. In *The Socialist Register, 1977*. London: Merlin Press, 1977.

Archives, Papers and Oral History

Archives on the Contemporary History of India, Jawaharlal Nehru University, New Delhi (cited as P. C. Joshi Archive [JNU]).

D. K. Barooah Papers, Nehru Memorial Museum and Library.
P. N. Haksar Papers, Nehru Memorial Museum and Library.
Bansi Lal Papers, Nehru Memorial Museum and Library.
Har Dev Sharma Papers, Nehru Memorial Museum and Library.
Oral History Transcripts, Nehru Memorial Museum and Library (K. S. Mehta, Gulzari Lal Nanda, Nirmal Kumar Mukarji, K. N. Vaswani, Janak Raj Jai, Sitaram Singh, Jha Bhogendra, Madhu Dandavate, Jyoti Basu, S. A. Dange).

Interviews

Professor C. P. Bhambri, 4 November 2014, JNU.
Gargi Chakravartty, 6 November 2014, New Delhi.
Sumit Chakravartty, 8 November 2014, New Delhi.
Arjun Dev, 15 January 2014, New Delhi.
Amarjit Kaur, 15 January 2014, New Delhi.

Periodicals

Indian Left Review, New Delhi.
Link, New Delhi.
Thought, New Delhi

Index

About the Author

David Lockwood is an Associate Professor of modern history at Flinders University, Adelaide, South Australia. He is a specialist in the modern history and politics of India and in Soviet history. He is especially interested in the role of the bourgeoisie in historical development. He combines this with work in the broad areas of the role of the state in economic development, the transition from state-controlled to market economies, and the effects of globalisation on national states.